KILLER DADS

The Twisted Drives That
Compel Fathers to Murder
Their Own Kids

MARY PAPENFUSS

Prometheus Books

59 John Glenn Drive
Amherst, New York 14228–2119

Published 2013 by Prometheus Books

Cover image © James Godman/Media Bakery
Cover design by Jacqueline Nasso Cooke

Inquiries should be addressed to
Prometheus Books
59 John Glenn Drive
Amherst, New York 14228–2119
VOICE: 716–691–0133 • FAX: 716–691–0137
WWW.PROMETHEUSBOOKS.COM

17 16 15 14 13   5 4 3 2 1

Library of Congress Cataloging-in-Publication Data

Papenfuss, Mary.
    Killer dads : the twisted drives that compel fathers to murder their own kids / by Mary Papenfuss.
        pages cm
    Includes bibliographical references and index.
    ISBN 978-1-61614-743-3 (pbk.)
    ISBN 978-1-61614-744-0 (ebook)
    1. Filicide—United States. 2. Children—Crimes against—United States.
3. Murder—United States. I. Title.

HV6542.P365 2013
364.152'3—dc23

2013007165

Printed in the United States of America

This book is dedicated to Clare, Susan, Charlie and Braden,
Laci and Conner, Betty, Stephanie and Catherine, and Jessica

. . . and to Roland, Leda, and Luke, who keep me warm through the sad times.

CONTENTS

ACKNOWLEDGMENTS

It's difficult to approach people and ask them to share the biggest tragedy of their lives with a complete stranger. It's far harder to agree to do it. I'm tremendously grateful to family, friends, and acquaintances whose lives have been rocked by the killing of a child. This book would not exist without their steadfast loyalty to the memory of their dead, and the strength and courage to revisit a heart-wrenching horror to try to make some sense of it. Chuck and Judy Cox, Wendy Wasinski, Julieanne Malley, Marianne Quinn, Lucille Messina, James, Kayla Chuba, and Kaija Hartiala not only shared painful, detailed information but gave me a small glimpse into the profound, shattering impact of such horrific crimes on the people left behind. Bruce Montague helped tremendously by providing details about Bill Parente's Ponzi scheme to help Parente's financial victims, but also to aid an effort to attempt to understand a tragedy that deeply affected him. Jonathan Bachrach, Joanne Schulter, and Susan Deluca offered intriguing insights into the Parente family. Melissa Garret of the Baltimore County Police Department was particularly helpful with information in the Parente murder-suicide. I also thank the many investigators, big gruff guys whose hearts ache for child victims, who dodged official channels to talk to me and slip me information on several cases. I apologize for any oversights or mistakes. I hope in some small way this book pays tribute to family and friends' willingness to share their pain, and to the memory of Clare Shelswell; Betty, Stephanie, and Catherine Parente; Susan, Charlie, and Braden Powell; Laci and Conner Peterson; and Jessica Mokdad, as well as all the other victims who died with far less notice or concern.

I'm also indebted to the research and perspectives of the scientists and activists who grapple with the issue of violence and child deaths at the hands of their parents. Work by Sarah Hrdy, Martin Daly (with Margo

Wilson), Richard Gelles, and Neil Websdale offered fascinating platforms from which to view violence against children, and I appreciate their patience walking me through the issues and their insights. Thanks, too, to Michael Petit of the Every Child Matters Education Fund, and Amanda Parker of the AHA Foundation for their help and information, and for fighting the good fight.

Mark Mooney, now at ABC, was the *New York Daily News* national editor who assigned me to cover the Scott Peterson trial in California, which is where the idea for this book was born. As painful as that story was to cover, I'll be forever grateful for that assignment. I was fueled throughout my endeavor by a supportive gang of pals and current and former colleagues willing to listen endlessly to my expositions on the problem of parents who kill their children and encourage me to keep churning through the work. It meant the world to me. You know who you are: Hannah, Mike, Elaine, Shaila and Madhav, Kipp, Patricia, Anna and Marcel, Adriana and Pablo, Livia, Linda H., Marilyn, Denise, Lisa and Lisa, Corinne, Deb and James, and even Lis, who said she'd have to read the book with her eyes closed.

Finally, I'm blessed with a family endlessly intrigued with my unusual interests. Leda kept me on my toes, Luke turned out to be a footnote meister, and Roland fortified me. This book is as much yours as mine, Rol.

INTRODUCTION

The kids are frozen in time: The boy with the impossibly wide grin, the shy student, the little one, the clown, the girl with the pink bow in her hair, the girl with pigtails. They crowd together in their first-grade class photo. All but one are dead now, cut down by a semi-automatic rifle fired by suicidal gunman Adam Lanza in their classroom in Sandy Hook Elementary in Connecticut. As I finish writing this book, we're still in the midst of the long, sad march of Connecticut funerals. One mom has talked of the "hole in her heart." A father said he hoped the death of his adventurous, creative girl with the infectious laugh would inspire us to be better, more compassionate, people.

I've been steeped in stories of horrific murders for a year. I've become friends with a killer; I've spent the night in a hotel room where a man described by a chum as "straight as an arrow" bludgeoned and suffocated his family before cutting his own throat; I've chalked up hours in court listening to accounts of a man who shot his stepdaughter in the head; I've learned the history of a kinky father-in-law who took Peeping-Tom photos of his son's wife, who vanished and is presumed dead somewhere in the desert ranges near Salt Lake City. As I drove home from my last interview, I learned of the Sandy Hook shootings on the car radio and was struck, again, by how unimaginably annihilating the human soul can be.

I've focused on child murders. Unlike the Sandy Hook victims, the children in this book were murdered by people they loved and people they thought loved them. And unlike the Sandy Hook victims, most of them died with little notice from the public, even though the toll from child abuse and neglect and homicide across the nation claims each week at least the same number of victims as the school shootings.

The toll is obvious in news reports. In the office where I write, I have a bulletin board of some of the victims' faces. One of them, a photo of four-year-old Emma Thompson, reminds me of my daughter at the same age. It's the time when a young child is truly aware of the impact she can have on adults. In her snapshot, Emma mugs for the camera, full of herself in the particular way little girls can be, delighted. Her top lip is curled above her baby teeth in a giggling grin. She was killed that same year the photo was taken, 2009, in her home in Spring, Texas, north of Houston. She had been raped, her ribs broken, her skull fractured, her lips bloodied, and her face covered with bruises. Her mom's live-in lover, Lukas Cole, was sentenced to life in prison for the attack. Emma's mother, Abigail Young, was handed 20 years for failing to protect her daughter. Weeks before Emma was killed, a pediatrician discovered she had a sexually transmitted disease, but the local Child Protective Services office didn't remove her from her home.

There aren't many pictures of happy kids on my bulletin board. In their photos, Jonathan Ramsey and Osman Irias Salguero already have the eyes of world-weary 80-year-old men, as if they can sense the dirt pressing around their graves. Jonathan died at the age of ten in his home in Ellis County, Texas, starved to death by his dad, Aaron Ramsey, who withheld food to discipline him for acting up. Doctors discovered that Osman, two years old, had more than 86 bruises, fractures, and contusions when he was rushed to a Texas hospital in 2012 after an apparent beating in his Houston home. His dad, 21-year-old Osman Irias, was charged in the toddler's death. Snapshots don't exist in the worst cases of abused kids; no one has bothered posing them for photos until their autopsy pictures are taken.

Emma Thompson, Jonathan Ramsey, and Osman Irias Salguero are the largely forgotten names of a stream of victims of a battle within the homes of many American families. I've read about and covered stories of battered and murdered children for more than 20 years as a journalist, including several horrific cases at the *New York Post* and *New York Daily News*. One summer, both papers featured one story after another, each more heart wrenching than the last, of a child injury or death at the hands of a parent. The *Village Voice* pointed out that there was no unusual epidemic of child abuse that summer, even though the coverage made it appear so—only that it was a "slow news" time when fewer stories competed for coverage with the usual incidents of child abuse.

In 2005, I covered the northern California trial of Scott Peterson for the *New York Daily News*. Peterson killed his wife, Laci, who was eight months pregnant at the time, the day before Christmas or possibly the night before that, drove her body to the Berkeley Marina, then dumped her corpse offshore from his boat. He's now on death row in San Quentin. The case riveted the public. A young, pretty, missing pregnant wife—her family desperately searching for her at Christmas—moved people at a time when they were profoundly connecting with their own loved ones over the holidays. I was struck by how annoyed many male reporters were at being assigned to cover the trial. They preferred stories with more "impact"—yearned instead to cover Congress or battles in the state legislature or a war. Though the Peterson case only dealt directly with a handful of people and the death of a lone mother-to-be, it stood as a particularly compelling example of domestic violence.

Some criticized the fact that Laci's case, because it involved a white woman (of Portuguese ancestry) of upper-moderate means, drew media and public attention while other similar murders were ignored. San Franciscan Evelyn Hernandez was a 24-year-old Salvadoran immigrant and single mother who was nine months pregnant when she vanished with her six-year-old son the same year Laci disappeared, and her body also washed up in San Francisco Bay. African-American Lisa Eatmon, 33, of Brooklyn was also eight months pregnant when she went missing. She was shot in the head, and her body dumped in the Hudson River. Her corpse was found as Scott Peterson was about to go on trial. Her married lover and the father of her baby, New York City sanitation worker Roscoe Glinton II, 42, was sentenced to 25 years to life in prison for the murder (his first wife also vanished, and her death was ruled a homicide, but no one was ever charged in the crime). But as one of the three cases, Laci's, drew attention, it led to coverage of the other killings. More typically, none of them would have drawn much notice.

If budget is a gauge, America's biggest fear is terrorism and other foreign threats. The US military budget has increased from $300 billion in 2000 to some $750 billion in 2011, close to 20 percent of the federal budget,[1] and the Department of Homeland Security commanded funds close to $46 billion in 2011.[2] But the closest most of us will likely ever come to terrorism is dealing with long, inconvenient security lines at airports. Most of us, however, live in towns and cities where children are being hurt and terrorized—or have been killed—by an adult in their home. As many as 20,000 children have been killed at home in the last ten years, more than three times as many Americans killed in the Iraq and Afghanistan wars.[3] Such violence against society's most vulnerable at the hands of adults they love and trust in the cradle of their home is particularly crushing. We should be striving mightily to protect these children. Yet we aren't even discussing the problem. The battle over abortion rights rocked the 2012 presidential election, with a powerful political faction pushing for more life to be brought into the world, regardless of the desires of pregnant women. But there was little or no discussion of protection for or support of children once they morphed from unborn to born.

New studies in the wake of the 2008 recession have shown that economic stresses are boosting violence at home, which is already surprisingly high in America.[4] Unlike during the Great Depression, when the public believed Wall Streeters were jumping from windows following economic ruin, the toll this time around could be more bruised, battered, and murdered children. A particularly disturbing development has been an increase in "familicides" by dads who kill everyone in their families, sometimes before committing suicide. The number of children killed has increased at least 10 percent in the last four years.[5] Though they represent a small subset of child fatalities, the puzzling murders hold clues to the stresses families face and hint at the troubling potential for deadly violence.

It's the particularly confounding cases that I've focused on in this book. Child abuse and murder by parents grappling with drug or alcohol abuse, mental problems, poverty, and rage is less puzzling than that by parents who appear to be caring, good providers who suddenly "snap" and abuse their children or murder them. Examinations of these "extreme" cases hold some of the most dramatic clues to dynamics within families and within men that can explode into violence. I've focused on child homicides, only some of which were preceded by abuse, and I've picked homicides by fathers because I believe their role in child killings has captured less media attention than deadly mothers.

I've chosen key cases based on "types" of fathers who kill, including a father who kills his stepdaughter, a suicidal family annihilator driven by apparent concern for his loved ones, a family annihilator driven by rage, the murder of a pregnant wife by a psychopath, and a killing in heartland America initially branded by law enforcement officials as an honor killing. I've also focused on studies and theories of family violence by experts, and possible strategies proposed by those battling to save children's lives to stem the tide of violence at home. What activists fighting to protect kids from violence fear now is that the economic upheavals that may be triggering increased violence against children and fatalities are at the same time constricting budgets for social services, policing, and court supervision that could save lives.

It's been a long year. I gathered the information in this book by interviewing more than 65 people and reaching out to scores of others. I've talked to friends, family, co-workers, neighbors, investigators, scammed clients, and experts who daily confront the face of child murder by parents. I've racked up trial hours, pored over news reports, police reports, court transcripts, and stats on international and US child abuse and homicides. I talked to one of the killers in depth, and we're still e-mailing and phoning each other in a continuing relationship that has taken me by surprise. One of the victims—the wife of a suicidal husband who killed their two children—who is missing and presumed dead, has spoken to me from beyond the grave in a series of compelling e-mails that reveal her as a strong, articulate, intelligent woman who wanted desperately to save her marriage, but not at any cost. Throughout it all I've seen the little ghosts and grieved their lost faces, the lost years, and the lost promise of children who should not have died.

ONE

RAGE

I'M A NORMAL GUY WHO MADE A BIG, BIG MISTAKE.

—James, 2012 phone interview with the author

James is a soft, hulking man with a boyish face who spends afternoons and evenings bent over a tiny seed-bead jewelry loom on a desk or on his metal frame bed at the state prison that's his home for the next several decades. Beneath a bright, cold overhead light and the warmish glow of a tiny desk lamp on his wispy brown hair, the 31-year-old convict carefully threads minuscule pieces of colored glass or rainbow-hued plastic on a needle and line, meticulously adding bit by bit of red or gold, green and blue in intricate patterns to create bracelets and pendants in a ten-by-twelve-foot room behind electronic doors and a tiny window that he shares with his "cellie." He uses beading patterns the convicts trade, or those he has gleaned from books, and he sometimes sketches his own patterns to re-create an arresting image he sees during the day, like the spiky yellows of the heavy dahlia heads that recently lined a row of one of the gardens in the sunny field where prison cattle used to graze. He has made a tiny American-flag pendant, an iris-patterned bracelet, and earrings using Native American designs provided by an inmate member of the Crow nation.

The intensive labor on the loom is James's calm after a murderous storm, an emotional tsunami that seems now like a half-remembered dream. The beading quiets his mind. "I'm usually too fidgety to read," he tells me in one of several phone conversations we've had about his crime and his life behind bars. "It focuses my brain and I'm calmer and can think about things." Not everyone can do seed-beading in the prison, where crafts are a necessity for inmates killing endless years in stir. It takes keen eyesight, and dexterity not well suited to the many thick fingers in the prison. He's worried about what he'll do if he gets arthritis later on in his 55-year sentence. It runs in his family. James spends other hours picking up litter, sweeping the cement pathways outside, and cutting the grass on the prison field. In winter he shovels snow. It's a cherry job at the prison because it affords several extra hours outdoors. He has to watch his back, though, because his particular work assignment is so coveted that other prisoners might tell lies about him to get him bounced off the detail so they can get it for themselves. As appealing as the job is, for months at a time, he usually works less than 20 hours a week, which still leaves long stretches of time to fill when remorse can suddenly fill James with dread. "I can't shake this feeling of sadness," he tells me.

James enjoys talking to the guards, seeing what's happening in their lives. Most are civil, though some are "meaner and more ill-mannered than the inmates they look after," James believes. His fellow cons gets annoyed when he chats up the guards. "There's a real us-and-them attitude here, and some inmates get mad at me because I'm friendly to the guards. I don't get it. Why make things uglier than they have to be?" he asks me. One guard told James recently that he "doesn't seem to be the kind of guy who belongs behind bars," James recounted. "I didn't tell him what I was in for." James considers himself a "normal" person with "control issues" who made a "big, big mistake." He's on antidepressants because "my life here is pretty depressing," he notes. The other inmates often confound him. They're hard to read because, he suspects, many of them are grappling with severe mental illnesses. "They're your best friend one minute, then trying to beat the crap out of you the next," he explains. He had a cellmate for a time who was "too hyper; he made me nervous," says James, so he asked to move out. He gets along with his current cellie, who has been in one prison or another since the age of 16. James has taught him how to string seed beads. The two never talk about their crimes.

James communicates with his elderly mom, who lives in Kelowna, British Columbia, but it's hard for her to travel to see him. He never hears from his sister, Tammy, who stood by helplessly when James's young victim died. Before the murder, they used to talk weekly, and he was closer to her as an adult than to any of his other three siblings and stepbrother. "It's hard for me," says James. "But it's probably much harder for her to deal with what happened."

James is being held in the protective custody West Block section of his prison, some five acres from the 1,500-man "mainline" facility, because his crime was so horrible his co-convicts want to murder him. He has asked me to use only the name James to identify him in case a copy of this book gets into the hands of fellow inmates. He knows his crime would be easily discovered through an Internet search, but cons at his prison have only e-mail access and can't search the Web. He also believes prisoners won't easily identify him from photos reprinted here because he's slightly older now and his appearance has changed. From his first day alone behind bars in an intake prison facility, other inmates, told of his crime by the prison guards, shouted to James from inside their cells what they planned to do to him when they got the chance.

Clare Shelswell (Wilson)

Figure 1.1. A mourner at Clare Shelswell's funeral holds a photo of the five-year-old murder victim after services. *Reprinted by permission from the Canadian Press/Darryl Dyck.*

James cut the throat of his five-year-old stepdaughter, Clare Shelswell, a heart-wrenchingly cute, skinny, blonde kid, who liked pickles and had an impish smile. He used a knife snatched off a kitchen counter in a cottage near Lake Cushman in Hoodsport, Washington, where he and his family were vacationing in 2010. His stunned, frantic wife, Sarah, a nurse, raced into the kitchen when she heard her baby scream. She desperately called 911 as she clutched Clare's throat, struggling to keep the life-saving blood inside the girl's limp body. James hung back, trying, too late, to be helpful and stay out of the way as Sarah screamed for help from the emergency dispatcher.

> *911 Operator: What's going on, Ma'am?*
>
> *Sarah (screaming): Oh my God, my baby, you need to send an ambulance right now.*
>
> *Operator: You need to tell me what's happening and calm down.*
>
> *Sarah: My daughter's throat has just been cut. I need you to come right now! I can't stop the bleeding!*
>
> *. . .*
>
> *Operator: Keep pressure on that cut now, keep pressure on it, please.*
>
> *. . .*
>
> *Sarah: (sobbing) You have to come now, please. Oh my God, please. I don't think she's breathing. Please, please, please . . .*
>
> *Operator: How's she doing, Ma'am?*
>
> *Sarah: She's barely breathing, she's barely breathing.*
>
> *Operator: OK, get her on the floor, on her back.*
>
> *Sarah: She is on her back, but I've got her head up, the cut is on her throat. You have to hurry up! Please, you need to come now!*
>
> *Operator: They are on their way, Ma'am. I dispatched them out.*
>
> *Sarah: You need to send the police, too.*
>
> *Operator: They are getting there, Ma'am.*
>
> *Sarah: She's breathing, but it's really, really ragged and infrequent.*
>
> *Operator: Is she changing color?*
>
> *Sarah: She's really pale. I'm cradling her.*
>
> *Operator: OK, I want you to keep pressure on that wound, whatever you do, don't take the rag off. If it gets soaked through, put another on top of that.*

Sarah: OK, I started on that.

Operator: OK, keep doing that. We have people en route now. If she stops breathing I need to know right away. Is she conscious and alert?

Sarah: No, she is unconscious, not alert of anything. Respiratory rate is four to six a minute.

Operator: Does anyone there know CPR in case she stops breathing?

Sarah: I'm a nurse, but the gash on her throat is so big there's no way it would work. I don't know if [the bleeding] is under control.

Operator: How did this happen?

Sarah: My husband took a knife to her throat.

Operator: Your husb— . . . purposely?

Sarah: Yes.

Operator: We need law enforcement on that call. Where is he now?

Sarah: He's here, but he's away from her. This is what I said: You need to send police, too. I haven't really examined the wound, she's still breathing. Hang in there, Baby, hang in there.

(Talks to someone in the background.)

Operator: What's going on with her right now?

Sarah: Her respiratory rate seems to have improved a little bit. She's still pale, but conforming with the rest of the color of her body.

. . .

Operator: Does he still have the weapon, Ma'am?

Sarah: No, he does not.

Operator: OK, where is the weapon?

Sarah: It's on the floor in the kitchen—where I am, not where he is.

Operator: OK, where is he in the house?

Sarah: He's sitting in the next room, but he's pretty docile right now.

Operator: OK, why is he so docile?

Sarah: Probably because he's in shock over what he just did.

Operator: How's she doing now?

Sarah: Breathing is becoming faster, but definitely more shallow. You need to move right now!

Figure 1.2. Pallbearers take the coffin carrying Clare Shelswell's body from a local church in her hometown of Abbotsford, British Columbia. *Reprinted by permission from the Canadian Press/Darryl Dyck.*

Operator: Is there any way they can get him out of the house?

Sarah: Probably. Why?

Operator: Because we don't need him the house.

Sarah: OK, the only complication with that is if we do that, there might be a second . . .

Operator: If you don't think that's safe to try and get him out of the house, I don't want you to do that. I'm just giving you some ideas.

Sarah: She is not breathing.

Operator: OK, then you're going to get her some air then. Is there anybody else there who can hold that bandage on while you tilt the head back and give her CPR?

Sarah: Yeah, but I'm going to have to keep the phone down.

Operator: OK, just keep it as close to you as you can, and let me know what's going on.

(Sarah's sister-in-law, Tammy, takes the phone while Sarah continues to attend to Clare.)

Tammy: It doesn't look like she's breathing.

Operator: So dad is in the other room?

Tammy: Yeah . . . the air is just coming right through her throat.

. . .

Sarah (in background): Oh my God! They have to hurry now!

Operator: What happened when you tried to attempt CPR?

Sarah (in the background): It sounds like the air is going right through her throat . . . I can't feel her chest rising. (Crying.) Nothing is getting into her chest when I breathe through her mouth, it's all exiting in the gash in her throat! She is not breathing, she is not breathing. Hurry up, Goddamnit! You have to hurry!

Operator: Ma'am, we are getting there as fast as we can. Please try to get some air into her. Is there someone helping you? Can you feel a pulse, a heartbeat, anything?

Sarah (in the background): Her chest is not rising at all, the gash in her throat is too big, they have to hurry up!

Operator: They are coming as fast as they can.

Sarah (in the background): Give me another rag! Oh my God, my baby . . .

. . .

Operator: What started this?

Tammy: I don't even know, I was gone, I just got back here.

Sarah (in the background): Please, they have to hurry!

Operator: Ma'am do you feel comfortable moving her out of the house at all?

Tammy: I don't think that's a good idea.

Sarah (in the background): There's no difference, she's dying!

Operator: Is the dad still in the house?

Tammy: Yes.

Operator: What is he doing?

Tammy: Sitting on the floor.

Operator: Is he alert at all?

Sarah (in the background): It's not him, you need to get the ambulance here for her!

Operator: Can you get her outside? If you can get her outside away from dad, we have a better chance of aid coming in without law enforcement.

Tammy: That's not important, that's not relevant!

Operator: Ma'am, can you get her outside?

Tammy: There's no point in that.

Operator: Why is that?

Tammy: He's not doing anything, he's just sitting on the floor.

Sarah (in the background): Where are the paramedics?

Operator: I can't make my units come in without law enforcement being there.

Tammy: There's nobody here!

Operator: We need to do something to try and save her.

Tammy: If he leaves, can you come in?

Operator: Yes.

Tammy (speaking to James): Can you leave?

Tammy (speaking to operator): He's leaving.

Operator: Tell him to get as far as he can but stay in the area.

. . .

Operator: Someone needs to tell me where dad went now.

Tammy: He went to other side of property, he's sitting outside.

Operator: How far away?

Tammy: He's literally non-coherent.

Operator: I know. Please answer my question. How far away from the house is he?

Tammy: The next lot over. Listen to me: She has not been breathing for approximately ten minutes at this point. If the paramedics don't get there STAT she is not going to survive. How far out are they?

Operator: I've advised paramedics dad is out of the house. Does he have any weapons on him?

Tammy: No, he has nothing.

Operator: OK, stand by. What's going on with her now?

Tammy: She's dead. We're doing CPR but she's effectively dead unless they're here now.

. . .

Sarah (in the background): How far out are they?!

Operator: Can you give me [a] description of [the] male?

Tammy: 5'8", 250 pounds, brown hair, shorts and a polo shirt. I can't tell from here. I really wasn't paying attention.

Operator: You were not there when this started?

Tammy: I was not there, no one witnessed it.

Operator: Is the dad still on the other property?

Tammy: Yes.

Sarah (in the background): We can deal with legal ramifications later! Can we please not have this be about a homicide?

Tammy: Sarah, the mom, is doing CPR.

Operator: How many people are in the house?

Tammy: Two of us, Clare, and two people upstairs.

Operator: What are the people upstairs doing?

Tammy: There's another daughter. She's upstairs with my sister-in-law, trying to keep her away from this scene.

Operator: How old is the daughter?

Tammy: Clare is five.

Operator: Is that the one with injury?

Tammy: Yes.

Tammy (speaking to James): They want you to stay where you are.

Operator: Who's there, Ma'am?

Tammy: The paramedics and police.

(Sobbing in the background.)

When police and paramedics arrived, James was sitting on a swing in a gazebo outside the cottage. James was "stoic," a responding officer noted in the police report, and he told them Clare was inside, and that he had just cut her throat. His wife later told investigators that the attack occurred after an angry argument about disciplining the children, Clare and her eight-year-old sister, Suzy. Finally, James told his wife "not to worry," that he would "take care of things," before walking Clare downstairs to the kitchen. He told police that when he took Clare's small hand into his own to lead her to the kitchen, he knew that he was going to kill her. James was booked into Mason County Jail, charged with first-degree murder, and held on $3 million bail.

The brutality of the crime riveted the public and the police who responded to the scene. "In 37 years, this is the most horrific, senseless crime I've ever seen," County Sheriff Chief Deputy Dean Byrd told CBC-TV News in British Columbia, where the family was living at the time.[1] "How does a person make the decision to take the life of a five-year-old girl in such a violent and horrific way? How does that happen?"

Sarah avoided the reporters who clamored for her reactions, asking that she and her family be "left in peace" to grieve "our beautiful baby girl. My daughter Clare has been killed. Anyone with a heart will be affected by this story, especially due to the brutal way in which she died," she said in a statement released to the media. "Asking us how we are doing is unhelpful. Put yourself in our shoes and give yourself an answer."

Hundreds of mourners turned out for Clare's funeral at the family's local church in Abbotsford, British Columbia, that featured photos of Clare and her worn green teddy bear, "Baby," which sat forlornly next to a drawing of a rainbow by Clare. Pastor Terry Kaethler recalled Clare as an "engaging girl" with a rare sensitivity and compassion beyond her years. She had a generous soul and "saw beauty where few other people would see it," he said. The principal of her kindergarten said Clare often waited to start playing at recess until everyone who wanted to join in was part of the group. Clare's sister, Suzy, talked of her joy reading books to her little sister, noting that in her glasses Clare had "quite the look." Sarah, who sat in the front row of the church with Suzy, said in a statement read for her that the family was struggling with a new life seen "through a glass darkly. This past week has been the most difficult of our lives. We have said good-bye to our beautiful baby girl and have today begun to look at what life without Clare might look like," she added.

Figure 1.3. James, in a bulletproof vest and handcuffs, is led into a Washington State court to face murder charges for killing his five-year-old stepdaughter, Clare. *Courtesy of the Mason County Journal/Kevan Moore.*

It was difficult to imagine James committing such a crime. Even his ex-wife spoke up for him. He had no arrest record. He briefly pleaded not guilty, offering a mental illness defense based on his struggles with bipolar disorder and anger issues. Sarah would say in an interview months later with Canadian broadcaster CTV that before the attack on Clare, James never exhibited any significant signs of violence, never threatened to hurt anyone, and "faithfully" took his medications for his disorder.[2] James quickly changed his plea to guilty to first-degree murder with aggravating circumstances to "spare his family the anguish of a trial," his attorney said in court. "He has apologized to his wife and family. He loved his family," said lawyer Ron Sergi. "He lost control. He never saw this type of conduct coming; he was as surprised as anyone else by this. He asked for forgiveness, well aware he wasn't deserving of it." As James entered his plea before the judge, sobbing, he said he wished he could trade his life for Clare's. Mason County Superior Court Judge Toni Sheldon sentenced him to the maximum time allowed in prison, citing Clare's vulnerability, the stepfather's abuse of trust, and the destructive nature of the crime for the family.

"Clare's death has been shocking and devastating beyond comprehension to me and my family," Sarah said to the court in her victim impact statement. "As I was preparing this, I realized how impossible it is for me to truly describe who Clare was, the spark that made her uniquely Clare, the essence of the little person that she was. Clare was a bubbly, smart, loving, creative, vibrant five-year-old girl. She was cheeky and had a fabulous sense of humor, even though she couldn't quite figure out how knock-knock jokes were supposed to go. Her laugh was infectious." Her mom recalled how her daughter "saw beauty" everywhere, especially in "wild flowers most would call weeds, or in caterpillar-bitten leaves. When beach-combing with my parents, Clare wanted to keep all of the broken shells she had picked up because they were all special."

Clare "never got to see her sixth birthday, or celebrate the first party she would have had with classmates instead of just family," Sarah added. "I'll never get to take her dress-shopping, and she'll never attend her prom. I won't get to teach her how to drive. I will never see her off on her first date or help heal her heart with a bowl of ice cream after her first breakup with a boyfriend. What remains of my baby girl this side of eternity is a bag of ashes inside a pretty urn, photographs and memories.

"The life and experiences that James has robbed from Clare, and the joy that he has taken from me and my family by ending her young life are irreplaceable. All I can do is trust that the sentence James receives today will reflect the significant and devastating impact of his actions and our tremendous loss," she said.

Sarah's sister, Helen Hutt, also read a statement in court about the tragedy that turned her life "upside down." Hutt had been friends with James for several years before he fell in love with her sister, he explained to me. James was introduced to Hutt by a cousin, who wanted to put him in touch with other young people when he first moved to Vancouver. He grew so close to Hutt's parents that he called them Mom and Dad and walked into their house without knocking, just as if he was one of their kids, he recalled.

"My faith has been shaken to the core," Hutt said in court. "Nothing people do, or are capable of doing, will shock me ever again." In a particularly poignant note, she mourned not only the loss of Clare, but of James as well. "In one night, my family lost two people that we loved and cared about," she said. Sarah, too, was devastated not only by the vacuum left in her life by Clare's murder, but also by the loss of James. "I have lost a daughter and husband," she said in her statement. "Suzy lost her little sister and the man both she and Clare called Dad."

THE TIMES TUESDAY, JANUARY 4, 2011 A3

Upfront

Today's
**SWARMJAM
DEAL** see page 13
"Get in on the Buzz"

Little Clare captured our hearts

CLARE, *from page A1*

Wilson's defence attorney, said his client fully acknowledged his responsibility for the crime and pleaded guilty to first-degree murder with aggravating circumstances to spare his family the anguish of a trial." He apologized to his wife and family," Ron Sergi said. "He lost control. He never saw this type of conduct coming; he was as surprised as anyone else by this . . . he asked for forgiveness, well aware he wasn't deserving of it."

Sergi said Wilson had bipolar disorder, but the condition was not deemed an adequate defence for the crime.

Sarah Wilson made it clear she never hinged her healing on a long sentence for her husband.

She is looking to her faith in God, positive memories of Clare and her eldest Suzy for that.

Despite the evil perpetrated against her daughter, Wilson still maintains hope for humanity.

Since Clare's death she has experienced repeated acts of goodness from her church, family, friends and perfect strangers.

> "[She's] . . . a reason to seek goodness and not get sucked into the darkness because if I go there, she gets sucked down with me."
>
> – Sarah Wilson, Clare's mother

Suzy also gives a powerful reason to get out of bed and put one foot in front of the other.

"[She's]. . . a reason to seek goodness and not get sucked into the darkness because if I go there, she gets sucked down with me," said Sarah.

"I could become jaded and give into bitterness, but it's a choice.

"And I have to make that choice every day."

–WITH FILES FROM RAFE ARNOTT AND CHRISTINA TOTH

RIGHT: Godson Elementary teacher Allison Smith wept as she recalled Clare Shelswell's sunny character, just before the little girl's celebration of life service at Mountain Park Community Church during Clare's funeral in

ABOVE: Sarah Wilson recalled how Clare lit up any room she entered and how difficult it continues to be for her and the family to cope with Clare's death.

– JEAN KONDA-WITTE/TIMES

Figure 1.4. The local *Abbotsford-Mission Times* revisits the murder that rattled a nation, and recalls a community stunned by a horrific crime that ended the life of a special little girl. *Courtesy of the* Abbotsford-Mission Times.

Among Sarah's most gut-wrenching struggles in the aftermath of her daughter's murder was the relentlessly recurrent image in her mind of Clare bleeding to death on the kitchen floor of the cottage, she told CTV News in an interview months later.[3] Sarah, a deeply religious woman, is convinced she'll see her daughter in the afterlife, and that's the "biggest thing" that keeps her going, she said. Her daughter Suzy also remains a "powerful reason to get out of bed and put one foot in front of the other," Sarah told the *Abbotsford-Mission Times.*[4] "She's a reason to seek goodness and not get sucked into the darkness because if I go there, she gets sucked down with me. I could become jaded and give in to bitterness, but it's a choice, and I have to make that choice every day."

Long after she presented her victim statement in court, Sarah laid bare the particularly agonizing pain of a mother who loved and trusted, and thought she knew, a warm, affectionate man who would inexplicably murder her daughter. Sarah recalled that the day she spoke in court "the one piece I could not prepare for in any way was my emotional response at seeing him again. That was pretty hard," she said, crying.[5] "I haven't just lost a daughter, I've lost my husband, too."

James, who still routinely refers to "my wife," would tell me two years later that far harder than going to prison for 55 years was losing Sarah.

TWO

JAMES TELLS HIS STORY

James's crime grabbed international media notice because of its particular brutality, but also because it was especially perplexing given his history with his family. I decided to reach out to him by e-mail in prison to ask if he would be willing to talk to me about what happened and maybe write an account of his life and his crime for this book. To my surprise, he agreed. "My story is a sad one, but, yes, if it will help you with your book and hopefully help others in the future then I would gladly like to help you," he wrote back. After that, we e-mailed and talked on the phone frequently for several months, and, periodically, pages of his handwritten "chapter" appeared in my mailbox. James is a friendly, intelligent, articulate, apparently compassionate man who still seems stunned by what happened. He's aware that he has a "problem with rage," as he puts it, and has been treated for bipolar disorder, yet he repeatedly emphasizes that he "makes no excuses" for what happened. He seems devastated by his crime and is desperately seeking some kind of redemption, which he fears he'll never find. He chose to summarize his background, highlighting events that may have influenced him or offer some kind of insight into who he is and what he did. Everything that follows was written by him, except for the account of the actual murder, which he recounted to me over the phone because it was difficult for him to put it on paper.

To start at the beginning, I was born in Vernon, British Columbia, in 1980. We moved to Spokane two years later, shortly after my little sister was born. My first memories are from our first house in Spokane when I was about four years old. I remember sharing a bedroom in the basement with one of my brothers, and I have vague memories of climbing trees in our backyard.

We moved to Biloxi in Mississippi when I was still four. I remember very little of the drive, but I know we left a box of crayons in the back window and they melted into a lump of very pretty colors. While in Mississippi, I had my fifth birthday. We had spinach with dinner, and I liked it. I split my head on a slide at the park while we lived there—one of many injuries I had during childhood. My dad told me that I liked to stand on the edge of the tub after a bath and would inevitably fall off and smack my head on the wall. My dad was stationed at the Keesler Air Force Base in Biloxi for hurricane season as he was in the Air National Guard.

About six months after moving to Biloxi, we moved back to Spokane and stopped on the way to see the Grand Canyon, Carlsbad Caverns, and the Petrified Forest. We moved into a two-bedroom house in Spokane. During that time, life as a kid was pretty normal. My mom helped with our schoolwork and kept us in line most of the time. Spankings were dished out for serious transgressions, and most of those were handled by my dad. We went to school, camped in the summer, and sometimes traveled to visit grandparents around holidays.

My mom left my dad when I was nine years old. She packed all four of us kids into the car and went to my aunt's house in British Columbia. My parents were divorced when I was ten, and my dad was remarried later that year.

A quick aside: There were four children when my parents were together. Number Five died before I was born. The order of the four of us goes as follows: Ray (six years older), Steven (one-and-a-half years older), me, and Tammy (two years younger and the only girl). Ray, being a few years older, was like an overseer, and generally wanted the other three of us to leave him alone. Steven, Tammy and I were the "Terrible Trio." If one of us was caught in trouble, then the other two were around the corner. We played as a group and were punished as a group.

Steven moved down to Washington to live with my dad, his new wife, and her son, Arthur (seven years younger than me). This happened when I was ten, and I moved down the following year because I missed my dad and brother. I lived with my dad in Spokane until 1995 when I then moved back north to live with my mom, and her new husband; and all four original children were back home. My brother Steven moved with me due to events that took place in Spokane.

Figure 2.1. A photo of a younger Clare Shelswell shows her smiling while wearing her glasses, which her big sister, Suzy, said gave her "quite the look." James (right), her stepfather and the man she called "Dad," was convicted of her murder. Courtesy of KOMO 4 News, Seattle.

My dad and stepmom, K, fought constantly over the three children in their care. Dad took Steven's and my side, while K defended Arthur. Because of this, K was mean to Steven and me, but for some reason, she really took it out on me. I even recall her telling me that their fighting was my fault. And, on a separate occasion, she told me that my bed-wetting problem was done on purpose to cause them to fight. I had started wetting the bed about a month after moving in with my dad in Spokane and continued until I moved back in with my mom. I maintain that it was stress-related. Not only did K blame me, but she also used to tell me that I was fat and stupid. She even hit me on rare occasions when I was about 13. I never told my dad or anyone else besides Steven about any of it. It wasn't until adulthood that it occurred to me that her behavior was inappropriate.

Basically, life in Spokane at that time was hell for me. The only reason my brother and I stayed was because both my mom and dad said they didn't want us jumping between parents every couple of years. In the end, Steven was the one to push K over the edge, and she kicked us both out. So by 1995, Steven and I were back at my mom's house, now in Kelowna, British Columbia.

Life in Kelowna was mostly fine, though my stepdad was a rough guy to deal with. He never had kids of his own, so to live with four teenagers was stressful for him. Ray was the first one of us to leave home. He moved to Vancouver by himself and started working full-time. Also at this time, our Terrible Trio lost a member as Steven started trying to act mature and felt that entailed keeping Tammy and me out of trouble.

Tammy was the next to move out the following summer due to problems she was having [with our stepdad and mom].

Quick fill-in: My mom and stepdad would start drinking from the time he came home from work until they went to bed. This caused its own tensions, and a lot of *fighting between my mom and stepdad. I remember a family get-together in 1996 when my stepdad started yelling at me for no reason that anyone but he understood. I tried defending myself, but I wasn't sure what was going on, and he sent me to bed at seven o'clock with family and friends still all partying around the house. I know quite a few people left because of this, and my mom had to calm me down because I was hysterical and on the verge of hyperventilating.*

Things were fine between my stepdad and me for the remainder of that school year. He spent the majority of his energy fighting with Steven then, so Steven moved in with my grandparents to finish high school (Steven and I were in the same grade all through school because our parents held him back a year right from the first grade). So for my senior year I was alone with mom and my stepdad. I had a job with a farmer down the road since 1995, and also babysat three or four neighborhood kids. When I wasn't working, I was hanging out with friends, hiking, and riding mountain bikes.

To recall a few key moments of my teens when I was thirteen or fourteen years old, I remember K making me so mad and frustrated that I tried to strangle myself with my sheets. My brother Steven put that to a stop. Another time I pushed Steven down a flight of stairs for locking me out of the house. My sister let me in, and I went straight for my brother, and pushed him down the stairs. He tumbled to the first landing, and got up, furious. We ended up fighting around the living room with Tammy screaming at us to stop. Steven was bruised and a couple of my mom's knick-knacks were broken, and that was all the damage. But I sometimes thought of that day later because I was so very angry and I wanted to get even with my brother so badly.

A couple of years later while working for the farmer, we were in the bed of his truck, throwing pruning clippings onto a mulch pile. The farmer thought it would be funny to push me out of the truck. I wasn't hurt, but I was so mad that I pulled a knife on him that I always carried while working. He talked me down and apologized for pushing me, and work continued as usual.

Oh, and I also ran away from home once when I was about fourteen because K hit me. My dad was at work late so I called him from a neighbor's house to come and get me when he was on his way home. I also ran away from school in fifth grade because my classmates were picking on me, and the teacher didn't stop them. I was missing for four hours, and my mom was frantic when I returned to the school. All I did was hide in the trees at the park down the block from school.

As you can see, I have a history of irrational overreactions.

I moved out of my mom's place right after I graduated from high school, at the very end of June 1998. I moved from Kelowna down to Vancouver to live with my oldest brother, Ray. I got a job working in a hydraulic repair shop, cleaning up and assisting the mechanics. It was a good job but it only lasted eight months before I was laid off due to a slowdown in business. About a month before my layoff, Ray and I moved to the suburb of Maple Ridge, . . . but a couple of months after my layoff he asked me to move out. So I was out on my own in the world.

It was at a Halloween party of 1998 that I met my first wife, Sherri, and we started dating. She was only a few months younger than me, and very smart and focused on her education at the time. She worked hard at her job and on her schoolwork. She was taking some extra courses at the local high school to make the college jump easier the next year. The qualities I found most attractive in Sherri were her drive, her work ethic, intelligence, and her heart. She loved helping people. Over our eight-year relationship her drive and work ethic seemed to fade, and for the last four years I supported our household almost 100 percent. She dropped out of college before finishing her degree, so we had a boatload of debt and only one income.

I attended college from the fall of 1999 to the end of the winter 2002 semester. I worked full-time during the summer and worked part-time while attending college full-time. I worked at a gas station as an assistant manager during this time, although without the title and without the extra pay—just the extra work and responsibility. I quit my job there at the end of 2001 because my hours were cut. I understand why they did it. I had numerous outbursts costing them both money and customers. I only recall one such incident, but I know there were more. I was never written up or warned after any one of them; they just moved to edge me out. The one incident I remember was in the summer of 2001. I went outside to fill up a customer's barbecue propane bottle; I checked the date stamp to make sure the seals were good. It's illegal to refill them past the date stamp. I informed the fellow that his tank had expired and offered to sell him a new one. The man got frustrated and tried to talk me into filling it anyway. I said I couldn't, as it would be risking my job and his safety. The man got mad and started to climb into his car. I told him that he would have to pay to dispose of his propane tank, and he told me to go fuck myself. From my angle, I only started becoming angry when he acted up. He kept telling me I was ruining his barbeque party and that I was trying to rip him off. Now, I've done some dishonest things in my past (lying, shoplifting, etc.), but I always prided myself on my work ethic. I took offense at his comments. I didn't even think about what I was doing. I just grabbed his propane bottle and threw it at his car and dented it. He had just started to drive away so he, of course, stopped, and that was when realization and panic hit me. I ran for the store and phoned the owner immediately. The customer walked in after me and I handed him the phone to speak to the owner. The company ended up covering the cost to repair his car. (I've tried to remember my feelings on some of these other issues, but they aren't coming to me.)

I was with Sherri from 1998 to 2006. We were married in 2004. It was a weird engagement, and it makes me look like a total ass, but I guess I was. I had told Sherri numerous times that I wasn't interested in marriage because of the way both of my parents' marriages had gone. On Valentine's Day 2002, I gave Sherri a promise ring just meant as a token. Well, she called her best friend to say we were engaged. She was so excited that I just went along with it. Upon reflection, yes, I should have clarified things, but I wasn't ready for that yet.

Our relationship was pretty easy-going. We both had similar interests, so fighting was fairly rare. Money was a hot topic, though. She spent it, and I yelled at her for it, but the cycle continued. The one spot where our relationship was far from normal was our sex life. I'd rather not even mention it, but it is pertinent to the main incident in my life. Sherri and I had an "open" marriage. Our parents were made aware of this after our marriage dissolved, because that's the reason it fell apart.

Even before I met Sherri, shortly after I moved to Vancouver, a cousin introduced me to some people around my age. Ray, being six years older than me and much more mature, hung out with an older crowd. My cousin introduced me to her daycare provider's daughter, and some of her friends. This would be my connection to Sherri and then, eventually, to Sarah (my second wife, and the mother of Clare, my stepdaughter who I killed). Helen was another of the girls I met through that first introduction. We became good friends, and I spent a lot of time hanging out at her house, and even called her parents Mom and Dad. Sarah was their other daughter, but she was never around, so I didn't meet her until 2006. But throughout that time, from the day I first met Sherri to the time I met Sarah, we kept in touch with Helen, so when Helen was married in 2006 we were invited to the wedding. Sherri dragged me along to the bachelorette part for Helen, which is where I finally met Sarah. Things by then between Sherri and I had already digressed to being pretty much roommates, just sharing a bed. In 2005 I had applied to become a police officer, but was turned down in 2006 because they said the debts incurred by my spouse displayed a lack of financial control on my part. This concerned them as they felt it would make me susceptible to bribes. That was the final straw in my relation-ship with Sherri.

When I met Sarah, I felt a connection with her that I had never felt with Sherri. I had never put much credit to the idea of "soul mates" before then, but Sarah was defi-nitely my soul mate. After just my first phone call with Sarah, I knew I loved her. We dated behind Sherri's back for a month before Sarah and I admitted to each other how we felt. I told Sherri I wanted to separate. She was crushed, and that was the end of my first marriage. It was your typical "you cheating bastard" break-up, and I was the bastard. I felt terrible about it, but as my relationship with Sarah was just taking off, all the other great things I was feeling squashed the ugliness with Sherri. Six years later, I still remember almost every minute Sarah and I spent together. But I've hurt her so terribly.

Even though Sarah filed for divorce after what I did to Clare, and remarried, in my heart she is still my wife. I loved her with every fiber of my being, and my ultimate punishment is living with the knowledge that I betrayed her and broke her heart. I took away one of her precious little babies, along with her best friend and husband. I was the one person who could have comforted her through such a tragic loss, yet I was the one who caused it. It's like a knife through my heart. I left behind two families, my own and my parents', with broken hearts.

I don't quite understand what happened the day I killed Clare. I was very, very angry. It sounds strange to say, but part of it was related to how much I loved Sarah. She was everything to me. But because of that she could hit all of my nerve centers. I sometimes think it would have been better for me to be with a woman I wasn't so wrapped [up] in. We had a perfect life the first year or so we were married. We had laughs and fun times, Sarah and me and the girls. The girls were nuts about me, and I loved them. Things started bothering me the next year. There were times I would feel sad or angry for no really clear reason.

I tried to commit suicide, twice. The first time I overdosed on medication with painkillers, any pills I could find in the house, after Sarah and I had a huge fight. I emailed my goodbyes from the living room while Sarah was sleeping in the bedroom. But I didn't know her email would ping on her phone, and she woke up and came in the living room, and said, "What's going on?" and called an ambulance and they pumped my stomach in the emergency room. After another suicide attempt a while later I ended up staying with her parents for about three or four months. I think I was overwhelmed by the family. I loved Sarah's girls, Suzy and Clare, and considered them my daughters. Clare especially was so excited to see me when I came home from work every day. She was the one who would run to the door, excited, with a smile on her face. But they were a lot of work, and Clare could be a troublemaker. Sarah and I were both working full-time. Sarah was working as a nurse, and I was selling parts for [a trucking company]. But somehow, I felt like I was getting stuck with more of the kid work. I was always the go-to guy. Sarah rolled out of bed in the morning and went straight to work, earlier than I did, and I had to get the girls up and ready for school, then drop them off. I usually picked them up from school, too. I felt like I was being taken advantage of. I thought that Sarah could have been more appreciative. I felt she didn't pay me in kind for everything I was doing, and I thought [I] was entitled to more. Actually, I don't think I was ready for kids then; I was too immature. Of course, no one would ever let me get close to children now.

At one point Sarah suggested I see a psychiatrist because she thought I had some of the same symptoms as bipolar people she had seen at the hospital. So I did see a doctor who diagnosed me as a bipolar, but not too enthusiastically, I guess. He gave me a prescription for Depakote, a mood stabilizer, which seemed to help sometimes. But he didn't really help me in any other way, besides writing out prescriptions. So I went to a counselor for anger management. But he eventually told me that he thought we were done, and I didn't really feel like I got anything out of it. It was costing a lot of money and it wasn't helping.

So I kept being angry and anxious, and I was getting worried. Sarah told me if I tried to commit suicide again I couldn't stay with her parents, and that made me feel trapped. I was worried about how angry I could get with the girls. I reminded myself of how my dad acted sometimes. [My dad and I have] talked about this. Sometimes you start out angry, then get angry with yourself because of the way you're behaving, and that just makes you angrier. Sarah and I fought about disciplining the girls. We both spanked the girls, but Sarah was upset because I hit them harder, and when I spanked them I could be really angry. I used way more force than was necessary. One time I was in the living room, and the girls were making a lot of noise in their bedroom with the door shut. I told them to quiet down a few times, and they didn't. I stood up, walked over to the door and threw it open to yell at them. The door smashed Clare in the face and split her lip. Sarah had to take her to the emergency room. Poor kid. Clare was such a beautiful little girl, and there she was, at four years old, with a scar on her lip because

JAMES TELLS HIS STORY 39

of me. That's a way to make you feel like a monster. I felt horrible about that. Another time, I don't remember what was going on, but I was in the driveway with Clare and she blurted out, "I hate you, Daddy." I got so angry I slammed her against my truck and I told her never to say anything like that again. She was so scared she peed herself, and I had to take her inside to change her. When Sarah told her parents about that, they contacted Child Protective Services. They sent someone out to talk to Sarah and her parents, but they didn't talk to me because by that time I was back in the hospital after another suicide attempt, and nothing ever came of it.

Things seemed to be better for a while for a few months in early 2010, then in the spring I was getting angrier again. Maybe the medication wasn't working. I don't mean to say that I wasn't responsible for what I did and I don't want to blame the medication for what happened. But I was suddenly, sometimes surprisingly, livid about things. Once when Sarah and I were arguing, I suddenly hauled off and slapped her across the face, hard. And we both said, "Whoa, where did that come from?" I had never done anything like that, and it had never entered my mind to do it. I think I was feeling disrespected by Sarah because I felt like I was getting stuck with most of the home and kid responsibilities, and she didn't recognize that.

The weekend I killed Clare, we had decided to spend a few days in a cabin in Washington, and take the girls, my sister, Tammy, and my stepbrother, Arthur, and his girlfriend along. I don't do very well on vacations. I get anxious and irritable. I can't remember a vacation with Sarah when I didn't blow up over one thing or another. We were going to go to the cabin for the weekend and Monday, but Sarah talked me in to calling in sick for Friday, too, so we'd have an extra day. I did that, but I didn't like doing it; it made me feel guilty. Then, just as we were packing to go, I smelled smoke, and I looked outside and saw that a hedge next door was burning. Someone had set a bush on fire. But we just shut the windows and locked up and took off. I was already so upset about things that Sarah asked me if I wanted to cancel the vacation and just stay home, but I didn't want to disappoint my sister and brother, and I was looking forward to spending time with them.

I don't remember everything that happened that weekend. Things went pretty well at first. I had fun with everyone, and the adults spent time playing board games in the cottage and talking while the girls watched TV. Thinking back on it, it wasn't so great for the kids. They were just stuck in front of the TV while the adults talked. Things got ugly pretty quickly, and Sarah and I went at it. At one point while we were fighting,

I told Sarah it might be a good idea, and better for the girls, if we separated. Then she threatened to drive home with the kids and leave me behind. But after a while things calmed down and Sarah went upstairs to one of the bedrooms. Later, Tammy walked into the living room and asked Clare if she had been chewing on her shirt. We were having trouble then with Clare chewing on everything—on her toys and on her clothes. She told my sister, "No, I haven't been chewing on my shirt." But you could see Clare had been chewing on her shirt because it was all crumpled up and covered with slobber. That made me angry. I told her that Auntie Tammy couldn't walk her to the lake now because she couldn't trust her, and Clare got upset about that.

Before dinnertime, Arthur and I were getting the food together to grill, and I had a question about the corn, so I went up to the bedroom to ask Sarah about it. She was lying on the bed, and it turned out the fight wasn't over, after all, and she was still angry, so we started going at it again. Then Arthur shows up at the door with Clare in his arms; he had found her in the living room crying. So there she is with tears in her eyes, looking for more sympathy. I felt like I was surrounded by people who were targeting me as a bully and it made me angry. I grabbed Clare to take her back downstairs. I think my intention right then was to kill her. I kept saying in my head: "If Clare's not here, then Sarah and I can't argue. If Clare's not here, then Sarah and I can't argue." I took Clare into the kitchen, and grabbed a knife on the counter. I held her down on the floor and cut her throat with the knife. I wanted everyone to hurt. I assumed it would be an instant death. But it wasn't. Clare was still breathing and I screamed up to Sarah to call 911. Sarah ran into the kitchen and started screaming: "My baby! What did you do to my baby?"

I stayed out of the way then, and hoped that Sarah could save Clare's life. I saw Tammy walking up to the house with Suzy and told her to go around the back and take her upstairs so Suzy couldn't see what was happening. I think there was a problem on the 911 call because they were afraid to send someone right away because I was there. I ended up going outside and sat on a porch swing next door and waited for the ambulance to arrive. When the police came, one of them drew a gun on me and put me down on the ground. He dug his knee into my back and handcuffed me and put me in a police car for six hours.

I think of that day every day, and I dream about it at night. It eats me alive. I wish I could take it back. But that's impossible.

———

As I lie here and think about my current life situation, it occurs to me that while it may be difficult in some aspects, life has become so much simpler. My freedoms are restricted and, because of cost, my contact with my family is severely limited. I have no money on my phone account so I can't call my dad, and I know from his last letter that is what he's waiting for. He's so busy that writing to me takes too much time, and is usually forgotten, even though it's my only method of contact right now. I have even less contact with the rest of my family. It's even harder for them to visit me as they are all in Canada. Of course, most of them don't want to contact me. I haven't heard from Tammy since Clare's death. But I manage as I can.

As for the simpler side of things . . . my meals are prepared for me, and I don't have to clean up after myself, other than throwing out my garbage. I have a bed and a roof over my head, and plenty of time to contemplate anything I happen to focus on. This is both good and bad, of course. Bad because of the sorrow and pain it brings me for what I've done, but I look at it as penance for the suffering I have caused my family and friends. In my case, that also includes Clare's family and friends, as they were one and the same before this tragedy. The benefit in having lots of time to think comes from reflection on my faults and allows the time to consider how I can improve myself.

Since I cannot rewind time and take back what happened, I figure the best way to show Clare I still love her and think of her is to make myself a better person. And what truly hurts me the most is that I know she would hug me right now and tell me she loves me. She was a special girl with a big heart. She loved everyone and was always quick to forgive any hurts against her no matter who caused it. I wish I had recognized sooner what a light she was in my life. My biggest comfort now is knowing she is safe from any further harm, and she can finally have that tea party with Jesus that she used to pretend to have.

I find it curious that, after a reasonably good day with no problems, I can still be depressed on antidepressants. I was content all day, happily working away on a beading project. Now, here it is after dinner, and I can't shake this feeling of sadness. No particular thoughts or memories come with it. It's just a sense of sadness and loss. I can understand why I would feel that, but why only sometimes?

Abbotsford • Mission

times

TUESDAY
January 4, 2011

18 Sports Year in
Review Part Two

f 🐦 **» NEWS, SPORTS, WEATHER & ENTERTAINMENT »** abbotsfordtimes.com

Tragedy unfolds for Abby family

Slaying of child rallies local community

ROCHELLE BAKER
rbaker@abbotsfordtimes.com

News story OF THE YEAR **2010**

Sadly, perhaps the most notable story of the year involved the violent death of five-year-old Clare Shelswell this summer at the hands of her stepfather.

The whole community of Abbotsford, and people living on both sides of the border were horrified by the death of the young girl, who by all accounts had nothing but smiles and hugs for everyone she knew.

Peter James Wilson, 30, slashed his stepdaughter's throat with a knife June 27 while the family was on vacation in Hoodsport, Wash. after an argument with his wife about disciplining Clare and her older sister Suzy.

The little girl's body was discovered after police received a frantic 911 call from her mother, Sarah Wilson.

Wilson — who has both U.S. and Canadian citizenship — was arrested without incident at the scene by Mason County sheriffs and held in jail pending $3 million bail.

Immediately following her death those who knew Clare and her family, or those in Abbotsford who felt for their pain, rallied to support the survivors of the crime.

Mountain Park Community Church, where the family is part of the congregation, established a trust fund.

There had been an outpouring of support, prayers and offers of help for the family both in Abbotsford, and from the first responders and community in Washington, stated officials with the church.

Grief counsellors were sent in to help students and staff at the elementary school that Clare and her sister attended.

More than 300 people packed Mountain Park Community Church for the young girl's memorial service on July 7.

Mourners viewed coloured crayon portraits of smiling butterflies and rainbows on a memory table, where among the photos of Clare, sat a well-loved, slightly worn green teddy called "Baby."

Senior pastor Terry Kaethler, who remembered Clare as an "engaging girl," with a compassionate nature beyond her years said.

"She picked the flowers no one else wanted. She'd keep the shells that were broken, the leaves eaten by caterpillars. She transformed broken things that others didn't want into things of beauty."

On October 22, Wilson was sentenced to more than 55 years in a U.S. prison for his crime.

Mason County Superior Court Judge Toni Sheldon outlined the reasons for Wilson's "exceptional sentence," citing Clare's vulnerability, the stepfather's abuse of trust and the destructive nature

> "She picked the flowers no one else wanted. She'd keep the shells that were broken, the leaves eaten by caterpillars. She transformed broken things that others didn't want into things of beauty."
>
> — Terry Kaethler pastor

of the crime for the family.

During her victim-impact statement, Sarah Wilson told an emotional courtroom about losing her young daughter described as a bub-

bly, smart, loving, creative, vibrant five-year-old girl whose favourite food was pickles.

"Clare's death has been shocking and devastating beyond compre-

hension to me and my family," she said, noting her daughter would never celebrate her sixth birthday.

see CLARE, page 42

Clare Shelswell's death in June, 2010 rocked the community of Abbotsford which responded with an outpouring of support to try and help the family cope with her brutal slaying at the hand's of her stepfather Peter James Wilson. Wilson pleaded guilty to first-degree murder in a Washington State courtroom in October and was sentenced to more than 55 years in prison.

Figure 2.2. The front page of the *Abbotsford-Mission Times*, the newspaper in Clare Shelswell's British Columbia hometown, marks her murder as the story with the greatest impact in the community in 2010. *Courtesy of the Abbotsford-Mission Times.*

From my experience with similar states of mind, it's usually brought on by a bad occurrence such as arguing with someone, being yelled at, or receiving bad news. There's no rhyme or reason to this one now, though, and such has been the case over the last few months—hence the reason for getting back on antidepressants to begin with.

I had a valuable thought yesterday that I shared with my cellmate. I think it would be a good addition here. While my crime was a tragedy and caused tremendous harm to family and friends, I am a better person now than I was before. The last couple of years before Clare's murder, I had turned into a prideful, self-centered ass. I was worried only about my own happiness, and making more money to add to my happiness.

I sit in a jail cell now with nothing, no family, nothing to do all day but think about what happened. All of it humbled me. I still have weak moments when my ego flares up and gets me in trouble, but mostly I am stripped of pride. The biggest reason is that I recognize that ego/pride only lead a person to conflict. Every single instance of arguing or fighting that I have witnessed since coming to prison is a result of one, or usually both, parties feeling slighted or that their manly persona was threatened. Everyone wants their ego stroked. The point is that my own pride was my downfall, and now I recognize that I am able to prevent most trouble that has arisen involving me.

Secondly, with a number of books I have read about Buddhism, yoga, and Christianity, I find the biggest rule that stands out is to love. Love everyone: your-self, your enemies and your friends. The Buddha teaches to let go of your attachments whether they are possessions, grudges, or whatever you cling to. I find that I am happier when I can help others. It could be as simple as someone needing to talk to about something bothering them, or it could needing a bar of soap or some coffee. The old me would have said, "No, I worked hard for my money and I'm going to enjoy it." Now I enjoy things I worked for just as much by giving them away.

And grudges! What a burden we all carry around by being mad at someone for some wrong against us. All we do is stress over it and get mad all over again every time you see that person. And for what? I have been wronged many times since coming to prison, and every time I forgive one of those people I feel better about it. A while ago I had another inmate harassing me because I stood up for someone he had been picking on. He then focused on me instead. He kept telling me to kill myself, and since he was in the cell beside mine, I couldn't get away from it. He was finally moved, and I was moved. I didn't speak to him for months, even when he tried to apologize. Then something was said at a chapel service that got my attention: God can only forgive you if you forgive others. I would definitely like to be forgiven after all the wrongs I've done in my life— whether they come from God or the people I've wronged. So I forgave this guy face-to-face and told him it was water under the bridge. We are slowly becoming friends again.

When I practiced as a Christian, I never felt a drive to encourage others to come to church or "save" themselves. I don't know if I would refer to myself as a Buddhist now but I think it most closely reflects my beliefs. Now I want to share what I feel and connect with people. As a group, inmates can definitely use the help; we have all violated someone's rights, and left a trail of pain behind us.

I wish I could do something to make amends, but I know nothing I do would ever come close to making up for my crime. I don't have any money, but I have all the time in the world to volunteer. Since no such program exists in prison, especially with the length of my sentence, I sit in a ten-by-twelve-foot cell for a minimum of sixteen hours a day, beading, reading, sleeping, and thinking. I can get really down. But I still think that over all, I'm a better person now than I was before. If only my baby girl didn't have to pay with her life to change me.

THREE

MUG'S GAME

Thousands of miles away and decades earlier, California anthropologist Sarah Hrdy was captivated by a different domestic-violence situation in the steamy hills of India.[1] In this case, Mug was determined to have the newly single Itch, but Itch was wary; Mug was a bit of a knuckle-dragger. Besides, Itch had a baby to care for, and there was little love lost between the brawny, boisterous male and her clingy infant, Scratch. Itch shunned Mug, stayed well out of reach of his grasping hands. Still, Mug remained determined. He hung around whenever he could, showed off his posture, stared intently at Itch, and vocalized his feelings as best as he could.

Itch was right to be wary. One afternoon, the impatient Mug charged straight at Itch and snatched at the baby clinging to her belly. Itch and fellow females of the Hillside troop screamed and pummeled Mug with their fists until he fled, leaving Scratch flecked with blood and shaken, but largely unharmed. Weeks later, a sudden, slashing attack at Scratch's thigh by Mug crippled the baby, and shortly after, Scratch vanished, never to be seen again.

This behavior—which would end up resounding through research into human violence—was exactly what Hrdy had traveled so far to witness in her study of the langur monkeys of India. A year earlier, when Mug was ousted from the Hillside troop by a rival male (only to return again), the same systematic attacks by the new leader on the troop's young had occurred. At that time, the offspring were dispatched by a usurping alpha male Hrdy had named Shifty Leftless. "Here was the phenomenon, the bizarre aberration of adult males attacking infants, that had brought me," Hrdy writes in her book *The Langurs of Abu: Female and Male Strategies of Reproduction.*[2]

Hrdy was fascinated by the midsized silver-gray primates with black

45

faces, long tails (*langur* means "long tail" in Sanskrit), and the "grace of a grey-hound," as she describes them in her book. She had pored over research for years about the animals, one of several species of the Colobine subfamily of Old World monkeys—consuming studies concerning their social structures, parenting, and relationship between the sexes—since she was an undergraduate at Radcliffe. Like humans, langurs are extremely adaptable primates. They're found throughout India from sea level at the southern tip of the subcontinent to high in the Himalayas in the north. Primarily herbivores, they feed on fruit, flowers, and leaves, as well as handouts from humans when offered. The langurs of India—which number close to 300,000—are widely known for their urban lifestyles, sharing alleyways with human city-dwellers and sleeping in parks at night; digging into garbage; raiding gardens, farms, and food markets; and swiping food off unguarded outdoor tables. Named for the monkey god Hanuman, Hanuman langurs are considered sacred in the Hindu religion, and it's illegal in India to capture or kill them. So humans, usually, tolerate them, though sometimes with shouts and well-aimed stones.

The largely terrestrial langurs, relatively easily observed, especially in and around the urban areas of India and other Asian cities, have been a subject of serious scientific study as far back as 1834. They also became a growing focus of research and debate because of their disturbing behavior. Unremarkable in many ways among the vast species of primates, scientists and residents who shared the monkeys' living areas were shocked to witness infanticide by the animals. The observation threatened to shatter a myth about ourselves and other animals—that humans are the only creatures who murder members of their own species. The langur killings were so startling to witnesses, and so difficult to explain, that they were generally dismissed by researchers who initially described them as aberrant behavior without any logical explanation. Even mere fighting among adult males was dismissed as "bizarre, certainly not typical, behavior," by researcher Phyllis Jay in a 1963 study.[3] Some scientists attributed witnessed langur infanticide to the stresses and "social pathology" of overpopulation, likely linked at least in part to their urban living situations that recalled a classic early study by John Calhoun conducted for the National Institute of Health. In his now-famous experiments, Calhoun allowed a population of confined rats to grow until the jam-packed animals began to express what he called a "behavioral sink" of activities with a range of pathological behaviors, including infanticide and cannibalism.[4]

Hrdy first heard of the langur infanticides in a popular undergraduate class on primate behavior, taught by anthropologist and evolutionary biologist Irven DeVore. When Hrdy attended Harvard to pursue a doctorate in anthropology, she came back to the puzzle of adult langur violence against infants. Her first graduate paper, "Infant-Biting and Deserting among Langurs," in a class about the evolution of sex differences, failed to convince an important reader. The teaching assistant who graded her paper wrote that it had "nothing to do with sex," she recalled later in her book.[5] But before Hrdy earned her doctorate, she would begin to make a powerful case that violence had almost everything to do with sex. She would end up exploding traditional theories on sex, gender, violence, and parenting with a revolutionary perception that deadly violence against offspring could, surprisingly, serve an evolutionary goal, and was fueled by the powerful drive of competition for mates explained in Darwin's classic theory of selection. The idea that infanticidal behavior might be adaptive for the perpetrators rather than an aberration provided a seminal insight that would help galvanize a growing body of research seeking to understand domestic violence by human males.

———

The lushly forested hills of Mount Abu rise from the worn plains of Rajasthan in northern India, some 455 miles southwest of Delhi. The key hilltop town is Abu, nestled next to Lake Nakhi, where the community's population of 8,000 swells at various times with tourists and pilgrims who make the trek to the area's sacred caves and the twelfth-century Hindu temple of Dilwara. Langur activity in Abu and the surrounding region was Hrdy's focus during 1,500 hours of research in five visits during different seasons from 1971 to 1975, when she tracked the behavior of dozens of langurs in seven different troops. Langur bisexual troops are relatively stable bands of females and their offspring, usually headed by a succession of lone males, whose reigns are challenged or usurped by other single males. Young, weaned males, or "sub adults," are typically ejected from the troops by the king male to find their own way, either to eventually attempt to head another troop, or cruise the region with bands of "extratroop" males, which may sometimes include immature females without young.

By 1975 Hrdy's study included 242 langurs living in either breeding bands or with extratroop males. She focused on a subset of individually identified langurs that lived in seven troops, which she named Arbuda Devi Temple, Bazaar, Hillside, Chippaberi, I. P. S., Toad Rock, and School, after their territories. Her troops had different levels of human interaction. The Chippaberi and Bazaar troops obtained a "substantial" portion of their daily food from humans—either scavenged by the animals, or, in the case of the Chippaberi troop, fed chickpeas, peanuts, and chapatti directly by travelers at nearby bus stops, she noted in *The Langurs of Abu*. Others obtained less food from humans, but most had some human contact. Like Jane Goodall, Hrdy named the langurs for noticeable physical characteristics—such as Splitear, Harelip, Cast-eye, T. T. (for "Tied Tail"), Elfin (for her pointed ears), and Pawlet (for a deformed right paw)—rather than as a collection of numbers or letters.

She wasn't particularly taken with the individual daily habits of the creatures, but was fascinated by their interactions. "I am no true naturalist," she remarked in her book. "It was the high drama of their lives, the next episode of the Colobine soap opera that got me out of bed in the morning and kept me out under the Indian sun, tramping about their haunts for eleven hours at a stretch."[6]

Although Hrdy had traveled to India expressly to witness and try to tease out why adult male langurs were killing infants, over time she expanded her study to include an examination of female, as well as male, "reproductive strategies." But when she finally encountered the violence that she had hoped to see, it was so shocking that Hrdy initially had a tough time coming to grips with it.

"Although infanticide was foremost on my mind when I decided to study langurs, its actual occurrence seemed totally implausible," she writes in *The*

Langurs of Abu.[7] Even though the Hillside troop's dominant male had been ousted by another, "despite the fact that all six infants were missing, despite reports by two local people who had seen an adult male langur kill infants in the Hillside troop's home range, I grasped at straws," Hrdy confessed in the book. "I spent a whole day trying to convince myself that this was a different troop, one without infants, which had somehow materialized out of the torrential rains and thick mist of that monsoon month. But the longer I peered through the mist at those rain-soaked, skittish females, the more I realized they were, unmistakably, Bilgay, Itch, Harrieta, Oedipa, Pawless, and Sol. The seventh female and the six infants were never seen again."

Hrdy gradually came to terms with the infanticides and eventually reached the startling conclusion that not only were the killings not unusual at Abu, and, according to reports, at nearby Dharwari and Jodhpur as well, but they were, in fact, routine after an alpha male was ousted by another. In the Abu region, infanticides by males turned out to be the "single greatest cause of mortality," Hrdy discovered.[8] Infant deaths varied among the troops she observed, from almost none in Toad Rock where the troop was ruled for a significant period of time by the same male, to an astounding 83 percent during a period in the Hillside troop when the alpha male changed three times. The females in Hillside were subjected to a particularly thankless task of birthing and rearing young before their offspring were killed due to a revolving door of males in their lives. When Hrdy first began observing the Hillside troop, it was ruled by Mug, who had taken over from Shifty Leftless and methodically destroyed Shifty's offspring before impregnating the females to populate the troop with his own young. Shifty later returned to oust Mug, destroying Mug's young in turn. But as Shifty attempted to dominate both Hillside and the nearby Bazaar troop, Mug took advantage of Shifty's absences to again take over Hillside and start the infant killings over again, confronting once more his former paramour Itch.

The cycles of infanticide were the catalyst for a theory by Hrdy that would revolutionize perceptions about adult langur violence against the young. Hrdy argued that the killings were far from an aberration. Instead, they could be expected when a new male took over a troop. Infanticide was a priority for usurping males who had driven out an old leader. The ousted male's offspring were quickly dispatched. The females fled or banded together to protect their offspring as long as they could. The infants had few protective resources other than clinging to their mothers, and usually didn't survive for very long, Hrdy noted. Mothers tended to stave off the inevitable for only a limited period. They were hunted by the males out to destroy their infants. Some mothers quickly lost their young to the murderous new leader, some mothers vanished. But some also weaned their young early, speeding up the time they would come into estrous again and mate with the new male. Others still with young might come into a "false estrous" and mate. In cases Hrdy observed where females still with young quickly mated or became pregnant, "leftover" young from a previous male were usually allowed to survive by the new leaders, apparently confused about the paternity of the offspring of females they were mounting.

In Hrdy's analysis, the infanticides were part of a clear strategy for male access to females and served the goal of evolutionary fitness, or reproductive success, for a troop's new dominant male. Male langurs tend to have a small window of opportunity to procreate and add their own genes to the langur pool before they're ousted by another younger, stronger, challenging male and relegated to the community of lower-ranked males whose chances at procreation are significantly reduced if not eliminated. Dominating a troop is a langur's drive for a kind of monkey immortality, at least for a male's genes. The killing of progeny of previous leaders serves to make the world safer for themselves and their own infants, and helps to ensure the evolutionary fitness of their offspring, who would be more likely to procreate themselves in a world where more rivals are eliminated. By killing infants, males also ensure that mothers come into estrous quickly for new mating, and their nurturing resources are immediately freed to tend to the new males' offspring. Because male langur domination of a troop can be relatively short-lived, leaders can't waste time waiting for existing offspring to grow and become independent before adult females become willing sex partners and new mothers for their own baby langurs. Of course, none of this goes through a langur male's mind when he kills an infant in his new troop; all he cares about is mounting a female, and she won't be in the mood if she has a baby clinging to her belly.

Hrdy's perspective rocked the study of the social, sexual, and parental relationships among langurs and sparked a fresh look at and analysis of infanticides not only of the primates but also among other species. The process Hrdy discerned involved a brutally pragmatic behavior linked, however unconsciously by the langurs, to an evolutionary cost-benefit drive. It was immediately controversial, and not a little disturbing to humans whose self-image as generous, caring adults and parents didn't fare so well in the bloody reflection of animals close to us on the evolutionary ladder. It was tough for many anthropologists to swallow. One critic sniped at the time that Hrdy's monkeys were deranged. A male colleague recommended she spend more time raising her own children, managing at the same time to highlight our possible links to Neanderthals. Despite the attacks, Hrdy's theory would soon become the orthodoxy of anthropologists and biologists as researchers began recording the same system of infanticides among several species. Hrdy's work is a stark example of how a reality can exist for decades yet remain unknown simply because scientists have not recognized it. While a long list of researchers had failed to make sense of langur infanticide, Hrdy's focus on the female position in langur troops and sensitivity to reproductive strategies led her to a startling, remarkable insight that soon became an accepted principal of animal science.

Several researchers before Hrdy had viewed langur and other primate societies as almost idyllic communities in which each individual did its bit to help ensure the survival of as many members of its own species as possible. Young male vervet monkeys who hung around the periphery of troops, for example, were even seen by some researchers as placing themselves as willing "buffer" primate sacrifices to predators stalking a troop to protect the more valuable members. "Not surprisingly," wrote Hrdy in *Langurs of Abu*, "when we first began to intensively study our closest nonhuman relatives, the monkeys and the apes, an idealization of our own society was extended to theirs."[9] Monkeys, like humans, appeared to "maintain complex social systems geared towards ensuring the group's survival," wrote Hrdy, convinced that the perception of such societies was more wish fulfillment than science. In a much later book, *Mother Nature*, Hrdy pointed out that, as a mother of three in the modern world, she's "partial" to a "companionate monogamous marriage" as the most satisfying for her and the most beneficial for her children.[10] Yet, she admits, that's not necessarily the case for primates, early man, nor even for modern human moms in different situations. "It would scarcely be wise, or fair, to extrapolate my self-interested priorities to them," she adds, referring to early mothers. "Nevertheless, from Victorian times to the present, this is what many anthropologists and evolutionists have done."

Far from the idealized visions of primate societies popular at the time she made her discovery, Hrdy realized that an individual's drive toward evolutionary fitness could be so selfish that it could even potentially threaten the survival of a community of langurs, such as in the Hillside troop, whose population was decimated by mass baby murder.

Righting idealized misconceptions in theories about primates and early man is critical because it promises to help us more effectively understand some of our own drives, Hrdy argued in *The Langurs of Abu*. It is exactly our "peculiar misconception about ourselves, and about primates, that lends the history of langur studies its significance," Hrdy wrote.[11] "By revealing our misconceptions about other primates, the langur saga may unmask misconceptions about ourselves."

If langurs provide an insight into human community, it's clearly not a touchy-feely vision of male baby love—nor does it argue for an easy relationship between the sexes, whose evolutionary interests are so disparate they're almost "two different species," Hrdy noted.[12] Rarely, she wrote, "do the best interests of the female langur coincide" with those of her consort. "Sexuality means conflict," Hrdy matter-of-factly added, quoting playwright August Strindberg. "Apart from insemination, langur females have little use for males except to protect them from other males."

Other scientists intrigued by Hrdy's research and analysis began to look out for, and record, a system of infanticide by males—and some by domineering females—among several other species, particularly among the Colobine subfamily of primates. Similar behavior is also well known today among lions, wild dogs, rhinos, mice, ducks, hippos, bears, rats, rabbits, and wolves, among scores of other species.

Within a few short years after Hrdy developed her theory, other primate researchers were witnessing infanticides with increasing frequency. Silverback gorillas, perhaps most notably observed by primatologist Dian Fossey, can be attentive fathers, and may even take over care for their young in cases of maternal death or rare desertion. Imposing, long-living silverbacks have an advantage of being in charge of a troop for extended periods of time, sometimes up to 30 years, so they don't have to deal with frequent challenges to their dominance. Nevertheless, Fossey alone documented nine cases of infanticide of offspring of a rival male.[13]

After studying chimpanzees in Tanzania's Gombe Park for ten years, Jane Goodall witnessed her first infanticide—but this time, it was by a mother and daughter team of chimps Goodall had named Passion and Pom. The pair hunted down and killed at least five (possibly as many as eight) infants of rival females in their troop by biting them in the neck—and then eating them. The "barbarous murders" so appalled Goodall that she very unscientifically chased the deadly duo away in the middle of one attempted infant-kill mission by yelling.[14] The killings stopped when Pom had a baby, whom Goodall named Pax. But Goodall was unnerved by what she had witnessed, and it rattled her view of pleasant chimp life as an idealized view of a simpler, pre-human parenting and community. "I had believed . . . that the Gombe chimpanzees were, for the most part, rather nicer than human beings. Then, suddenly, we found that chimpanzees could be brutal—that they, like us, had a dark side to their nature," she noted later in her book *Reason for Hope: A Spiritual Journey.*[15] The infanticide she witnessed rattled her view of the essential nature of chimps—and man—and she recognized for the first time that human capacity for aggression and violence was as deeply rooted in our evolutionary past as our ability for cooperation and compassion. It was a lesson many didn't want to learn. When she first published her findings in "Life and Death at Gombe" in *National Geographic* in 1979, the magazine was attacked for the graphic description and photos of the killings. Again, the behavior was viewed as aberrant, just as the langur killings were initially regarded, and Goodall's eyewitness accounts were criticized as merely "anecdotal," she recounts.[16] This was "patently absurd," Goodall wrote. "We had watched, at close range, not just one but five brutal attacks. Even more significantly, other field researchers had observed similar aggressive territorial behaviors in other parts of the chimpanzees' range across Africa."

Goodall continued her research into infanticide by females, which she determined was fueled by an evolutionary drive similar to males. Higher-ranking chimp females, similar to Pom and her daughter, were witnessed in several cases killing the young of rival females at a time when the offspring could be easily dispatched and before they could pose any threat to a ranking female's young, whose own evolutionary fitness would be bolstered by the elimination of rivals.

Hrdy reassures readers in *The Langurs of Abu* that such behavior is far in our own evolutionary past, and that alpha humans aren't out to murder other males' offspring. Human males don't have to kill a rival male's baby to win access to and have sex with a woman or to live with her; countless men share a home with a woman and a child or children from previous relationships. "What are the implications of this infanticidal heritage for humans?" she wondered in her book.[17] "There is little reliable evidence to support the hypothesis that human males have been selected to murder infants in order to increase their own reproductive success." Some kinds of culturally sanctioned infanticides do occur, rarely, and usually only if a baby's chances of survival are small and resources limited, she noted. Among "most preindustrial human societies," infanticide was "primarily practical," and often involved the acquiescence or even participation of the mother—which, by the time Hrdy began work on *Mother Nature*, would be another focus of her research. Infant abandonment or even outright infanticide by a mother is usually linked to "economic constraints, the probability of infant survival and future marriage potentialities," Hrdy added. In modern times, men of the Yanamamo in Brazil have been witnessed killing children when they raid another community. Mothers may also be kidnapped and their infants left behind, which is "functionally equivalent to infanticide" by males because the children can no longer nurse and are more likely to starve to death, noted Hrdy in *The Langurs of Abu*. Still, she emphasized in her book, "nothing resembling a genetic imperative for infanticide can be found" among humans. Hrdy does, however, in passing, point to the biblical account of Herod's order of mass murder to slay male toddlers and babies to eliminate an expected challenge to his rule by the recently born Jesus. Interestingly, she also begins her book referring to the feared murderous jealousy of a Roman ruler in Shakespeare's *Titus Andronicus* over his wife's "blackamoore baby," clearly fathered by her Moorish lover.[18] The mother begs her lover to destroy the baby to save her. He refuses, explaining: "My mistress is my mistress," but the baby "my self." If "more primatologists had seen this play before going off into the field, they might better have understood the behavior unfolding before them in the savannas and forests where monkeys are studied," Hrdy wryly noted.

In 1982 Hrdy, together with zoologist Glenn Hausfater, convened in Cornell a conference of researchers studying infanticide, which resulted in the book, *Infanticide: Comparative and Evolutionary Perspectives.* Hrdy was confident that the evidence presented would convince any remaining skeptics that infanticide could serve an evolutionary-fitness goal. In the introduction to their book, Hrdy and Hausfater stressed how far science had traveled concerning the view of infanticide in a few short years since Hrdy's langur study. "Over the past decade, the intellectual pendulum in behavioral biology and related disciplines has swung from an earlier view that infanticide could not possibly represent anything other than abnormal and aberrant behavior to the current view that in many populations, infanticide is a normal and individually adaptive activity," they wrote.[19] In fact, researchers have "begun to interpret an ever expanding list of behaviors as subtle forms of infanticide or counter-strategies to infanticide," they added. Scientists were initially resistant to the idea of infanticide in the animal world in part because it's considered such "an abhorrent practice in our own society," wrote Hrdy and Hausfater. But they also didn't understand what possible role it could play in survival of the species. "Once infanticide began to be explained in evolutionary terms" by Hrdy, "published reports of infanticide in mammals increased dramatically," they wrote. The pendulum had swung so far, the authors noted, that "quite possibly, readers ten years from now may take for granted the occurrence of infanticide in various animal species, and may even be unaware of the controversies and occasionally heated debate that have marked the last decade of research on this topic."

Although the matter was settled as far as most evolutionary biologists were concerned, however, some controversy persisted decades longer within anthropology. There was even a learning curve for Hrdy concerning infanticide among all species, including humans. "From the 1980s onward, there was increasing awareness that infant abuse, neglect, abandonment, and infanticide were far more widespread than even those of us who studied such phenomena had realized," she wrote in *Mother Nature*.[20] "I already knew that abandonment and infanticide—both in humans and other animals—stretched far back in evolutionary time. I just had not realized the magnitude of what was going on." Despite the grim statistics, Hrdy is surprised there isn't even more infanticide among humans. "Given how prevalent infanticide by males is among primates—reported now for over 50 different species, often with much the same pattern as predicted by the 'sexual selection' hypothesis I first proposed in 1974—and given how much access to other men's infants men have in our species, what really surprises me is how uncommon infanticide by males turns out to be in humans," Hrdy wrote to me in a 2012 e-mail. She attributes that to how "different the breeding systems of humans are compared to those of some of our closest Great Ape relations—gorillas and chimpanzees"—as well as the development of human male emotion and the reproductive strategies of women.

These reproductive strategies became a key focus of Hrdy's study over the years. She was one of the few women scientists in anthropology when she began her research, and was drawn to an important player in evolution that her male colleagues tended to ignore: females. Most researchers, just as Darwin did, regarded females as passive players in the evolutionary drama unfolding around them. They were viewed generally as sitting by coyly as they were chosen by strong males. Then they did what they were biologically destined to do: have babies and raise them. From this perspective, Hrdy quipped, it was as though females had never really evolved. Yet she had witnessed how intently and strategically females protected their young. Langur females banded together in attempts to shield offspring from murderous new alpha males. This shared protective parenting—which Hrdy later termed "allo-parenting—was cultivated throughout life as female langurs young to old cared for other females' infants, sometimes within minutes after birth. She also witnessed mothers seeking sex with a range of mates, she surmised, to confuse males about the paternity of their young, which would likely serve as protection since males only attacked infants being carried by females with whom they hadn't mated.

Human mothers, Hrdy argued, sometimes rely on a similar strategy, by building bonds through sex with more than one interested male, who may then feel protective about her babies, or, at least, view a future when she is carrying their own baby. In such a way, an assertively sexual women can use a man's uncertainty about paternity to her and her child's advantage, and, in addition, have available men "at hand" in the event her primary partner deserts her (she may also deliberately seek out a nurturing good provider mate unlikely to desert her, rather than males with the obvious knock-out handsome, strength or intelligence genes). But the breeding tactic "best suited to the goose will often look different from the one preferred by the gander," added Hrdy.[21] The female "many possible fathers" strategy may particularly frustrate a male, who, while he may himself be interested in sex with a number of women, can become obsessed with his partner's fidelity because he doesn't want to be caught expending resources on an infant secretly plopped in his nest by a rival male. Because fertilization takes place inside a woman's body, a male can only know for certain he fathered her child if he has a guard "eunuch at the gate" or a DNA "lab at his disposal," she notes in *Mother Nature*.[22]

Hrdy acknowledged in later books the important parenting role that fathers play, not only in helping to begin life, but also in raising their children. Human males are loving, attentive parents usually in for the long haul. Fathers have powerful biological drives to nurture their young, much like mothers, and react similarly to women in responding to cues like the crying of their babies much like their wives. Yet men tend to respond less frequently at a lower threshold of crying. Hrdy argues that tiny differences in parental responsiveness during infancy tend to lead to a significant difference in parent-child relationships over time as a deeper bond develops between a child and the more responsive parent, typically the mother. Still, a man's continuing presence in a family as his child grows is vitally important to the well-being of a child, from modern America to the Brazilian Ache tribes, where an infant who loses his father is four times more likely to die before the age of two than a cohort with a dad, Hrdy noted in *Mother Nature*.[23]

If Hrdy's early discovery about parenting among the langurs and their infanticide shocked many, her later findings reassured. Her work underscored how deep the Pleistocene legacy of shared care and provisioning of the young—our evolved parenting as "cooperative breeders"—has shaped our better natures, she has argued in *Mothers and Others: The Evolutionary Origin of Mutual Understanding*. It is parenting, not gathering together for warfare, that is the elemental force behind our more "other-regarding" and cooperative selves, she maintains. Langurs may murder an infant, but evolutionary eons later, a human infant can melt a man's heart. Human babies are so dependent for so long that it takes a village to raise them. They could not have survived without a cooperative community of parents along with what she calls "allo mothers" or "allo parents," people of either sex who help care for the young. Our relative pacifism, our ability to empathize, our capacities to read one another's intentions, and our eagerness to help and please others were forged while infants were developing to elicit care not just from mothers, but from others as well, Hrdy argues. It's a life-saving evolutionary legacy that sets humans well apart from other apes. Chimpanzees may be pretty smart, she notes in her chapter "Apes on a Plane," but if we flew with a planeload of them from New York to Los Angeles, we'd be "lucky to disembark with all 10 fingers and toes still attached."[24] Even among "famously peaceful bonobos, a type of chimpanzee so rare and difficult to access in the wild that most observations come from zoos, veterinarians sometimes have to be called in following altercations to stitch back on a scrotum or a penis," she notes.

Paleontologist Richard Leakey emphasized the "profound homologies between us and other apes," while a psychiatrist like Peter Hobson "is more struck by differences between closely related species," Hrdy noted in *Mothers and Others*.[25] "Both are right." But from a "tender age and without special training, modern humans identify with the plights of others and, without being asked, volunteer to help and share, even with strangers. In these respects, our line of apes is in a class by itself," writes Hrdy.[26]

It was a far different view of interaction among members of a community from what Hrdy had first encountered on Mount Abu. But researchers weren't done yet exploring darker aspects of our kind of primate.

FOUR

HOMO SAPS

Canadian research partners Martin Daly and Margo Wilson talked excitedly of Hrdy's work at a 1976 California seminar while Daly was teaching psychology at the University of California in Riverside. The seminar featured Harvard entomologist Edward O. Wilson's provocative book, *Sociobiology*, a tome on the field of study that links social interaction to evolutionary development. Hrdy's name came up because Wilson cited her langur studies in his book, pointing it out as an example of "routine" infanticide by usurping male animals that served an evolutionary goal. His perspectives and Hrdy's theory fascinated the academics. They found E. O. Wilson's and Hrdy's behavioral interpretations far more convincing than the then-trendy view of what they labeled as social scientists' "greater good-ism" view of animal societies as designed to preserve and "reproduce the species" rather than a recognition of the powerfully competitive drive within each individual to mate and procreate. Like Hrdy, Daly and Margo Wilson believed animal studies were often contaminated by researcher bias; scientists tended to see what they unconsciously hoped to discover: an altruistic society. Such a society didn't ring true for them. They were convinced by Hrdy's theory behind langur infanticide. In light of her analysis, as "horrifying" as animal infanticide appears to the human observer, it is "clearly not pathological," they would write later in *The Truth about Cinderella: A Darwinian View of Parental Love.*[1] In fact, Hrdy's insight that langur infanticide served an evolutionary goal "is so compelling that the interesting question is why it was not investigated and understood sooner," they noted. Hrdy's proposition that evolutionary "selection will favor infanticidal males over non-infanticidal males" is almost "inescapable," they concluded.[2]

59

Daly and Wilson, however, weren't as quick as Hrdy was initially in *The Langurs of Abu* to dismiss her theory's possible implications for human behavior. Clearly, human males aren't systematically eliminating their stepchildren as part of a subconscious, instinctive drive toward evolutionary fitness, they acknowledged, but the essence of the evolutionary drive to survive, mate, and successfully raise our own young, who in turn find partners to create families, infuses a significant well of human behavior. Human fathers aren't langurs or lions, intent on killing a rival's offspring, but they have been forged by evolution, like langurs, to reproduce and discriminate in favor of their own offspring, which can have significant consequences for stepchildren. "Indiscriminate allocation of parental benefits without regard to cues of actual parentage would be an evolutionary anomaly," Daly and Wilson noted.[3] "Although sexually selected infanticide is clearly not a human adaptation, discriminative parental solicitude just as clearly is." These "child-specific bonds" make it possible for adults to shoulder and enjoy what the two scientists described as the "onerous burden" of parenthood. Because of the nature of relationships forged by evolution, "stepparents do not, on average, feel the same child-specific love and commitment as genetic parents, and therefore do not reap the same emotional rewards from unreciprocated 'parental' investment," they added. The upshot is that parents would predictably tend to be more careless with or more likely to express anger against a stepchild. Or a husband might be annoyed, even lash out in anger, when a wife seems to favor her child from a previous relationship over his biological offspring.

Given this perspective, and Hrdy's intriguing findings, Wilson and Daly couldn't help but wonder about rates of violence in families with stepchildren. As they mulled possible effects among humans, they noted the overwhelming number of stories of evil human stepmothers, and stepfathers, in cross-cultural myths and fairy tales. The "abused stepchild is one of the stock characters of folklore," they pointed out, with "hundreds of variants" of Cinderella's plight in a home ruled by an evil stepparent throughout the world.[4] A dad under pressure from his new wife, Hansel and Gretel's stepmom, abandons them in the dangerous woods to be kidnapped and nearly cooked by a witch (who could also represent the stepmother). In the Juniper Tree, a woman beheads her stepson and feeds him in a stew to his father, to protect the family's assets for her own biological child. In the Indian fairy tale Murimong and Thanian, a brother and sister flee home, sick of ingesting rotting food fed to them by their evil stepmom. The image of an evil stepmother has even infected language. In Dutch, bad treatment by someone may be referred to as *steifmoederlijke behandling,* or "stepmother treatment."[5] Wilson and Daly theorized that most of the evil stepparent fables focus on stepmothers because moms tend to be the traditional family storytellers, and the tales passed down through generations served as a warning from mother to child about the dangers of a stepparent coming into their lives in the event of their own mother's death or desertion by a husband. But stepfathers also present as evil doers. A French proverb warns: "The mother of babes who elects to wed has taken their enemy into her bed."[6] Gruesome tales of stepparents "would not persist where their themes had no resonance" with humans, noted the research couple, concluding that they "must have something to do with the human condition."

Why, they wondered, was there no research into the risks to children posed by stepparents in modern human society in light of the folklore and especially in the wake of Hrdy's langur research and further studies by other anthropologists? That oversight, as well as the curiosity Hrdy's work triggered, convinced the two to veer from their rodent and primate studies to concentrate instead on violence, particularly family violence, this time among the infinitely intriguing populations of *Homo sapiens.*

When Wilson and Daly began their studies of human violence and homicide, the field was generally dominated by sociologists looking at social impacts, such as poverty, on human actions, or psychologists examining abnormal behavior of perpetrators, noted Daly. The researchers were more concerned with the specific relations between killer and victim, and in possible evolutionary rationales for such violence. Like Hrdy's research, the stepparent studies they launched rattled the orthodoxy on theories about family violence. In their first major examination of child-abuse rates in step-families compared with intact birth families, Wilson and Daly made a stunning discovery: "Enormous differentials in the risk of violence" turned out to be "a particularly dramatic consequence" of the "predictable difference" in parents' feelings toward stepchildren.[7] In fact, they discovered, having a stepparent turned out to be the single greatest risk factor for severe child maltreatment.[8]

The scientists' remarkable findings on violence against stepchildren—revealing rates of abuse of stepkids nearly unimaginably higher than among biological children—sealed their reputations as two of the foremost researchers in evolutionary psychology—a descendant of E. O. Wilson's sociobiology view of behavior. "Ev Psych," as its students like to refer to it, involves a through-the-looking-glass vision of us as more apelike and driven by evolutionary pasts than we might like to believe. For all of our vast differences from our ape ancestors, we are also, still, surprisingly similar. We are preoccupied with sex, finding a mate, and raising children. We can watch a Shakespeare play and marvel at the sixteenth-century language, but we're captivated by plots that deal with "universal" concerns about chastity, fidelity, jealousy, and paternity molded far earlier in our jungle pasts. It's a convincing vision that, once truly viewed and embraced, is impossible to ever dismiss. It's not the complete explanation for human behavior, but it provides a key piece of the puzzle, and one that can be used to help shape valid approaches to dealing with lethal violence in a continually evolving humanity.

Margo Wilson died in 2009, but Daly continues to explore the evolutionary fuel of human violence (and recently paid homage to Wilson in a presentation of his latest work on motivations behind homicide at a May 2012 conference at McMaster University in Hamilton, Ontario, where he's now emeritus professor). He took a break from the Ontario Ecology, Ethology, and Evolution Colloquium—which featured studies on behavior of zebra finches to bees to Atlantic salmon, as well as mink, Pacific coast dune plants, and humans—to talk to me about his work. The rangy, bespectacled Canadian with a shock of white hair and a wry sense of humor seems to constantly view the world around him through a jungle prism. He talks of the violence "risk factors" of a friend's relationship with a threatening young male, and refers to humans as "Homo saps." He corrects me when I ask about how animals (as opposed to human beings) would react in a certain situation. "You mean *other* animals," he amends. He recognizes his own conflicts as a modern human with animal drives, an intellectual who struggles with an evolutionary-selected sense of "male entitlement."

Viewing men largely as apes in suits (or, in the case of academia, apes in blazers or rolled-up shirt sleeves) is an attitude that can infuriate people, most notably a faction of the American public battling to replace the teaching of evolution in schools with the theory of a God-directed "Intelligent Design." While working on this book and explaining my examination of "types" of fathers who kill their children to anyone who would listen, the most "understandable" to many was a situation in which a father kills a stepchild. But that wasn't the response Daly and Wilson first received when they published their findings. The scientists were sharply attacked by many researchers, horrified by the view that humans marched to dictates of their brutal inner ape (while, bizarrely, others criticized them for research conclusions that were blindingly obvious). Daly lamented that the findings triggered more than their share of skepticism despite "abundant confirmatory research" that followed. Some of the response seemed colored by the same anti-Darwinist perspective of fundamentalist Christians that man is unique, and could not have evolved from apes. "There is that view that man is somehow special, with a touch of the divine," Daly explained to me at the conference. "The response to our work initially was vicious." E. O. Wilson's sociobiology and the subsequent field of evolutionary psychology were also attacked in academia for giving far too much weight to a presumed elemental human nature, versus the potential of familial and cultural nurture, and for being deterministic and ultimately conservative—that humans are destined with little choice to behave a particular way because of evolutionary dictates. "The human brain allows for a wide range of behavior," argued Harvard paleontologist Stephen Jay Gould in the early days of the debate.[9] "Violence, sexism, and general nastiness are biological since they represent one subset of a possible range of behaviors. But peacefulness, equality, and kindness are just as biological—and we may see their influence increase if we can create social structures that permit them to flourish."

Daly recognizes that humans have tremendous freedom of choice, and emphasizes that other outstanding aspects of the human personality like kindness and cooperation are just as influenced by evolution as violence is, but he believes evolutionary forces had been largely ignored as a fundamental platform for human behavior when he began his research. Much of the controversy has died down since its height in the 1970s. The influence of our animal history on our behavior is now far more widely accepted, Daly believes. "There's a recognition that some 'human nature' exists," supported dramatically over the years largely by neuroscientists, who have discovered physical and hormonal effects that come with the body reaching back through evolution, he told me at the conference.

When Daly and Wilson launched their first stepchild study, battered-child syndrome was already being studied, along with some examination of conflict in families with stepchildren. Early research on stepparent families found higher levels of conflict within such families, higher rates of children leaving home at earlier ages, and higher rates of divorce among couples parenting stepchildren rather than biological children. "The picture made sense to us as evolutionists," explained Daly.[10]

In their first study, Daly and Wilson turned for statistics to a registry of battered-child figures kept by the American Humane Association (AHA), which tallied legally mandated child-abuse reports along with basic demographic information about victim and perpetrator, relationships between the two, details of the abuse, and any follow-up investigation. For comparison of age-specific rates of abuse for stepchildren versus biological children, available data was pitiably sparse. The US census didn't (and still doesn't) tally genetic, adoptive, and stepparenthood, so they used instead estimates based on limited surveys, which they judged to overestimate the number of stepparent families, and such estimates, they surmised, would therefore give them conservative, rather than exaggerated, findings on possible abuse rates of stepchildren. Early results were stunning. By Daly and Wilson's calculations, based on the data, an American child under the age of three living with one biological parent and one stepparent was about seven times more likely to become a "validated child-abuse case" in the AHA records than a child living with two genetic parents.[11] For the recorded fatal child-abuse cases they analyzed, per capita rates were 100 times higher for victims who lived with a genetic parent and stepparent, compared with those who lived with two genetic parents.[12] The differences could conceivably be attributed to the stress and possible marital conflict complicated by situations such as poverty, but Daly and Wilson found that rates of stepparenthood and the consequent abuse risk factor to children were similar in all income levels.

A future study bolstered their first findings. Statistics in their home metropolitan area of Hamilton-Wentworth in Canada revealed that preschool children living with a stepparent were 40 times more likely to be reported as a victim to the Ontario child-abuse registry in 1983.[13] Even more chilling, Daly and Wilson discovered that a co-residing stepparent in Canada was nearly 70 times more likely to kill a child under two years old than a co-residing biological parent.[14] Again, poverty—and factors such as family size and maternal age—did not appear to significantly impact the figures. "Stepparenthood held its place as the most important predictor, and its influence was scarcely diminished when the statistical impacts of all the other risk factors were controlled," wrote Daly and Wilson.[15] Other researchers would discover similar situations in studies around the world.

That's not to say stepparents can't or don't love their stepchildren (or adopted children) profoundly—or that stepchildren's lives aren't "enriched immeasurably" by the love and care of a stepparent, the scientists noted. Nurturing a stepchild can even fulfill an evolutionary drive. But in Daly and Wilson's no-nonsense interpretation informed by evolution, a stepparent may "trade" care for a stepchild in expectation of expanding a family with his or her own biological children, they pointed out. In their pragmatic explanation: "Step-parental investment is evidently the price paid for future breeding opportunities with the genetic parent."[16]

It's a view of the human animal that has drawn criticism from those who regard *Homo sapiens* as far "more evolved" and capable of the finer points of love, compassion, charity, and selflessness. Daly stresses that those attributes, too, have been developed through evolution. But the researchers have prodded us to recognize all the evolutionary forces that may be impacting us, regardless of how unconscious we may be while following these primal motivations. Recognizing all these drives, no matter how uncomfortable they may be to acknowledge in some cases, is a key step in understanding violence in human society, wrote Daly and Wilson. "We would suggest that more realistic world-views invite more humane attitudes and practices than fantastic ones, because they entail better models of human nature, and hence greater sensitivity to human needs and desires," they noted.[17]

Wilson and Daly offered no concrete solutions to the dilemma of violence in stepparent families. Daly believes a positive step is to simply recognize that it's perfectly natural to struggle with mixed feelings about a stepchild. "The expectation that a father coming into a family will immediately embrace another man's child as his own is unrealistic, and can bring an added strain that only makes the relationship more difficult," he told me.

———

Daly and Wilson built a reputation with their "Cinderella Effect" theory and research. The theory became the go-to idea for reporters seeking some rationale on domestic-violence tragedies in which stepchildren were singled out for abuse or even death in reconstituted families. Daly was quoted in newspaper articles about the Clare Shelswell murder, which he remarked was "particularly brutal" (his studies also indicated that abuse tends to be more severe for stepchildren compared with abuse of a genetic child). He did not, however, speculate on James's behavior. James's situation involved several important complex factors which could have contributed to his crime, including his struggle with bipolar disorder, problems with rage and impulse control, a troubled childhood, and fury with his wife—as well as his status as Clare's stepdad.

Daly and Wilson's Cinderella Effect theory and studies were only one part of a lifetime of investigation by the professors as they linked the kind of behavior and influence interpreted by Hrdy into analyses of other kinds of violence among humans and in families. If violence against a stepchild was influenced by our evolutionary past, it was logical to assume that other domestic violence—and violence throughout society—had a strong Darwinian link as well. Criminology theory is "overwhelmingly and appropriately" framed in sociological terms, conceded Wilson and Daly, but it also necessarily "entails assumptions" about such aspects of a criminal's psychological makeup as human nature and desires, molded, they emphasize, by evolutionary drives.[18] Evolutionary fitness is not a conscious goal of humans, but it "explains why certain goals have come to control behavior," the researchers wrote in their book *Homicide*.[19] Childhood abuse, alcohol-induced psychosis, hormonal imbalances, access to guns, rage over social inequities may all contribute to crime and murder, acknowledged Wilson and Daly, but the importance of Darwin's theory of natural selection to social sciences and its ability to provide a platform from which to analyze basic human nature remained "shamefully underappreciated," they argued in the book.[20] Hypotheses about what spurs human violence "can be derived from an evolutionary psychological perspective on human emotions, motives and information-processing mechanisms," they wrote in their 1995 study "Familicide: The Killing of Spouse and Children." [21] A Darwinian perspective is vital to answering the question of why people kill one another, but an analysis of homicides can also help unlock our understanding of all human conflict, the authors noted. Killings, as an extreme example of conflict, provide a "valuable window on the psychology of interpersonal conflict," they added. A Darwinian perspective means that violence and murder are usually not merely crimes of opportunity by a rageful or addled killer, but are sparked by situations and relationships; and any useful analysis of violence must incorporate an examination of those factors in light of evolutionary forces.

Daly and Wilson also examined uxoricides, the murder of women by their mate, through the looking glass of Darwinism. Again, inspired by insights gained from an evolutionary psychological perspective, they postulated that, like our primate ancestors, men are driven to "possess" the "reproductive capacities" of their chosen mates, and will jealously guard a wife against rivals. When rivals move in, or a mate wanders, that's when the ape in us steps in. As Sarah Hrdy emphasized, human conception hidden inside a woman's body can lead to questions about paternity, particularly for a nervous man with an alluring, flirtatious wife. Men killing wives at first glance appears to be a ludicrous example of a reproductive evolutionary drive. It's hard to impregnate a dead woman. Killing "often oversteps the bounds of utility," Daly and Wilson wryly acknowledge in their 1996 study "Male Sexual Proprietariness and Violence against Wives."[22] Yet the researchers also argued that even violence that ends in death is triggered by evolutionary drives and relates to men's sexual relationship to a mate.

When family members are murdered by a household member, wives are the most frequent targets. Family members can be targeted, many believe, because the victims are closest at hand when adult, mainly male, tempers explode. But that's not a scenario Daly and Wilson bought into. "Although it is often supposed that wives are assaulted mainly because they are accessible . . . targets when men are frustrated or angry, mere opportunity cannot account for the differential risk of violent victimization within households," Daly and Wilson wrote.[23] Rather, human "evolutionary history" better explains violence against wives, they concluded. Because men are driven to mate and reproduce, their "possessiveness" of females and their access to the "reproductive capacities" of a mate are critical to men, the academics argued. The determination to control a mate can drive to violence a man whose jealousy has been aroused, even to the point of murder. There's a "cross-culturally ubiquitous connection between men's sexual possessiveness and men's violence," they noted in their study. Resentment of suspected infidelity and women's attempts to leave a marriage "is everywhere implicated as the dominant precipitating factor" in a large majority of uxoricides, they note. "Wifely infidelity is viewed as an exceptional provocation, likely to elicit a violent rage, both in societies where such a reaction is considered a reprehensible loss of control and in those where it is considered a praiseworthy redemption of honor." Such infidelity is often seen to "mitigate the responsibility of even homicidal cuckolds."

Wilson and Daly developed their "reproductive control" theory of violence against wives based on questionnaires filled out by women who had been assaulted by their husbands. The higher the incidents of violence, the higher the percentage of responses to questions concerning a husband's jealousy and attempts at controlling his wife's actions and relationships with outsiders. Almost all attacked wives answered yes to statements such as: "He is jealous and doesn't want you to talk to other men," "He tries to limit your contact with family or friends," "He prevents you from knowing about or having access to the family income, even if you ask." Such "autonomy-limiting" threats of violence to females serve to keep wives from sleeping around and ultimately leaving their partners, and also help a male from expending resources on offspring that may not be his, brought into the world by a secretly unfaithful wife, Daly and Wilson noted in the study. Wives are killed at higher rates when they are young and at childbearing ages, which adds support to Wilson and Daly's theory. Females ages 15 to 24 have the highest rates among all age groups of murder by boyfriends or husbands. While the ultimate murder of a mate is a "maladaptation" that serves no evolutionary goal (other than to remove a potential mate for a rival male), "brinkmanship" in a relationship can get out of hand. The threat of violence or its non-lethal use can serve to corral a wandering lover. But it's difficult to control violence or call it back once it's unleashed. A threat has to be convincing or it loses its power, argued Wilson and Daly. "A threat is an effective social tool, and usually an inexpensive one, but it loses its effectiveness if the threatening party is seen to be bluffing. Vengeful follow-through may appear counterproductive . . . but effective threats cannot 'leak' signs of bluff," they observed.[24]

Women who leave their husbands tend to face the greatest risks of violence, which is further support for Daly and Wilson's view. Separated wives are killed by their mates at higher rates than those who live with their husbands. This is also the time, other researchers have discovered, that children face the greatest risk of violence from their own fathers. In such cases, fathers may kill their own children as a way to punish their deserting wives in the most painful manner imaginable. Ultimately, the "link between male sexual proprietariness and violent inclinations has presumably been selected for because violence and threat work to deter sexual rivals and limit female autonomy," the researchers concluded.[25] This evolutionary male inclination to control women is frustrated not only by women seeking increasing autonomy, but also by changing times and mores that encourage female independence.

Wilson and Daly further expanded their family-violence research to "familicides" or "family annihilations" in which fathers kill their spouse and one or more children, often also before committing suicide. They studied 109 familicides in Canada, England, and Wales (with a total of 249 victims) that occurred from 1974 to 1990.[26] The murders in those cases were almost exclusively committed by men, and half of the men committed suicide— a far higher rate than males who kill only their wives or children (though fewer men who killed their stepchildren in a family annihilation also killed themselves compared to fathers who killed biological children in family annihilations). Guns were used in almost half the Canadian cases and close to a third of the killings in England and Wales. Again, Wilson and Daly make a case that evolutionary drives are behind the murders even though, clearly, there's ultimately no fitness benefit for a father who kills himself after wiping out what's left of his gene pool. It's obviously a "maladaptation," but it's fueled by evolution, just as in uxoricides, they argued. Some of the same jealousies that drive men to murder their wives can extend to the children in a familicide, wrote the researchers. If men suspect their wives have been unfaithful, they may also strongly suspect the children are not theirs. In this type of rage-driven familicide, the killer "professes a grievance against his wife, usually with respect to alleged infidelities and/or her intending or acting to terminate the marriage," wrote Daly and Wilson.[27] As for the wife, the man's thinking goes—the scientists believe—"If I can't have her, nobody can." These "accusatory" familicides are often preceded by threats and actual violence against a wife, noted Daly and Wilson, who cited the case of a suicidal Canadian father who killed his wife and two young daughters after repeated violence to his wife and a threat to kill her and the children "if you ever leave me."

Yet far from all family annihilations are driven by anger. Some, if not most, may be, strangely, inspired by a twisted idea of love and devotion to a family.[28] The killers in these cases are often inordinately devoted family men and "good providers" before their crimes. This type of familicidal male tends to command an organized, successful life that tends to serve the family exceptionally well until his "care" is mangled by the dark trajectory of machismo in some kind of distress. These men tend to be "depressed and brooding" after suffering some kind of setback or failure and humiliation, such as a pending bankruptcy or discovery of a financial crime. "Expressions of hostility toward the victims are generally absent" in these cases, noted Wilson and Daly, and there's often no known history of violence. The killer dads tend to see a family annihilation as the only way out. The fathers' logic, sometimes expressed in letters left behind, is: "No one can care for them the way I do." Daly and Wilson cite a number of examples, including the case of a 55-year-old American man who used a hammer to fatally bludgeon his wife and son in their beds, but bungled his own suicide attempt. He explained: "I kept thinking about the bills coming, the house taxes, piling up, piling up in my mind. I thought everything was going to fall around my head. I knew it could be a catastrophe in a short time. My son wouldn't be able to stand the stigma, my wife wouldn't have the things she was used to." In another case, a suicidal South African killer dad left behind a note saying: "I cannot let my family suffer the degradation of losing everything we possess and being thrown penniless onto the street."

Despite their differences, murderers in both categories of family annihilation subscribe to a rationale that "invokes a proprietary conception of wife and family," noted Wilson and Daly.[29] "In either case, the killer apparently feels entitled to decide his victims' fates." In 2008, Manhattan lawyer William Parente, who was about to suffer a devastating economic setback, humiliation, and almost certainly prison time, took it upon himself to sentence his family to death and arranged a special trip to his daughter's college so they could all die together.

FIVE

POSSESSION

STEPHANIE IS WITH HER FAMILY.
—William Parente, on the phone to his
daughter's college roommate after
killing his wife and children

New York attorney William Parente had a habit of sitting extremely still and staring intently when he was collecting his thoughts.[1] He did that two days after Easter in 2009, at his desk in his Manhattan law office on Lexington Avenue. Parente was pale, sweating slightly; he didn't look well. In the previous two weeks he had written several bad checks for hundreds of thousands of dollars. So he was considering his future, slowly moving a palm over the top of his head, staring into the distance. His midlength hair was receding, neatly trimmed, dyed brown to cover most of the gray, and had a tendency to be slightly unruly. Parente, 59, was not, unruly—usually—and it annoyed him when his hair didn't follow suit. But that day, his demeanor matched his hair. He was frazzled, on edge. He had just confessed to Dorothy Schimel, a friend of his late mother and a woman he had known since he was a boy growing up in Bay Ridge, Brooklyn, that he had lost millions she had entrusted to him to invest. He told her that "someone" had threatened his life. The shaken Schimel, who had come to Parente's office with tax forms in hand so he could complete and file them for her just days before the deadline, would later tell police that he had become involved with the "wrong kind of people."

Bill usually kept it together. The unassuming, slightly nerdy, bespectacled lawyer with kindly, almost-grandfatherly eyes had a reputation as a bit of square—but that worked to his advantage in his business. His suits were expensive, but understated and traditional, nothing flamboyant, nothing that shouted the net worth most believed he had earned after decades of hard work in a lucrative practice on Manhattan's East Side. He dined well, vacationed in his condo in the Hamptons, lived in a spacious, white clapboard Long Island home in upscale Garden City, but he had the quiet, modest manner of a boy with a respectable middle-class upbringing, the only child of a New York State trooper and a stay-at-home mom, both of them Italian immigrants. He was under five foot ten and thick, tending toward pudgy. He was the kind of guy who usually kept his suit coat on, even sitting alone in his office and not expecting visitors. "You never, ever, saw him with his shirt out," said Jonathan Bachrach, a lawyer who once shared a suite of law offices with Parente. "If anything, he was a bit too much on the side of uptight and organized."

People trusted Bill. He had a reputation as a devoted family man and frequently stood out as the sober, meticulous adult in any situation. He rarely socialized with colleagues, opting whenever he could to head home instead to be with his family. "The only thing he was passionate about was his family," said Bachrach. "It was always his girls. They were his life. I've never seen a man as proud of his family as Bill was." In a previous workplace, Parente was responsible for collecting the rent from 12 lawyers who shared offices along with secretaries and a receptionist. Each month he tracked down the dollars from each suitemate, meeting the rent deadlines, carefully accounting for what was paid and what was owed. "Bill was considered the most trustworthy, and certainly the most reliable among our group of attorneys," said Bachrach. "We looked to him as the final word on suite management. As far as the other lawyers were concerned, whatever Bill said was solid." As for his own work, Parente rarely pushed, rarely appeared to be selling anything, a facet of his personality that, paradoxically, tended to boost his business.

He started out soon after graduation from Brooklyn Law School with his own practice begun with another attorney, Alan Kornblau, whom he had been introduced to by a cousin. The men eventually struck out on their own with separate businesses but stayed lifelong friends. Parente started out as a real estate and tax attorney, but soon also served as an investment advisor to scores of clients. Most of his investment customers were referred to him by others, and he gave investment advice matter-of-factly, at times, reluctantly.

"I had to press him to talk about stocks," said Bachrach. "The only time he put the bite on me was to buy church raffle tickets. Every few months there would be tickets to something."

Figure 5.1. A young Stephanie poses with her little sister in 2003 for a holiday shot that would become their Christmas card that year. *Reprinted by permission from Portraits by Joanne.*

By 2009 Parente was managing millions of investment dollars entrusted to him by a growing pool of clients. Parente pitched penny stocks to some investors, but also "bridge loans" earmarked for developers, particularly mall builders, unable to get quick capital from banks, he explained to his clients. He supplied launch money from his stable of investors, and the grateful, successful mall developers repaid the loans—plus lucrative interest—as soon as their bank funds came through, which tended to be very quickly, according to Parente. Each loan was secured by reliable developer securities worth at least 150 percent of the loan—securities not acceptable to conventional banks for some reason—so the loans were risk-free, Parente assured his clients. The investments consistently paid a return of at least 12 percent. His investors were pleased. The real estate market had been booming for years, and the financial statements from Parente always showed a tidy profit.

Queens attorney Bruce Montague was one of Parente's happy clients—happy for a time, that is, until his nagging doubts slowly grew into a deep concern. He was referred to Parente by Kornblau, who invested in the bridge loan operation himself and was thrilled with the money he was making. "Everything Parente said made sense when I met with him," Montague told me in an interview at a Garden City diner. "He came highly recommended, and he was a serious, sober kind of guy, who fully explained all the details of what he was doing. It sounded like a safe bet. I got regular statements showing a 12 percent return on my investment, and he provided full records and 1099s on the income. But my accountant was suspicious, and he urged me to take some money out of the operation to make certain it was legitimate. When I asked Bill to cash out some of my investment, he did. Sometimes there was a delay, but he always came through."

But the situation continued to bother Montague. He knew it was too good to be true. "No investment consistently provides that kind of return," he said. "I always advise my own clients that something too good to be true is a scam. But I didn't listen to my own advice. I always used to think, 'How can people be so stupid?' But I was just that stupid. I wanted to believe in something that was too good to be true. It was a humbling experience."

The buzz of concern in Montague's mind became impossible to ignore in the wake of the massive Bernard Madoff Ponzi scheme that blew up in late

2008. Madoff ripped off thousands of investors for billions of dollars in the largest financial fraud in US history. Other Parente investors whom Montague knew were also getting increasingly squeamish after the Madoff news broke. The economy was weakening and many of them now needed cash, and Madoff had made them nervous about their invisible funds. Parente's clients began calling back their money. "I wanted to pull back, and so did others," said Montague, who had entrusted Parente with close to $1 million. "But Bill put a lot of us on hold, on hold, on hold. He paid out some checks, but told people not to cash them. I started to get a really bad feeling." Montague was persistent about his funds. Parente finally, reluctantly, wrote out two checks worth $400,000 each to Montague, telling him not to cash them until tax day. That was just days before Dorothy Schimel came into Parente's office to have her taxes done, and found the lawyer looking "awful," she would later tell police. Alan Kornblau, too, turned up with his tax forms in hand about the same time and was alarmed by Parente's uncharacteristic, nervous behavior.

So there was Parente, finally, alone, just days after signing the Montague checks and soon after dropping the Schimel bombshell, sitting at his desk, staring into the distance, making decisions. He faced what a colleague once described as an "explosion" of family photos—on his desk, his bookshelf, his credenza. There was the professional family Christmas portrait of the four of them, the girls, Catherine, then 11, and 19-year-old Stephanie in red gowns, Bill and wife, Betty, in elegant black; a shot of Catherine's First Communion; a photo of a beaming Stephanie in cap and gown at graduation at Garden City High School; a picture of Betty at the annual Sugar and Spice motherdaughter dinner and dance to raise money for a local cerebral-palsy fundraising association; a snap of Betty and the kids at a backyard barbecue.

In five days they would all be dead.

————

Parente left the following day with Betty and Catherine to visit Stephanie at Loyola University outside Baltimore, where she was a sophomore studying to be a speech therapist. The family made the trip frequently, often driving Stephanie there simply to drop her off after one of her visits home, then turning around and heading back to Long Island. Steph was a member of the crew team freshman year, and one of her teammates noted how often her family turned up to watch her. "They would always come to the regattas," said the sailor. "It was weird for a family to be at every single regatta. But they wanted to see Stephanie."

Catherine was a quiet, gangly athlete who was beginning to make a mark on her middle-school basketball and soccer teams and had recently played Pamina in her fifth-grade production of the *Magic Flute*. She was wearing a removable boot cast on her foot because of a growth-plate crack in a bone from playing soccer, but she was going to Loyola because the Parentes always made the trip together; they did nearly everything as a family. They were extremely close. Betty's best friend, Marianne Quinn, said the women rarely saw each other weekends because that was "family time."

Figure 5.2. "Two Santas," Stephanie and Catherine go cheek-to-cheek in a 2008 photo. *Reprinted by permission from Portraits by Joanne.*

Betty Mazzarella Parente, 58, was as gregarious as her husband was quiet. She had a musical voice, had a frequent laugh, and touched people often, resting a hand on an arm, grasping a friend's shoulder. She met Bill in a Bay Ridge bar; Bill asked her for her phone number the second time they saw each other there. They married soon after. Betty worked as Bill's secretary for years until she became pregnant with Stephanie after several rounds of fertility treatments. Eight years later, she was stunned to find she was pregnant with Catherine at the age of 46. She doted on her daughters, was active in Girl Scouts, volunteered for most of their school events, attended every activity. She also quickly became a social force when the family moved to Garden City from Bay Ridge. She was the queen bee of the local Bunko club, which functioned as a kind of welcoming committee to wives moving to town. "Betty was one of the first friends I made when I came to Garden City, and we were still close ten years later," said Lucille Messina. Lucille shared her heartache with Betty over her late daughter, Jacklyn, who suffered from severe disabilities, and Betty eventually pitched in to help Messina with her work when Messina became president of the Tri-Town Auxiliary of the United Cerebral Palsy Association of Nassau County. Betty was also a Eucharistic minister at St. Joe's Catholic Church in town. She continued to nurture her past friendships, and frequently drove back to her old neighborhood and returned with Italian pastries to share with her Garden City pals. Betty was known for showering her friends with notes—thank you cards and "buck up" jottings. "Betty truly cared about people; she had a way making each one feel like they were special to her," explained Messina. "You are a dream come true as a friend, you bring out the best in me," Betty wrote to Quinn, thanking her for a framed photo she had given Betty as a birthday gift. "As the kids say, you ROCK. Love you to pieces, Betty."

But she wasn't a pushover. Betty had survived an ugly bout with breast cancer, and she had the strength to help others who were diagnosed. Quinn introduced her to a friend diagnosed with cancer a second time, and the three women had dinner together. They talked about difficulties the friend was having with her husband. "Betty said, 'That's your cancer stick. Get rid of him,'" Quinn recalls. "She could call the shots."

Trouble with a husband was not Betty's problem. "Bill was just a quiet guy, and always good to her, as far as I could tell," says Quinn. "He frequently watched Catherine at night when Betty and I had some commitment on a week night. He went with her on all her doctor appointments when she had cancer. He was there for her on her journey."

Figure 5.3. Catherine Parente smiles as she stands alone on a cruise ship stairway for a photo during a cruise with her mom in early 2009. She would be murdered by her father two months later. *Courtesy of Marianne E. Quinn.*

Like Bill, the rest of the family appeared to be well off without being particularly flashy. Betty and Bill did each drive a Mercedes—a four-door sedan for Bill, and a sports utility wagon for Betty, that were updated every few years—but their home was relatively modest, though elegant. Betty and the girls spent summers at their condo in West Hampton, and Bill commuted there when he could. The family also took a major annual vacation on top of the summer getaway. Betty and Catherine took a cruise to Jamaica early in 2009, but Bill didn't accompany them that year because, Betty explained to Quinn, he had "lost a very big client" and wanted to save the cost of his passageway and spend the extra time working. Besides the disappointing loss of a client, Bill was also struggling with the death of his mother the previous year, Betty confided to Marianne. The first anniversary of her death was nearing, and he seemed more dejected about losing her than ever. Betty asked Marianne if she thought it was a good idea to still take the cruise, given the circumstances. "Go, have fun with Catherine," Quinn advised her. "Life is short." Parente's sadness over his mother's death was also an issue at his meetings with a Long Island psychic. Both Betty and Bill had been seeing the woman in Hicksville for about 10 years, visiting her separately every six months or so. Bill would usually arrive from work still in his suit. He was a "brilliant, good-hearted, generous man who loved his family very much," recalled the family's psychic in an interview. But shortly after Betty and Catherine returned from the cruise, he confided to the psychic that he was worried about his business and was scrambling to move money around to save it. He asked her about heaven and if she thought God was forgiving. "I told him people have to suffer everything they've done to others in life, but then God forgives all," she told me. "I assumed he was talking about his mother and the afterlife."

Quinn was surprised just two months after the cruise, the week of Bill's building crisis, that the Parentes were on the road again to visit Stephanie just two days after their daughter had returned to school from Easter break. Betty had hosted a party for Bill's relatives on Easter Sunday, and Stephanie went back to school on Monday. The day before the party, Betty called Quinn to ask if she wanted some pasta from a special Italian store Betty still shopped at in Bay Ridge. "She always made pasta and a ham for Easter," said Quinn. Though Quinn turned down the pasta offer, Betty and Bill drove up to her curb later that day. It was pouring rain, so Bill ran out of the car alone with flowers for Quinn and chocolate Easter eggs for Quinn's two sons. They hugged and wished each other a happy Easter. It was the last time she would see Bill and her longtime friend. Betty's face through the car window was blurred by the rain on the glass.

Figure 5.4. Catherine, Bill, Betty, and Stephanie Parente pose for a Christmas photo in 2006. The family did a holiday photograph with the same studio each year for 18 years the day after Thanksgiving. *Reprinted by permission from Portraits by Joanne.*

Quinn spent hours gabbing with Betty on her cell phone the Tuesday after Easter as Marianne drove to Boston to visit colleges with her high-school-aged son, and Betty never mentioned plans for the family's trip to Loyola the following day. "The only thing odd was our conversation about sharing a baby gift for the grandchild of a friend of ours," recalled Quinn. "I suggested a small swing you can set up in the house, which would have cost us about $50 apiece. But she said it was too expensive—the kind of thing I had never heard from her—and that she wanted to spend half that amount." The following day, the Parentes were on the road to collect Stephanie. "She never mentioned anything to me about going to Loyola," recalled Quinn.

———

Someone else surprised by the family's trip was the college sophomore. Stephanie was perturbed when she got the call that her parents and sister were coming down. She had just left home Monday, and the family was already back on the road to visit her 48 hours later. She was settling in to classes after the Easter break and had a major chemistry exam coming up after the weekend. It was unusual for Stephanie to ever be testy. The high-voltage, long-haired brunette was almost always up, and her peals of laughter could be heard across campus. She was sassy and funny. While so many female students wore the standard college "uniform" of black North Face jackets, Stephanie had opted for the hot-pink version of the parka. She liked to stand out, and she did, even though she barely tipped the scales at 90 pounds and wasn't nearly 5 feet tall (though insisted she was). She was so petite that her nickname was "Little Steph," which distinguished her from "Big Stephanie," another of five Loyola suitemates who called themselves "The Mates."

Stephanie liked to party, enjoyed dressing up in a "naughty nurse" costume for Halloween one year, and, just like her mom, threw herself into activities and connected deeply with her pals. She warned friends their work lives could be a grind, so they should enjoy life whenever they could. But Stephanie was also a serious student, and serious about a career, as were each of her suitemates, and they shared their plans for the future. They were each preparing to spend junior year abroad, and Stephanie intended to go to Newcastle, England. In fact, there was a meeting for students and families the following week at Loyola about spending junior year abroad, which made it even odder that her parents were coming down just days after Easter.

Julieanne Malley, one of Steph's closest friends of their group, seemed to have a sixth sense that week about something troubling. She watched out for her roomie. She knew Stephanie needed some extra sleep, needed to study, and needed to relax because she was nervous about the chem test. But she also knew Stephanie wanted to please her parents. Julieanne kept tabs on her friend's plans and spoke briefly with the Parentes Saturday morning at breakfast at a campus cafeteria. She knew Steph's mom slightly more than her dad because Betty was so outgoing. Bill Parente was quieter, but polite and friendly. He worked along with Julieanne's dad getting their daughters settled when they had first moved into their suite. That Saturday, Steph planned to spend a few hours with her family, watch a Loyola lacrosse game, then return to study. That had generally been the routine since the family arrived on Wednesday. Stephanie would attend classes and study, then meet up with them for shopping or meals, and would head back to her own suite to spend the night in. Saturday afternoon in Garden City, meanwhile, Quinn stopped at the Parentes' house to show Betty some magazine clippings on alternate baby gifts to buy together. She was surprised Betty wasn't at home, and noticed newspapers and a bill for an awning outside the front door, indicating the Parentes hadn't been home for days. Quinn rang her pal on her cell phone. Betty explained they had suddenly decided to take a trip to visit "the sister," referring to Steph. She "sounded happy, a bit rushed and breathless, and mentioned they were going to some kind of game," said Quinn.

On Sunday morning Stephanie accompanied her family to Shirley's Café near Loyola. A restaurant video shows the family walking in, sitting quietly at a table, and eating breakfast in the crowded restaurant. Steph returned to her suite later and began studying for her chemistry exam. She took off again after noon, leaving her chem book open on her desk. When she didn't return, Julieanne called her a short time later, but Stephanie's cell phone had been turned off. She told police later that Bill Parente must have picked up his daughter again that day to return to the Sheraton Hotel in nearby Towson, where they were staying. Stephanie had no car at Loyola, and there was no convenient public transit to the suburban Sheraton.

By late Sunday night, Stephanie still hadn't returned. Julieanne called the hotel to see if the Parentes had checked out, and was mortified when the desk rang her call through to their room. "I knew it was too late to call," she told me. "It was close to midnight. If the family was still there, I was afraid I would wake them up." Bill Parente picked up the phone and didn't sound like he had been asleep. He was uncharacteristically curt. Julieanne introduced herself and asked if Stephanie was with them, because she hadn't returned to her suite. "Stephanie is with her family. She's staying here," he responded. "Good night."

The next morning, Julieanne sent an e-mail to Stephanie's chem professor to make certain her roomie had turned up to take the test. She hadn't, which surprised the teacher, who knew Stephanie as the kind of student who would always send a note if she couldn't make an exam for any reason. Julieanne then called the Parentes' home in Garden City to talk to Stephanie's parents, or at least confirm that Bill Parente's voice, or a voice on his answering machine was the same one she had heard the night before. The message machine was nearly full, packed with increasingly frantic, repeated calls from investors whose checks were bouncing, police would later discover. The initially polite messages soon became curt, demanding. "Bill, I waited to deposit the check the way you asked, and it bounced," said one woman. "I'm not happy. Call me." Finally a banker from Chase, where Parente's account was, called. "Mr. Parente, please call me," he said. "It's actually rather urgent."

Figure 5.5. Stephanie, Betty, and Catherine attend a Garden City event in Long Island. Betty was active in several charities and her local church. *Courtesy of Marianne E. Quinn.*

After calling Steph's home, Julieanne then contacted student services, which contacted police, who called the hotel. A short time later, a hotel manager called 911. "We have a dead body in one of our rooms, ma'am," said a calm male voice.

"Any idea how this might have happened?" asked the operator.

"I don't know. I'm not going further into the room after what I just saw on the floor in the entrance," he responded.

When a school administrator called the hotel again to check on any news about Stephanie, she was told the hotel manager was "busy with the police."

What hotel manager Robert Least saw in the entry hall into room 1029 was the body of Bill Parente. He lay dead on his back just beyond the bathroom door. His eyes were open, his right leg was up, bent at the knee. He was wearing green corduroy pants, a white t-shirt, socks on his small feet, and a gold and silver watch on his wrist. He had two white handkerchiefs in his right back pocket. The 911 dispatcher reported a possible cardiac arrest, but the responding officer immediately called detectives when he entered the darkened room where all the curtains had been drawn and all the lamps unplugged. The only light came from the bathroom. Baltimore County Investigator John Tollen entered a short time later. He stepped around Parente's body, opened a curtain of one of the windows along Dulhaney Road next to the king-sized bed. He pulled back a white duvet and sheet to "reveal the three Parente women, all obviously deceased," the police report states.

The bodies of Betty Parente, Catherine, and Stephanie lay side by side on the bed. They appeared to have been posed. Betty was wearing black trousers, a pink shirt, and a light, zip-up black blazer. She wore only one silver hoop earring; the other was found on the floor. She lay on her back, her eyes closed, her right hand resting on her chest. Catherine, in orange shorts over gray sweatpants and a dark sweatshirt, lay next to her, also on her back. Her right hand rested beneath the pillow where Betty's head lay, and her other arm was bent, with her hand placed on her stomach. Stephanie, dressed in gray sweatpants and a blue hoodie, was lying on her side, facing her sister and her mother, her brown hair falling across her face.

The suspected murder weapons: "lamp and hands," the Baltimore County Police report states. "There was blood observed in the bathroom, the bed, and on the rug. There was a small amount of blood spatter on the wall and headboard of the bed. There were several knives observed in the room, which were just purchased. The suspect appeared to have several self-inflicted cuts: one in each wrist and one in the neck." A pair of eyeglasses, apparently smeared with blood, were spotted on the floor next to the foot of the bed.

Betty suffered the worst violence. The top of her face and head were bashed and bloodied. She was apparently struck with a heavy hotel table lamp with such force that it cracked the base of the lamp, whose decorative pattern left an impression on Betty's skull. Catherine showed "mild petechia"—red marks on her face—from apparent asphyxiation, spotted by the detective. Investigators believe a scuff mark on the wall may have been made by the pink cast on Catherine's foot as she kicked out while she was smothered. She also had an abrasion on her chin and bruising on her chest and forearms. Stephanie apparently fought hard for her life. Her death was attributed to "multiple injuries," like her mom. She had abrasions on both sides of her hips, the back of her left hand and forearm, abrasions and bruising on her left foot and left shin, lacerations on the top of her head, marks and scratches on her neck.

Amid the horror and destruction of the room were banal items that testified to the heartbreaking lost normalcy of their now-shattered lives. Betty had a safety pin attached to her bra with two charms: "One safety pin with two charms recovered from right bra strap of victim #1," the police report states. A plastic shopping bag, apparently Catherine's, held a bobby pin, a plastic penny, and a plastic snowflake. "One (1) pair tennis shoes, Reebok brand, size 9, and two (2) brown shoes, American Eagle brand" were catalogued by forensics investigators. Stephanie wore a blue-and-yellow elastic ponytail band on her right wrist. More ominously, a strand of her hair was found caught in Bill Parente's watch wristband. Police also spotted the usual casual detritus of a family on vacation. Clothes were strewn in the room, some on the floor, others folded over chairs. Suitcases, including two Louis Vuitton bags, hotel-door card keys, the keys to Betty's car, three cell phones, and two wallets with cash and credit cards lay about the room.

No one will ever know exactly what happened in the room. The blood told a tale, a sequence of attacks and murder, indications of resistance or of sudden, fatal submission. Much was made of the fact in newspaper accounts at the time that no one was restrained. Betty and Catherine were dead by the time Stephanie walked into the room. Betty was likely killed, or at least rendered unconscious, first, typical in such family annihilation cases so a mother can't help the children who are attacked next. Did Parente attack her as Catherine was in the shower? Did he cover Betty with the duvet to hide the fact from Catherine that her mother was dead before he smothered her? Did his daughter plead for her life? Did Parente respond? Did he try to make her understand whatever mangled logic he believed made sense of his mission? Did he attack Stephanie as she walked in the hotel door, or did she see her mother's and sister's bodies first? Was the idea that her father was a killer so unfathomable to her that she waited too many precious seconds to respond or run to save herself? And how could devoted family man Bill Parente continue to battle to kill a daughter fighting for her life?

Parente killed himself several hours later, likely shortly after midnight, investigators believe. He may have spent at least some of that time watching TV in the dark, the light from the screen flickering on his face, his thumb hitting the remote button, channel surfing. Two movies were rented on the hotel TV late that afternoon. Maybe he lay beside his family as he watched. When a worried Julieanne Malley spoke to Parente at midnight, Stephanie, her mom, and her sister were already dead.

Parente left the room after the murders of his family to walk across the street to the Towson Town Center Mall, where he purchased a boxed set of six black-handled Robert Welch kitchen knives at the Crate & Barrel store. Hours after he returned to the room, he used three of the knives to slash at his wrists, and finally stabbed himself in the neck in the bathroom, eventually collapsing just outside the bathroom door. Parente also had redness and discoloration on his nose and left eye, possibly from struggles with his victims. When police entered the room, the bathroom sink was partially filled with blood, and a blood-slicked knife lay on the counter. Blood spatter surrounded the sink and was on the floor. Several blood-soaked towels were folded and stacked on the edge of the bathtub. Tollen noted two partially eaten cookies in the trash can next to the desk in the room. An empty can of coke with apparent blood stains was also recovered from the garbage. The remaining four knives still lay in their box alongside the wide-screen TV, next to keys and cells phones and a half-eaten roll of Life Savers.

After the crime was publicized, local police were contacted by a couple who stayed one floor up from the Parentes and across the hall. They told investigators that they had reported to hotel management the afternoon of the murders that they had heard a woman scream, twice, followed by what sounded like gargled sounds of a strangulation. Hotel management confirmed that they investigated the report but were unable to determine which room the sounds had come from.

Quinn heard of the murders Monday morning from her husband, who called her as she was driving to work. He was on the local school board and had been informed early of the killings as board members discussed how to handle announcing the tragedy at Catherine's middle school. "Pull over. I have something to tell you, and you shouldn't be driving when you hear it," he said. She immediately called in to work at her insurance office to report she wouldn't be in that day, and sped to the Parentes' house, which was already surrounded by news trucks. She mistakenly believed they were vehicles for paramedics or some other kind of "rescuers"—a part of her still hoping someone could save her friend.

Julieanne Malley's mother called her the same day and told her to sit down. Police had found a murdered family in the Towson Sheraton, but the media initially incorrectly reported that two parents, a daughter and son were dead. "That's OK, Mom," Julieanne reassured her mother. "Stephanie didn't have a brother."

While the Parente family was in Baltimore County, Bruce Montague—and several other investors—were discovering that no funds existed to cover the post-dated checks Parente had written. He called Alan Kornblau that Monday. "Have you heard?" asked Kornblau, who had already been contacted by police. "The Parente family is dead."

Montague was devastated. "You can replace money, but you can't replace those lives," he said. "I felt horrible for his wife and daughters. In some twisted way he was he hoping to spare them pain. But to murder someone to save them is psychopathic. It's unfathomable to me how someone could commit murder, especially that kind of murder—to take the lives of your wife and children. As bad as things are, for him to believe that his family was better off dead was absolutely crazy."

Bizarrely, just days before the Parente murder-suicide, another dad in

Maryland shot to death his wife and three young children in their home an hour away from the Towson Sheraton. Christopher Wood, 34, who also committed suicide, was $450,000 in debt and suffering from depression at the time of the attack. He left behind six notes citing the family's financial problems and expressing remorse for what he had done.

Parente "was a good man who had a bad day," said the family's psychic. "I don't believe he ever meant to cheat anyone, but he became overwhelmed by the debts. Garden City is a competitive, very status-conscious community, and he didn't want to leave his family behind to deal with his humiliation and a financial crisis in that kind of atmosphere. Maybe he wouldn't have killed them if he had a sibling he could have counted on to take care of them, but he didn't."

The murders haunt Quinn, who first met Betty when she worked as an assistant teacher at a nursery school, and watched over a three-year-old Catherine. "What I want to believe is that he took them because he loved them so much. But the attacks were brutal. He hit Betty in the face with a hotel lamp—there was no open casket. Did he mean to kill her when he hit her? Or did they fight? Was it premeditated? Stephanie was the most bruised; she put up the biggest fight. The baby had bruising on her chin. And she was in a cast."

Perhaps those most profoundly affected by the bloodshed were Stephanie's roommates, who were drawn together even more closely after her death. They did travel abroad the following year, graduated from Loyola in 2011 and went on to careers without her. They began a scholarship in Stephanie's honor their senior year in college, and it has grown to one of the largest the school offers. "Not a day goes by that I don't think about Stephanie," says Malley, who still wonders if there was something else she could have done to save her friend's life. More than anything in the wake of Stephanie's murder, "the Mates" needed the one person who always had an uncanny ability to make them smile in any situation—Stephanie. "I miss you more than you know, Little Steph," wrote suitemate Lauren Gallieni on a Facebook page tribute to the Parente victims. "Keep an eye on us now because we need you more than ever."

———

I stayed in room 1029 at the Sheraton Towson, though it has been re-numbered because, as a maid explained, people are "superstitious about it." I don't like to think I'm superstitious, but I was hoping the room would give me an insight—or maybe I would sense something from the haunted souls there. The only thing it offered was a restless night, a fear that I would suddenly feel fingers on my shoulder, and a crushing, overwhelming sadness. I tried to imagine the blur of family members interacting in some sped-up time-machine past—with a dad slipping on his watchband, a sister ordering room service or telling her sibling to hurry up and get out of the bathroom so someone else could use it, a mother brushing her hair in front of the mirror, threading a silver hoop earring through her earlobe. I imagined the murmur of voices as they communicated the things families talk about in a hotel room as they share time away from home together. But they told me nothing.

SIX

DEVASTATION

The rest of Bill Parente's devastation became apparent after the bodies of his family were found in the Sheraton Hotel room. Bruce Montague was convinced Parente's failed investment operation triggered the murder-suicide. He met with his partners at his Queens law office to discuss what steps he should take. "Fortunately, I have a law firm," he explained. "I knew there were other investors out there facing the same losses—and in many cases, more—without the resources I had."[1] Montague and his partners decided to go public. A lawyer from Montague's firm contacted the New York attorney general, the Manhattan District Attorney's Office and local FBI officials to reveal what Montague suspected was a Ponzi scheme likely operated by Parente for several years. Montague and his partner Steven Drelich talked to the press about the tragedy and its suspected link to the investment scam. The next day Montague's office was inundated with calls from reporters—and pleas for help from investors now out millions of dollars. Montague's office began collecting affidavits from investors to pass on to law enforcement authorities. Many Parente investors were elderly and came to him through his mother or his mother's friends, like Dorothy Schimel. A number of them lost their life savings trusting Bill Parente. Montague's office collected 22 affidavits, though subsequent research during legal proceedings regarding Parente's estate would uncover some 66 investors. Not everyone lost money. Some earned more than they invested and, for a time, were considered targets in potential clawback actions in an operation that was estimated to have collected millions.

The unbelievability of the Parente family murders coupled with the decades-long scheme operated by the apparently super-straight, ultra-reliable Bill Parente spawned a bizarre myth about Parente's crimes. Because he told clients some investments went to Russian developers in Canada, some investors became convinced he and his family had been assassinated by thugs in the Russian mob. Even Alan Kornblau was convinced, for a time, that Parente had been the target of a mob hit. Some of that was a human need to make sense of the senseless. "We tell ourselves they're all in the witness protection program," said Susan Deluca, a co-owner of a Brooklyn photo studio that took the Parentes' Christmas photos for 18 years. "We know that's not really true, but it's a way for us to deal with it."

In fact, as far as authorities could determine, there were never any developers who received loans from Parente or his clients. After being contacted by Montague's office, the FBI seized files and computers from Parente's office. "There were no co-conspirators" uncovered, a New York FBI agent told me months after the investigation was completed. "He may have made some penny stock investments or some loans over the years, but nothing showed up in his accounts. He had no separate investment accounts for any of his clients. He even co-mingled his own personal and business funds." A police search of Parente public records showed some 30 different business names with a lower Manhattan address registered in his name, including Internal Resource Services (with the useful IRS acronym) and Flomar Accessories Corp., which Parente used to pose as investment or construction and mall-development operations. Other retail and restaurant business names registered by Parente likely served as paper fronts for imaginary distributors and stores in his imaginary malls.

A court judgment in the distribution of the assets of the Parente estate, which called the scam and murders a "tragedy of epic proportion," described the lawyer's operation as a classic Ponzi scheme in which money was never invested—only used to pay off earlier investors and Parente's own expenses.[2] Victims filed nearly $36 million in claims against Parente's estate.

Parente's tangled scheme became the focus of a macabre court battle over his assets. He had life insurance, including a $5 million irrevocable insurance trust he established in 2007 naming his wife and children as beneficiaries. The funds would be available even in the event of suicide. It's possible the insurance policy was part of Parente's Ponzi exit scheme.

Perhaps he considered committing suicide even then, and leaving his family the $5 million, but eventually opted instead to take Betty and his daughters with him.

Figure 6.1. The Parente family poses for one of their annual holiday studio photos in 2005. Bill didn't often have his photo taken with the family, but always accompanied his wife and daughters to watch them have their pictures taken. *Reprinted by permission from Portraits by Joanne.*

The insurance policy, and Parente's other assets, were the target of a court challenge by a cousin of Betty Parente, Joseph Mazzarella, the 81-year-old owner of the Mazzarella funeral home that prepared the Parente bodies and was the administrator of Betty's estate. Betty, Stephanie, and Catherine were buried together in a single grave, while Bill Parente was cremated separately at the insistence of friends and relatives furious with Bill. A suit by Mazzarella first challenged the determination of the heir in the suicide-murders. It demanded a hearing to determine definitively who was breathing last in Parente's rampage, because that would be the ultimate heir, and that person's "distributees" would get the estate's assets. "No evidence was presented as to the order of death among Betty, Catherine and Stephanie," the action stated.[3] "Arguably, based upon the death certificates and the police report, petitioner has made a prima facie showing that Betty, Catherine and Stephanie died before William, and that William killed them before committing suicide. However, the court must hold a hearing so that the respondent is given the opportunity to rebut the evidence presented, as these issues and the issue of the entitlement of William and his heirs to inherit from these three estates are inextricably linked."

Whatever the determination, officials should leapfrog over Parente as the final holder of the estate in any case because he was a murderer and neither he nor his "distributees" should profit from his crime, Mazzarella's suit further argued. "It is well established law that one who takes the life of another should not be permitted to profit from his own wrong and shall be barred from inheriting from the person slain . . . no one shall be permitted to profit by his own fraud, or to the advantage of his own wrong, or to found any claim upon his own iniquity, or to acquire property by his own crime," the suit said. The familicide required a hearing to officially determine Parente's status as a murderer, the lawsuit argued, a legal procedure usually skipped in such a situation once police determine what happened.

The court action was an attempt by Mazzarella to wrest away assets headed to Parente's defrauded investors and steer them to Betty's side of the family. The Nassau County probate court ultimately ruled against Mazzarella, and noted it's "undisputed Stephanie and Catherine predeceased William and that Betty died first, followed by Catherine, then Stephanie and finally William."[4] And regardless of William Parente's criminal actions, Betty's "collateral relatives could not have had any reasonable expectation of benefit from the insurance policy on William's life. It cannot be said that equity would be better served by directing the proceeds of the life insurance trust to Betty's relatives, leaving the victims of William's Ponzi scheme with no hope of recovering even a small portion of their losses."

Figure 6.2. Betty and Catherine pose for a photo on a vacation cruise early in 2009. Stephanie was away at Loyola and Bill decided to stay home to work because he was losing some important business and needed to put in extra hours, he told his wife, Betty confided to a friend. *Courtesy of Marianne E. Quinn.*

Figure 6.3. An angelic Stephanie Parente, 8, smiles down at her baby sister, Catherine, for the photo that would be their 1998 holiday card. *Reprinted by permission from Portraits by Joanne.*

Nevertheless, Mazzarella, as administrator of the estate of Betty and the girls, was granted control over some $500,000 in Parente family assets as part of a settlement with the Nassau County public administrator representing the Parente estate. That included proceeds from the family's properties—the Garden City home, the condo in Westhampton, and Parente's mother's Bay Ridge co-op—along with all personal effects, including the family cars, which hadn't yet been paid off. Part of the money would cover the $30,000 bill for the family funeral, and Mazzarella agreed to spend up to $15,000 to erect a "permanent memorial tribute dedicated to the memory of Betty Ann Parente, Stephanie Ann Parente and Catherine Ann Parente, in the form of a dignified plaque."[5] Most of the proceeds from the sale of the properties would go to the husband and two children of Betty's late sister. The $5 million life insurance trust as well as proceeds from other life insurance policies were directed to be divided among Parente's scammed investors to cover some of the losses, though funds had not yet been dispersed by the time of this writing, late 2012, as the estate administrator attempted to validate the size of each claim. The judge concluded after the settlement: "I would like to say this is a very tragic event and these things, not only do they have emotional and family and personal aspects, but they have legal aspects. And with respect to the legal aspects, perhaps, this is the end of that part of it. I know this will never be the end to the personal sorrow."[6]

For a man "ruined" by his schemes and driven to murder-suicide, after his death Bill Parente's estate held millions in life insurance, even though he had less than $5,000 in the bank, making Parente, like Willie Loman in *Death of a Salesman*, worth more in dollars dead than alive. But everyone had a claim on those dollars.

The Parente family possessions were distributed in a "tag sale" set up by the Mazzarella family at the Garden City house. Goods not purchased were distributed to charities. Marianne Quinn is left with memories of Betty and the kids, and notes from her pal. From the Mozzarellas' tag sale she managed to take home a photo of Betty that she had given her friend for her last birthday. The Lenox frame holding the photo urged: "Celebrate life."

SEVEN

DEATH BY THE NUMBERS

WE BLIND OURSELVES TO THE STRUCTURAL PROPERTIES OF A FAMILY AS A SOCIAL INSTITUTION THAT MAKES IT OUR MOST VIOLENT INSTITUTION WITH THE EXCEPTION OF THE MILITARY IN TIME OF WAR.
—Prof. Richard Gelles, dean of the School of Social Policy and Practice at the University of Pennsylvania[1]

A s confounding as William Parente's murder-suicide rampage was, it was hardly unique. It was part of a cluster of similar cases that year and others, and it bore an uncanny similarity to other family annihilations in the United States, and in other nations—so alike it's almost as if the murderous dads' fortunes were designed by a single mechanism, and their actions when fortunes fell were commanded by an unseen dictator. Parente's British "clone" pulled off his attack just eight months earlier across the ocean. Their personalities were dramatically different. British killer Christopher Foster was a bit of a blowhard and could be volatile, unlike Parente, and was also warmer, more charismatic, handsome, and athletic. But like the New York lawyer, Foster became a roaring success from a modest background, enjoyed his wealth, basked in the attention of his well-provided-for all-female household, and was utterly devoted to the family he annihilated.

Like Parente, Foster also had a dark secret. Before his murderous spree, his financial success had been rotted away by profligate spending, tax liens after years of evasion, and lost court judgments over slippery financial dealings, though his family had no idea how desperate his situation had become. Just weeks before his home was to be repossessed, he not only killed his wife, Jill, and 15-year-old daughter, Kirstie, but every living thing on his tony Shropshire farm.[2]

Foster was a proud, self-made millionaire who had traded up a nondescript home in Wolverhampton in England's East Midlands for his sixteen-acre multi-million-dollar Obaston House estate near Maesbrook when he made it big with an invention for fireproof insulation. Foster always went for broke. To prove to investors that his insulation worked, as he prepared to launch his company, he mortgaged his house (pre-Obaston) to pay for an expensive, dramatic demonstration to prove that his invention could withstand a dramatic blaze. If the insulation held, he had it made; if it burned, he lost everything. It worked. Within months he was boasting to his mom and pals that he was a multi-millionaire and had so much extra cash he couldn't spend it fast enough.

Foster reveled in his new life and was such a gregarious life of every gathering that he "sucked all the oxygen from the room," said a pal. "To come in second place wasn't his style," another friend recounted in a documentary about the crime, *The Millionaire and the Murder Mansion*.[3] "He had to be up front with the winners." Foster bought his palatial home—for cash—after his wife spotted it featured in a story in a country living magazine. He quickly donned the lifestyle of a wealthy gentleman farmer, collecting cars and guns, and traipsing through his property on hunting parties shooting pheasant with his Labrador retrievers. At various times he owned two Range Rovers, a silver Jaguar, a Mercedes, a Bentley, an Aston Martin, "his and hers" Porsches, and a collection of custom-made rifles, which he once told a friend could be Jill's "insurance policy" if anything happened to him because they were worth a small fortune.

But Foster could erupt unpredictably, too. He shot Jill's doves when they strayed into his multicar garage, and he shot Kirstie's beloved, but stubborn Lab, Holly, after the dog ran onto a neighboring farm and chased the sheep. He could be angry, headstrong, impulsive. That's when Jill and Kirstie steered clear. His housekeeper revealed in the documentary that she was unsettled by his obsession with guns; he always left one in the kitchen and in his bedroom.

Foster lost his company to liquidation shortly before his rampage. He never told Jill or Kirstie that the firm was gone. He still pretended to work every day and boasted at a party that he was close to signing a $17 million insulation deal with a Russian company. Creditors would never get his home, he vowed ominously to a friend. "They have to take me out in a box for that to happen," he said.

Before everything imploded, nothing seemed amiss, just like the day Bill Parente climbed in the car for the trip to Maryland to pick up his daughter. Foster had just turned 50 and was a bit more emotional than usual. He was looking though family photos and watched his wedding video, taken 21 years earlier, with Jill, and they both cried, according to their housekeeper. But otherwise, Chris was "in a cheerful mood and larking about" with his wife and daughter, the housekeeper told police in a videotaped interview.

Four days later, CCTV surveillance cameras Foster had installed on his estate show Jill and Kirstie hopping out of his Range Rover as Foster pulls it into their garage as they return home from a neighborhood barbecue bash. Kirstie disappears from the video frame, apparently to free the Labs from their kennels because the excited dogs suddenly appear on camera wagging their tails and simpering around Foster. Soon after, before bed that night, Kirstie texted a 16-year-old boy in her class, eventually telling him that her dad was about to "shut down the Internet," she wrote. "Night night. Bye. Love u," she signed off. By the predawn hours, Jill and Kristie were dead, killed with a single bullet to the head. The several dogs and five horses would also be shot dead, or perish in the fire set by Foster as he torched his farm and posh country home in an attack so massive that authorities initially thought kidnappers had struck Foster's home, or that it was some kind of "organized reprisal situation," recalled a detective on *The Millionaire and the Murder Mansion*. British media initially talked of possible terrorism. Twelve fire crews had responded to the blaze at the farm, where a horse trailer with its tires shot out initially blocked access to the gates. When the fire was finally extinguished, the house was a gutted shell and the expensive cars little more than charred metal hulks. Fire investigators would discover later that Foster had turned his home into a kind of funeral pyre by using a hose to pump hundreds of gallons of oil from a tank on the estate into the basement of the house before setting it ablaze.

Arriving investigators were perplexed. "When we first arrived, in a very few minutes we realized the extent of the damage. Everybody said someone's making a statement here rather than it being a straightforward fire or a murder," senior forensics investigator Paul Beeton explained from his office in the documentary. But footage from the CCTV cameras showed Foster calmly walking through his grounds in the predawn hours as he cradled one of his custom-made rifles, outfitted with a silencer, with his dogs. Blood spatters indicated he took the Labs into their kennels, where he shot them, then carried their bodies to lay them next to two horses he had shot earlier. Kirstie and Jill were likely already dead in their beds, though they wouldn't be found for days after the fire was extinguished because the house and their corpses were so ravaged by the blaze. "He shot the dogs in the head, shot the horses in the head, shot the wife and daughter in the head," remarked an investigator in *The Millionaire and the Murder Mansion.* "No distinction, is there?" Foster was found dead next to his wife's body, the rifle by his side. He had died of smoke inhalation.

"My worst nightmares are that in the spilt second before he shot her, Jill sensed him there or woke up and knew what was happening," Foster's brother, Andrew, explained on the film. But even more troubling to his brother was what Foster—viewed as a "bully" by Andrew long before the murder-suicide—stole from Kirstie. "It's what's been taken away from her that I find the most difficult to come to terms with," he said. "She was never given that choice. There were no questions asked; it was just taken away with the pull of a trigger."

Foster's mom was devastated by the actions of a murderous son she didn't recognize, but still desperately missed, as much as she mourned the loss of her daughter-in-law and grandchild. She was left grappling with her own shaken ideals of love and family. "Your whole concept of everything changes," said Enid Foster in the documentary. "But you always love your child, don't you? No matter what they did, you forgive them."

Such family annihilations, or familicides, are almost exclusively committed by fathers. This particular "brand" of murder-suicide, like William Parente's, usually involves white males of apparently moderate to well-to-do means. They're often committed with a gun and are frequently preceded by a financial fall, usually with some kind of extra humiliation—court cases, bankruptcy, charges of fraud, or a firing. Murder-suicides, including family annihilations—whether fueled by rage or a twisted sense of concern—are on the rise in the United States. The number of murder-suicides in the United States increased a third in six months of 2011,[4] compared to the same period in 2007,[5] from an average of nine incidents each week to 12 each week. The number of deaths jumped 34 percent to 691 in those months. In 2011, 80 percent of all murder-suicides in the nation occurred in the home,[6] and family annihilators accounted for most of all murder-suicide incidents with three or more victims.[7] Close to three-fourths of murder-suicides in the United States the last several years have involved the murder of an intimate partner or spouse, almost always by a male.[8] In 2008, 45 of the victims in murder-suicides in a sixth-month period were children, and 55 were kids in 2011.[9] Forty-four children witnessed some aspect of the crime in that time in 2008,[10] with 66 surviving child witnesses in 2011.[11]

An estimate of 1,382 murder-suicide deaths for all of 2011 is extrapolated only from media accounts tracked periodically since 2002 by the Violence Policy Center, a non-profit organization in Washington, DC. There are no official statistics for the phenomenon; no government agency tallies murder-suicides. The numbers are only part of the picture for another reason. Figures gleaned by the Violence Policy Center don't include family annihilations in which the father (at least 90 percent of familicides over the years have been committed by dads) either doesn't attempt to commit suicide or fails in a halfhearted attempt, a more common situation when intimate partners and children are killed in a rage, as opposed to what Parente or Foster might have rationalized as "mercy killings" committed out of a sense of love and protectiveness.

Family annihilations like Parente's are a tiny subset of homicides, and a small portion of child homicides, yet they draw the attention of domestic-violence experts because they are so confounding—generally committed by upstanding, devoted fathers with little or no history of domestic violence—

and because their secrets may help unlock a hidden, elemental vulnerability to violence and a susceptibility to social stresses that lie deep within even apparently strong, healthy families. "Even though familicides are relatively rare, they raise critical questions about the very fabric of modern social life," said Northern Arizona University sociology professor Neil Websdale, who has extensively studied the phenonmenon.[12]

Richard Gelles, one of the nation's leading experts on domestic violence, and currently the dean of the University of Pennsylvania's School of Social Policy and Practice, believes familicides demand attention. Family annihilators "either view their family members as possessions that they control, or don't see any boundaries between their identity, their wife, and their children. And so these are 'suicides' of the entire family, where the overly enmeshed individual can't bear to leave the pain behind and so takes his wife and children with him," Gelles explained at a 2010 videotaped conference focusing on research regarding domestic and sexual violence held in Arlington, Virginia, by the National Institute of Justice. "What commonality do you find in these guys? They're the atypical ones for whom there isn't much of a record of domestic violence or of child abuse. They're the ones where the neighbors typically say, 'He would be the last person on earth I would see doing that.'" Gelles has noted similarities between such a father and the leader of a cult: "It's a different kind of cult. It's a cult with the father/husband seeing himself as the head of the family, the king, the Jim Jones, and everybody's going to drink the Kool-Aid because Jim Jones doesn't want to be around any longer. Cult mass killings seem to also be male-driven. I can't think of the last female cult leader who had a mass killing involved with her."

Gelles has viewed such families as the "canaries in the violence mine shaft" of American society. He worried that an alarming cluster of the murder-suicides the last few years was an indication of the start of a surging domestic-violence and child-abuse problem across society that had yet to reveal itself due to the lag of statistical information behind actual occurrences, as well as the time it takes for families to fully experience and react to the impact of a faltering economy.

A 2012 study by the PolicyLab of the Children's Hospital of Philadelphia apparently discovered that very link from the economy to violence against children in the family.[13] In the largest study to examine child abuse within the recession, researchers discovered a significant increase over the last decade in the number of sons and daughters admitted to the nation's largest children's hospitals due to serious physical abuse. While admissions for accidental injury declined, researchers found that admissions at 38 hospitals for overall physical abuse of children under the age of six increased by 0.79 percent a year, with admissions for traumatic brain injury suspected of being linked to abuse increased an astounding 3 percent each year between 2000 and 2009. The study also tracked a corresponding increase in local mortgage foreclosures as a gauge of the economic downturn and a possible marker of economic stress. Each 1 percent increase in 90-day mortgage delinquencies over a one-year period in a specific community generally corresponded to a 5 percent increase in local hospital admissions due to traumatic brain injury suspected to be a result of child abuse.

"We were concerned that health care providers and child welfare workers anecdotally reported seeing more severe child physical abuse cases, yet national Child Protective Services (CPS) data indicated a downward trend," the study's lead author, Dr. Joanne Wood, an attending physician at the Children's Hospital of Philadelphia, said in a statement. "It's well known that economic stress has been linked to an increase in child physical abuse, so we wanted to get to the bottom of the contrasting reports by formally studying hospital data on a larger scale."

Results suggest that "housing concerns were a significant source of stress within communities and a harbinger for community maltreatment rates," her study concluded.[14] "This is not surprising given the magnitude of fore-closure and housing crisis that marked the recession." The data highlighted the value of using hospital-admission statistics along with child-welfare data to "ensure a more complete picture of child abuse rates both locally and nationally," noted Wood. The research also underscored the need to "better understand the stress that housing insecurity places on families" and its impact on violence in the home, she added.

Child abuse and fatalities in US homes are shockingly high. "We've got a problem, and it's a big one," Michael Petit, executive director of the Every

Child Matters Education Fund, a non-profit organization that battles abuse, told me. His organization estimates some 21,000 American children have died due to neglect, abuse, or outright homicide in the home over the past decade. That's three times the total number of US soldiers killed in Iraq and Afghanistan.[15]

The United States has one of the three highest rates of child-maltreatment deaths among wealthy nations, according to a 2003 study by the United Nations Children's Fund (UNICEF), the latest in a series of "report cards" on worldwide child fatalities, and that's before taking into account child homicides by parents that aren't registered as abuse deaths, such as those that occur in a William Parente kind of family annihilation.[16] The United States tallied 2.4 annual deaths per 100,000 children in 2002, compared to 1.4 for France, 1 in Japan, and 0.9 in Britain, according to the UNICEF calculations. The child-maltreatment death rate in the United States that year was triple Germany's and 11 times that of Italy. Rates in the United States, Mexico, and Portugal—the three nations with the worst records—were as much as 15 times higher than the average for the countries with the best records—Spain, Greece, Italy, Ireland, Norway, and the Netherlands.

As dispiriting as the statistics are, they under-represent the true problem because of gaps and inconsistencies in the way the figures are gathered. In the United States, child deaths are tallied very differently across the nation due to different protocols, definitions of abuse, and legal-reporting requirements in various states. The proportion of child deaths followed by autopsies to determine the exact cause of death, for example, can range from 13 percent to 82 percent, depending on different state requirements, indicating that many communities are likely missing many deaths caused by abuse, notes the UNICEF report.[17] Even when deaths are investigated, it can be difficult to determine exact cause. "Did the two-year-old fall from a window or was he dropped? Was the newborn baby a victim of Sudden Infant Death Syndrome or was she suffocated?" asks the report. "Did the month-old baby drown in a moment of inattention or was she held under? Was the broken neck the result of a trip or a push? Was the cerebral trauma caused by a fist or a fall?"

Poverty and stress, along with drug and alcohol abuse, "appear to be the factors most closely and consistently associated with child abuse and neglect," the report determined.[18] A pithier profile of the typical killer might be "jealous drunks with guns," author David Adams noted at the National Institute of Justice conference on domestic violence. His book, *Why Do They Kill? Men Who Murder Their Intimate Partners*, touches on child murder in family annihilations.

Child-maltreatment fatalities in nations tend to follow rates of adult homicides, the UNICEF study noted. "The three nations with very high levels of child deaths from maltreatment—the United States, Mexico and Portugal—also have exceptionally high adult homicide rates," while the "same small group of countries that have extremely low rates of child death from maltreatment also have very low rates of adult homicide," it concluded.[19] "In between these two extremes lie the bulk of industrialized nations, all with fairly low rates of child maltreatment deaths and variable rates of adult homicide."

In the most conservative estimates, nearly five children a day died from neglect or abuse in America in 2011.[20] The frightening vision of a young child snatched from a front yard or walking to school to meet his or her death at the hands of a stranger is a relatively rare occurrence, despite the fascination such situations holds for the public and for the media. The most lethal people in child victims' lives are their parents, relatives, or a parent's lover. There has been little improvement in the United States in the number of child fatalities due to abuse or neglect for years. That's a surprise, because despite the grim statistics—and the PolicyLab's findings and some other studies aside—federal data indicate that child abuse in the United States is the lowest it has been in two decades. But the statistics present problems in calculating both abuse and maltreatment deaths, and it's nearly impossible to find officials or experts who believe the national numbers represent an accurate picture, particularly in tracking child fatalities.

Abuse and abuse-fatality figures are gathered in the federal National Child Abuse and Neglect Data System (NCANDS) by the Children's Bureau of the Department of Health and Human Services, which has collated statistics voluntarily provided by state agencies since 1990. The numbers are linked to a hodgepodge of definitions of abuse that vary by state, and a variety of reporting requirements, though they meet basic federal standards set by law. NCANDS tabulates abuse and neglect cases addressed by local Child Protective Service agencies. States unable to provide this information for whatever reason generally submit aggregate counts of indicators of child maltreatment. An estimated 3 million children were the subjects of reports of suspected maltreatment or neglect in 2011.[21] Following investigations, approximately 681,000, children (more than one a minute) were determined to be victims of at least one incident of child abuse or neglect, or an average of 9.1 of every 1,000 American children. Babies, from birth to age one, had the highest rates of abuse or neglect, with 21.2 of every 1,000 children affected. Boys were affected at about the same rate as girls.[22]

Based on state reports, NCANDS estimated that 1,570 children died from abuse and neglect in 2011 (the highest estimate in the previous four years was 1,740 in 2009); that's 2.1 fatalities per 100,000 children, the same rate as the previous year (compared with 2.3 in 2009).[23] Four-fifths of the victims were under four years old, and boys had a higher fatality rate than girls. Four-fifths of the abuse and neglect deaths were caused by one or more parents. Mothers and fathers together were responsible for 22 percent of the deaths; a father alone was the perpetrator in 15.3 percent of the deaths, and a mother alone was responsible in 26.4 percent of the deaths.[24]

Both abuse and fatality figures are almost universally believed to miss much of the problem. As for abuse, the number of children "officially reported to child protection systems substantially undercounts the total population of children who experience abuse or neglect," according to a report for the national Centers for Disease Control.[25] A 2008 national survey of children's exposure to violence found that more than one in ten children surveyed suffered some form of maltreatment in the previous year,[26] which is ten times higher than the NCANDS statistics.

A statistical shortfall is also apparent in the number of maltreatment *fatalities* reported in the NCANDS stats, according to several experts and even many agencies that tally the numbers. A key issue is that a significant percentage of deaths never make it to the report because not all children killed by abuse have ever been part of a child welfare system, which in almost all cases is necessary to be included in data provided by individual states. Even if children are part of the system, it can be challenging to make a final determination that a child's death was caused by abuse or neglect, as the UNICEF report noted. The determination of cause of death can be further complicated because it requires complex coordination and agreement among social workers, medical professionals, police, and local district attorneys and courts, the 2011 NCANDS report observed.[27]

A 2011 study by the General Accounting Office (GAO) determined that NCANDS child-maltreatment fatality figures were likely significantly undercounted.[28] The GAO attributed the inaccuracy to a range of inconsistent definitions of abuse and reporting requirements across the nation, lack of training or experience in some communities dealing with or spotting abuse, and sometimes-inexplicable holes in data provided. The GAO found that three states didn't bother reporting their child abuse fatalities in 2009, and for some unknown reason 13 states didn't include statistics on children who died after they were returned home after a stint in foster care.[29]

Officials must deal with a daunting array of different legal requirements and definitions. "At the local level, lack of evidence and inconsistent interpretations of maltreatment challenge investigators—such as law enforcement, medical examiners, and child welfare officials—in determining whether a child's death was caused by maltreatment," noted the GAO in its assessment of the 1,770 fatalities in 2009 (up from 1,450 in 2005), when nearly six children a day died due to declared neglect or abuse.[30] Just as in the UNICEF report, the GAO also recognized the difficulty in determining when deaths are due to abuse or neglect. "Without medical evidence, it can be difficult to determine that a child's death was caused by abuse or neglect, such as in cases of shaken baby syndrome, when external injuries may not be readily visible," investigators observed.[31] In addition, "at the state level, limited coordination among jurisdictions and state agencies, in part due to confidentiality or privacy constraints, poses challenges for reporting data to NCANDS."[32] One study cited by the GAO found that maltreatment deaths in three states were undercounted by up to 75 percent.[33]

Even states themselves struggle with inconsistencies among their own communities. Michigan officials told GAO investigators that when a separate agency cross-checked 2005 child-maltreatment deaths reported by the local CPS with medical records for 186 cases, the analysis indicated that 37 child deaths labeled as natural, accidental, or undetermined should have been documented as maltreatment, noted the GAO researchers.[34] Officials from nearly half of the states told GAO investigators they needed more help to collect accurate data on child-maltreatment fatalities.[35]

The GAO report emphasized that any comprehensive strategy to combat child deaths in the United States is already missing an essential piece of the puzzle: complete, reliable statistics. Lack of accurate data makes it "difficult to develop prevention strategies. We should be doing everything in our collective power to end child deaths and near-deaths from maltreatment," the GAO concluded.[36] "The collection and reporting of comprehensive data on these tragic situations is an important step toward that goal."

Even if NCANDS statistics were vastly improved to offer more complete statistics, they don't even pretend to present the complete picture of children killed by their parents. Nearly half of the reporting states only provided data supplied by child-welfare agencies—even though many children who die from abuse never have contact with such an agency. A sudden, inexplicable murder of a child—often in cases with no known previous instances of abuse or neglect—will not be in the abuse-fatality-tracking figures. As a homicide without prior reported abuse, William Parente's murder of his daughters, for example, would not make the NCANDS statistics. In fact, it's unlikely most of the five major homicides reported in this book made NCANDS stats, though murder at the hands of a parent is the ultimate child abuse.

Child-homicide figures, including children killed by their parents, are tracked in FBI statistics, which are, again, a collation of local statistics, but in this case provided by police departments across the nation. According to FBI statistics, 445 sons and daughters were killed by their parents in 2011, though the victims are not categorized by age, nor do the numbers include most deaths due to abuse that are not likely considered "intentional" under the law. There is no comprehensive, systematic national tracking by the FBI of the murder of children by parents, nor is there complete national information available on such things as specific ages of murder victims and their relationships to their killers.

The closest federal authorities provide comes from the National Crime

Victimization Survey (NCVS) conducted by the Bureau of Justice Statistics. The unit, within the Department of Justice, analyzes crime based on a data sample obtained from 40,000 US households to determine the frequency, as well as characteristics, of criminal victimization in the United States. Members of the households are interviewed twice a year to determine if someone in the family has been a crime victim, and the information is used to estimate crime rates.

According to the 2008 NCVS findings on homicides within families, murder of a partner by a spouse or ex-spouse—which accounted for most family homicide—represented a decreasing percentage of all family homicides from 1980 through 2008.[37] In 1980, they made up half (52 percent) of all family homicides. By 2008, they accounted for just over a third (37 percent). But children, who are the second most frequent victims of family homicide, comprised an increasingly larger percentage of such murder, jumping from 15 percent of all family homicides in 1980 to 25 percent of all family homicides in 2008. And the boost was true for both black and white families. In 1980, 16.1 percent of white family homicides and 13.4 percent of black family homicides involved a parent who murdered a child. Yet by 2008, 23.5 percent of white family homicides and 30 percent of black family homicides involved a child killed by a parent. Interestingly, the percentage of parent victims killed by one of their children also increased, rising steadily from 9.7 percent of all family homicides in 1980 to 13 percent in 2008.[38]

Domestic-violence expert Richard Gelles believes the lines tracking homicide rates of children and wives in households may, at one point, "cross," as homicides of wives continue to decrease and child homicides remain relatively flat. He attributes that situation to the different manner that violence against children and women are handled in the United States. Domestic violence against women is dealt with in the criminal-justice system, while child abuse in all but the most extreme situations is still largely an issue for social-service agencies, he noted. "I like to quote Al Capone here, who said that you can get much farther with a kind word and a gun than you can with a kind word alone," Gelles told me. "That's the situation now with men who attack their wives or intimate partners. They're dealt with by law enforcement." The "kind word alone" from a social worker "doesn't seem to be as effective" in stemming fatal violence against children, he noted.

If statistics are to be more complete, and an effective tool for professionals battling the problem of domestic abuse, the system needs a "one-stop shopping" store of data, argues a report by the PolicyLab that grew in part out of its research contradicting NCANDS statistics. Different, sometimes contradictory, information can be "unsettling" for child-welfare administrators trying to use data to "better understand the prevalence of maltreatment in their jurisdiction, and more important, improve outcomes for children," notes a PolicyLab position paper.[39] The PolicyLab recommends combining the NCANDS figures with FBI homicide statistics, death certificate data, and hospital statistics. The International Classification of Diseases (ICD) system already exists for hospitals to track various diseases, injuries, medical conditions, and child abuse encountered by their staffs, but it's not included in national abuse statistics.

Some states already have such multisource abuse tracking in place. The Alaska Surveillance of Child Abuse and Neglect Program (Alaska SCAN), for example, builds reports based on input from Child Protective Service agencies, police, hospitals and clinics, child-advocacy centers, and child-death reviews. To effectively address child abuse "the problem must be as clearly defined as possible through surveillance," argues the PolicyLab.

EIGHT

TRAIL OF TEARS

I f all the statistics concerning child fatalities due to abuse, neglect, or homicide were reliably gathered and reported, would it shock us into taking more action to protect children? The fact is, some major cases aside—like Florida mom Casey Anthony's acquittal on first-degree murder charges after the remains of her two-year-old daughter, Caylee, were found, or Scott Peterson's murder of his pregnant wife, Laci—domestic violence and child abuse rarely trigger major alarm bells with the public. In two months during the summer of 2012 at least 40 children nationwide were killed by fathers in attacks considered horrific enough to make local headlines or national news. If the General Accounting Office is correct in concluding that national figures only tally a portion of abuse attacks, the number of child-maltreatment and child-neglect deaths at the hands of children's caregivers would have been *at least* 240 in two months. If 40 children had been shot or strangled at a local school, the story would have captivated the media for months, and would have made the floor of Congress as politicians discussed what to do to prevent the problem in the future, just as the horrific shootings at Sandy Hook Elementary did that same year in December. But because the earlier cases were separate incidents, or perhaps because they were domestic-abuse cases, the deaths were less riveting to the public. Two major mass killings that summer—the shooting deaths of 12 at a showing of the *Dark Knight Rises* in a movie theater in Aurora, Colorado, and the killing of seven in a Sikh temple in Wisconsin—burned up news pages. But in fact, familicides like Bill Parente's murderous attack usually account for the majority of murder-suicides involving at least three victims in the United States each year. Most Americans poring over news reports about shootings at a Batman movie were unaware of the trail of tears in homes across the nation while several American children met their death at the hands of their father in 2012:[1]

- Lewis Beatty, 40, admitted to police that he cut the throats of his six-year-old daughter, Sara, and eleven-year-old Amanda in his suburban Pittsburgh home June 1, then followed his estranged wife from work to her home to stab her to death there before setting the home ablaze. Beatty returned to his own home, where the bodies of his two girls still lay, to set it on fire as well. He was rescued from the blaze by a neighbor. He told police he became enraged when Sara casually mentioned while playing with her Barbie dolls following kindergarten graduation that her mom has been talking to another man. He also killed the family's pet pony, goat, and dog because, he explained to detectives, there wouldn't be anyone left to care for the animals. Beatty was sentenced to three consecutive life terms without parole. "This should never have happened," Beatty said in court.

- The body of James Butwin, 47, was found with his 40-year-old wife, Yafit, and their three children—seven-year-old Matthew, 14-year-old Daniel, and 16-year-old Malissa—all killed by bullets in a burned-out car in the Arizona desert close to the Mexican border. Police initially thought the bodies were the result of a drug deal gone bad because of known Mexican cartel activity in the Pinal County area. But investigators later discovered that Butwin, described by a friend as the "nicest guy," had left two notes indicating that he planned to commit suicide, including instructions to a friend about what to do with his real-estate holdings. He had lost his job, was deeply in debt, and had just been diagnosed with a brain tumor. The last evening of his life, he celebrated his 47th birthday with his family at their home, then they climbed in the car for a nighttime drive in the desert.

- Trucking Company owner Avtar Singh, 47, fatally shot his wife and three sons, ages three, 15, and 17, early June 9 before turning the gun on himself in the family's home in Selma, California. Singh appeared close to being extradited to India, where he was wanted for the 1996 kidnapping and murder of a Kashmiri activist and was a suspect in other murders while he was a general in the Indian army. Following an investigation about Singh's criminal history by a California journalist, his 36-year-old wife, Hervander, threatened to sue unless there was an apology. She said her husband was an honorable soldier who had bled for his country, but would never spill the blood of an innocent. Singh's background first came to the attention of local police weeks earlier when he was arrested and charged with felony domestic abuse after choking his wife. "He was a nice guy," said a truck driver who worked for Singh.

- On June 25, Marquis Garrison, 30, allegedly shook his two-month-old daughter and threw her on the ground when he said her fussing and crying "frustrated" him, according to the Denver District Attorney's Office. She later died of her injuries.

- Memphis dad Maurice Brown, 28, was charged with murdering his three-year-old son while babysitting July 1. He reported the toddler missing and said he feared the boy had been kidnapped by members of a rival gang. His son's body was later found nearby in a large trash bin. He had died from blunt-force trauma. Maurice Brown Jr., three feet tall and 65 pounds, was last seen alive wearing a Batman shirt and blue jeans. A witness told police he saw Brown leave his house at night with a child slung over his shoulder. "As the father of a small child, I can't even begin to imagine what could prompt somebody, or trigger somebody, to not only react violently to a small, three-year-old child, but to dispose of the body in such a manner," a police spokesman told News Channel 3 in Memphis.[2] The toddler's maternal grandmother had warned her daughter about Brown's temper. "Maurice was getting angrier and angrier," she said.

- The bodies of Randall Engels, 37, and his estranged 35-year-old wife, Amy, and their two children, Bailey, 13, and Jackson, 11, were found shot to death July 4 at the old family home in Dundee, about 25 miles south of Portland, Oregon. Amy had filed for divorce from Randall in late May, after 14 years of marriage, and had moved with the children to a new home in a nearby town. When Engels filed for divorce, she asked a Yamhill County judge to issue an emergency temporary custody and parenting order, citing an "immediate danger" to her children. Amy's friends became alarmed when Randall posted on his Facebook page: "If she's gone I can't go on," from the Beatles song, "You've Got to Hide Your Love Away." Police saw the same words written on a white board when they peered through a window to check on the family.

- North Dakota construction worker Aaron Schaffhausen was charged with murdering his three daughters in the Wisconsin home they shared with their mother, his estranged wife. Police said Schaffhausen asked for an unscheduled visit with his daughters July 10, and his ex-wife agreed; he showed up at their Minot house to be with the girls, and dismissed the babysitter. Two hours later, investigators said, he texted his wife: "Come and see your children. I killed them." Police found the dead girls lying together in a single bed. River Falls Police Investigator John Wilson described in court how he entered the house with a paramedic and discovered each girl—eleven-year-old Amara, eight-year-old Sophie, and five-year-old Cecilia—with covers pulled up to their necks, their eyes open and lifeless, and with what appeared to be dried blood on their mouths and cheeks. The walls of one bedroom were splattered with blood, and the carpet was covered with a large pool of blood. The girls had large, "gaping" wounds across their necks, Wilson testified. Schaffhausen has pleaded not guilty by reason of mental disease or defect, and his trial was slated for spring 2013.

- Indianapolis dad Johnny Bishop, 30, confessed to police that he violently shook and critically injured his nine-month-old son on July 11 because his wife was in the hospital and he was "stressed," according to police reports. "I shook him," he said. "It is my fault. I need to control my stupid temper." Bishop, also the dad of a three-year-old girl, had a previous conviction for injuring an infant, according to police. He pleaded guilty to two counts of aggravated battery, battery, and neglect. His baby survived.

- Jesse Adams, 3, was shot dead by his 34-year-old dad, Carey, who then fatally shot himself in the head in his North Carolina home in

Grifton on July 13. Police said the murder-suicide was the result of an ugly, ongoing domestic dispute with his wife. "The safest place in the world that a child should be is in his mom or dad's bed, cuddled up with them," Pitt County Deputy Mason Paramore told a local news program.[3] "And that was not the case this time. I took the mother to the hospital in hopes that maybe I could give her an opportunity to say good-bye. That was a long ride to the hospital, talking and praying together and a whole lot of crying together." A victim's rights advocate from the police department said mom Christy Adams "doesn't want everybody to make Carey out to be the worst person that ever walked the Earth. She wants us to know that once upon a time, he was a really good person. He had a very sweet little boy and Jesse loved him."

- Oregon dad Kaliq Mansor, 34, was sentenced to at least 28 years in prison for the July 13 death of his eleven-week-old son, Bryan, and the abuse of Bryan's twin, Ethan. Bryan suffered bruises, a fractured skull, broken ribs, and bleeding and swelling in his brain. Police found Internet searches on Mansor's computer including "father hates infant" and "How do I stop abusing my baby?" as well as a downloaded video game that involved images of abusing children, according to court records. "The man that I loved is not the man sitting here today," said Mansor's ex-wife, Angela Foster, in her victim impact statement the day he was sentenced. "That man died the day he started hurting my boys."

- Massachusetts dad Daryl Benway, 41, who had recently lost his job as a computer consultant and was estranged from his wife, shot his seven-year-old daughter, Abigail, and nine-year-old son, Owen, in the head July 28 before turning the gun on himself. After he was shot in the master bedroom of the family's Oxford house, Owen managed to crawl to the kitchen and was still alive when police found him. Abigail died.

- A dad in Dodge City, Kansas, was charged with killing his nine-month-old son, Brandon Villa, on July 21. Jonathan M. Villa-Ramirez was out on bail on aggravated robbery, attempted aggravated robbery, attempted robbery, and aggravated assault charges when he allegedly attacked the baby, according to court records.

- Pennsylvania dad Robert Heibert, 28, of New Brighton, was charged with killing his two-month-old daughter, Melanie Alexander, on July 26. He told police he was watching the baby while his girlfriend was out playing bingo, and that he might have shaken her to revive Melanie when he noticed she was unresponsive and her lips were blue. He later allegedly admitted shaking her to stop her from crying so vigorously that her chin bounced on her chest, according to police records.
- Kentucky police alerted by a burglary alarm set off on July 29 in Sadé Goldsmith's new Louisville home arrived to find Goldsmith, 26, and her sons, six-year-old John Jr. and five-year-old Jon'tee Devine, shot to death. The boys' dad and Goldsmith's estranged lover, John Devine, confessed to the murders at a local hospital where he was treated for a self-inflicted gunshot wound, according to police reports.
- The missing four-year-old daughter of Waynesboro, Pennsylvania, dad Kevin Cleeves, 35, was found unharmed with her father. But Cleeves was charged with shooting to death three people on July 27—his estranged wife, Brandi, her boyfriend, and the boyfriend's mom—then kidnapping his daughter. Cleeves told police he had "made a mistake" confronting his ex and her new lover, according to police reports.

Domestic-violence expert Richard Gelles believes the steady stream of child-abuse deaths isn't enough to pique the public's, or politicians', interest, except for an occasional super tragedy, and that the very numbers may work to the disadvantage of the attention the issue can draw. "'Josef Stalin said that one death is a tragedy, a million is a statistic," noted Gelles in a phone interview with me.[4] "That's how it is with domestic violence. The public reacts to a single dramatic tragedy but can't sustain an interest in the overall problem—unless it's presented as an 'epidemic.'"

Perhaps we tend to accept a certain level of family violence because we're convinced that society is largely powerless to protect children within their own homes—or that it's not society's place to interfere, even though Michael Petit of Every Child Matters is convinced that in the most extreme abuse cases, the "only thing standing between a child and death at the hands of a parent is the government." Part of American culture, Gelles believes, is the strong belief that parents have a right to raise their children without government interference. One of the reasons the United States (along with Somalia and the South Sudan) hasn't ratified the Convention on the Rights of the Child, a United Nations' human-rights treaty, is because conservative political factions argue that it conflicts with our constitution, which "keeps government at more than arm's length from how parents raise children," Gelles adds. Women abused by husbands have used civil-rights laws to win greater protection from courts and police, notes Gelles. "But children don't have anywhere near the same level of civil rights," he added.

Ironically, the same political factions that would block increased government supervision of or help for families are the same ones that would boost the number of children in the nation by restricting abortion. Like the langurs, maybe we're driven to bring as much life as possible into the world, but once it's here, we defer to a system that can be very hard on young life.

A respect for and interest in protecting children is nearly a non-issue in American political debate, even as the "personhood" of a fetus gains increasing recognition. "The rights of the unborn child are taking precedence over care of actual children," notes sociology professor Neil Websdale. Petit emphasizes that the "parental role is a stewardship role, not an ownership role," but it's a distinction not everyone recognizes. There is a sense in "some American communities, where religion might play a part, that parents own their children," he observed.

Why are child-abuse fatalities and murder so high in the United States? Reasons offered by experts range from lack of supportive social services, to poverty, to easy accessibility of guns, to an American culture of violence.

The United States has one of the highest rates of relative child poverty in the developed world, according to UNICEF calculations. Of the 35 wealthy countries examined by the agency, only Romania had a relative child poverty rate higher than the United States.[5] UNICEF based the rankings on an equation to gauge relative poverty established by the Organization for Economic Cooperation and Development. Under this definition, a child is deemed to be living in relative poverty if he or she is growing up in a household where disposable income, when adjusted for family size and composition, is less than 50 percent of the median disposable household income in a particular nation.

By this standard, the United States has a relative child poverty rate of 23.1, compared with 4.7 in Iceland, the best rate of 35 "economically advanced" countries examined by UNICEF.[6]

And just when families are suffering in the United States, budgets for support services are being cut by localities strapped for cash. "We haven't seen a big cut in national expenditures on social services—yet—though that could change," warned Petit. "We are seeing sharp reductions in services in cash-strapped states." As families "struggle and stress levels rise, child maltreatment becomes more of a risk," Jane Burstain of the Center for Public Policy Priorities, a think tank in Austin, Texas, testified before Congress.[7] "To cut programs that support struggling families in tough economic times is the very definition of penny wise and pound foolish and is a choice our children will pay for with their lives."

If child deaths aren't enough to stir our empathy and action, the costs of abuse have tremendous implications for society. The total lifetime toll of child maltreatment is estimated to be $124 billion each year, based on total costs linked to criminal justice, healthcare, child welfare, special-education expenses, and productivity losses, according to a 2008 study conducted for the Centers for Disease Control (CDC).[8] "Child maltreatment is a serious and prevalent public health problem in the United States, responsible for substantial morbidity and mortality," noted the study. Abuse ramifications aren't confined to a single child; the violence has an inevitable impact throughout society, with the kid who suffers today more likely to become the child abuser or the criminal of tomorrow. Child maltreatment has been shown to have lifelong adverse health, social, and economic consequences for survivors, including behavioral problems, increased delinquency risk and adult criminality, violent behavior, boosted risk of chronic diseases, and lasting impacts or disability from physical injury. Early abuse "gets under our skin," noted the CDC report, citing findings that maltreatment can affect brain development and learning, blood pressure, and the immune system.[9] The earlier the battle against abuse begins, the better, not only for the victim, but for a society that will be forced to deal with the fallout, notes the agency report, adding, "scientific evidence now shows that it's better and more efficient to 'get it right from the start' by preventing maltreatment rather than trying to fix the many problems that result from early trauma later in life."

NINE

CONTROL FREAK

JOSH ACTED LIKE A CULT LEADER; NOT THAT HE
HAD ANY TRUE FOLLOWERS, BUT HE THOUGHT
EVERYONE SHOULD BELIEVE IN HIS REALITY.
—Chuck Cox, father of Susan Cox Powell, who's
missing and presumed killed by her husband

Scads of houses in the massive pancake expanse of the Salt Lake Valley race west toward the foothills of the snow-peaked Oquirrh Mountains in Utah like jet-powered cars on the Bonneville Salt Flats. Save for a scattered, nomadic Ute settlement or a fur trapper's camp, the vast, 500-square-mile valley was empty when Brigham Young and his 148-person advance team of Latter-Day Saints arrived in 1847 to found what would soon be a massive religious settlement. The pregnant wife of Brigham's brother Lorenzo felt heartsick upon seeing the lonely, empty land as the faithful emerged from Emigration Valley on their trek to escape persecution from the east. But that didn't dissuade Brigham. "It is enough. This is the right place," he declared.[1] He was transfixed. The Mormon leader had "seen the valley before in vision, and upon this occasion he saw the future glory of Zion and of Israel," wrote an apostle. If the space was inhospitable, all the better, Brigham believed. It would dissuade settlement by the persecuting "Gentiles" the Mormons were fleeing. In line with their vision that Utah was the Promised Land, the Latter-Day Saints named the river that bisected the great valley after the Jordan River and set off a massive exodus of Mormons—nearly one million in a century—that would result in America's nearest example of a religious state. But even 165 years later, the jumbled developments, ribbons of highways, and hundreds of thousands of residents barely make a dent in an overwhelming sense of limitlessness and stark-raving blue sky in the heart of the vast space of the western United States.

A woman could feel lonely here, even in the midst of family within a neighborhood of warm community barbeques, screeching, laughing, bike-riding packs of kids, and a supportive local Mormon ward. The summer of 2009, Susan Cox Powell, 27, looked and acted just like other moms in the sunny community of young families in West Valley City, a booming town of 130,000 southwest of Salt Lake City, in the fastest-growing area in the state. She was a pretty blonde, sociable with neighbors and co-workers, and a fun, devoted mom to her two little boys, two-year-old Braden and four-year-old Charlie.[2] She went to work, biked with the kids, chatted with pals, made dinners, and weeded her garden just like moms down her street. But Susan lived a secret life behind the walls of her home. She feared for her life and for the welfare of her sons from her own husband, Josh, who had inexplicably and inexorably veered off the rails of normal behavior. Susan's once sweetly distracted spouse had become a prickly, threatening control freak who dictated how Susan should clean and organize their small, white ranch house; whom she could talk to and what she could say; and what groceries she was allowed to purchase. Susan was uprooted, hundreds of miles from the rest of her family, to find herself in a life so tightly controlled that it resembled existence in a small desert cult of four, ruled by a 32-year-old dictator, Josh.

The marriage hadn't turned out quite the way Susan had imagined. She had fallen hard eight years earlier for the charmingly loopy boy-man who ardently wooed Susan in Puyallup, Washington, where she lived with her parents and three sisters. Josh was slightly built, appeared far younger even then than his 24 years, with pouty lips and blue, puppy-dog eyes, spiky dark-brown hair, and a tiny mustache that looked like the type adolescents grow to look more manly. But to the 19-year-old Susan, Josh appeared as an attractive "older man"—mature and well on his way to a stable, successful life. He was aiming to finish up a business degree at the University of Washington, and he was already working as an on-call subcontractor hauling and installing furniture in various schools for a commercial industrial furniture company, a job he obtained through his dad, Steven Powell, who worked as a salesman for the operation. Even better in Susan's eyes was that Josh wanted to settle down. He regularly attended services at a Mormon "branch" congregation in Tacoma, which was only open to singles to give them a chance to meet partners within their faith, and he appeared to be focused on finding a mate, marrying, and starting a family. "It seemed like he had everything going for him," recalled Susan's dad, Charles "Chuck" Cox, a now-retired investigator with the Federal Aviation Administration, as he sat in the large, dark-shingled family home on a tucked-away street in Puyallup. Cox believes Josh was set on marrying a Mormon girl. Though Josh's mom was a devout Mormon, his dad, with whom he lived after his parents' divorce when he was 16, not so much. "Mormon wives tend to be more submissive," said Cox. "Husbands and wives are partners, but the man is the head of the household, and Josh wanted a wife who recognized that." In a short period of time, "Susan fell in love with Josh and wanted to be married," said her mom, Judy. But her dad amended: "She was in love with the idea of marriage." Nine years later, Susan would vanish and her sons would be murdered by her suicidal husband.

Figure 9.1. Young animal-lover Susan Cox relaxes outdoors, long before Josh Powell would become part of her life. *Courtesy of Charles and Judy Cox.*

Figure 9.2. Susan and Josh stop for a snapshot on a hiking date. *Courtesy of Charles and Judy Cox.*

Judy Cox never trusted Josh; he seemed rude and "off." Chuck had misgivings, too. Josh first hit on their oldest daughter, Mary, whom he also met at the singles Mormon congregation in Washington. He showed up at the Cox's Puyallup house, uninvited, the night of Mary's senior prom. She was getting ready to go out with her boyfriend as Josh sat in the living room talking to Judy. He was still there when a perturbed Mary returned home later that night, still with her date, and Chuck finally had to tell Josh to go.

"He was odd," said Judy. "There was something off about him." Unfazed that his attentions were rebuffed by Mary, he moved on a few years later to her younger sister, Susan. Judy didn't understand Susan's attraction to Josh. Both Judy and Chuck were troubled when a thrilled Susan accepted Josh's marriage proposal some five months after they began to date. "We weren't sure about this guy, but we believe in letting our kids live their own lives," explained Chuck.

The union nearly fell apart within hours of the young couple's wedding at the LDS Mormon Temple in Portland, Oregon. Susan overheard her father-in-law tell Josh: "Well, she's not a lawyer or a doctor, but she'll do." Josh just smiled. A stunned Susan, close to tears, rushed to tell her mother what she had overheard, and Judy seized a final opportunity to get Josh out of her daughter's life. Surrounded by the sound of wedding guests celebrating a marriage she felt sick about, Judy counseled: "Call it off right now. We'll make an announcement, apologize to people, return the gifts, and let them enjoy the rest of the reception." But Susan stuck by her man.

Figure 9.3. Susan Cox cuddles up with beau Josh Powell at the wedding reception for her big sister Denise. *Courtesy of Charles and Judy Cox.*

What seemed to be Josh's maturity and stability as he wooed Susan quickly dissolved over the following few years. He didn't finish his college degree and fell into a pattern of ditching or being fired from a series of jobs—sometimes as quickly as two weeks after starting—after he quit the contract work for the local schools. He jumped from work at a car dealership, Home Depot, an eldercare facility, Wells Fargo, and in real-estate sales. He was cantankerous about jobs he was able to find, inevitably complained about his bosses and colleagues, kvetched that the workers needed a union, and was often irritated that his work was "beneath" him. "He was Mr. Know Everything, and always had a complaint about where he worked," recalls Chuck. "He would call me up to complain, and I would tell him, 'Slow down, Josh, you don't want to lose this job, too.'" What the Coxes didn't know then about Josh—but would later learn from his parents' divorce documents—was that he had been a seriously troubled teen. The divorce proceedings years earlier revealed that Josh had tried to hang himself at the age of 13, killed his sister's pet gerbils, and once threatened his mother with a butcher knife. Steven Powell accused Josh's mom, Terrica, of practicing an ersatz Mormonism mixed with the occult that he described as "witchcraft and devil worship" that he said harmed their five children. Terrica accused Steven Powell in the same divorce proceedings of an obsession with pornography—material she said he shared with their three sons—and of mental and physical abuse. Terrica told the court she believed her husband needed "serious medical help" due to some mysterious "underlying problem." He proclaimed he had a "right" to take another wife and had his eye on a married woman, detailing sexual fantasies about her in his journal, according to Terrica's legal filings. Her husband also turned on the children "far more violently than was necessary or fair," including yelling, name-calling and spankings that were "too forceful or too long," when he became upset about their behavior, she charged in the court documents. Josh was a particular target of abuse by his father. "For years, he pointedly attacked Josh very frequently, nearly every day for a time," Terrica added. Steven admitted he found Josh difficult to discipline. "At times I have no idea how to handle Josh," he noted in divorce documents. "He is very independent, and he is now a little taller than I, and may, with his regular weight-lifting, be a little stronger and bulkier than I. I cannot spank him. Spanking didn't even help when he was younger."

Josh became withdrawn as a teenager, "unwilling to interact, even to make eye contact for a year or two," said Terrica in the divorce filings. "He seemed to have a soul-deep hurt because of his dad's erratic and explosive behavior." According to Josh's older sister Jennifer Graves, who believed he and his dad developed a twisted special relationship, Josh's behavior soon morphed into aggression, and he began to emulate his father's cocky, demanding attitude, particularly toward women, she would testify years later in a court case against her father. The males in her family, especially Josh, frightened Terrica, Josh's mom argued in her divorce deposition. "There have been times when I have been afraid of Steve and/or the boys because of their extremely hateful behavior," Terrica said. "They group together and stir each other up to almost a fever pitch at times. Their vehemence has often flashed in their eyes and body language, making me feel threatened." When she once asked Josh to show her more respect, he responded: "You have to earn respect, Mom. What have you done to earn my respect?" But even worse, Terrica said, Josh and his brother, John, then 15, pushed and hit her. Once, when she tried to get Josh to wash the dinner dishes, he turned to her with a butcher knife in his hand, flashed it near her face and warned: "Don't push it, Mom." Terrica recalled, "I felt extreme fear when Josh made a veiled threat at me with a butcher knife in his hand. His demeanor was menacing."

While the Coxes knew nothing at the time about the disturbing descriptions of Josh in the divorce proceedings, they continued to be troubled by Josh's behavior and found him curiously disconnected. He expected strict organization from Susan, but was distracted and disorganized himself. He had a habit of showing up to appointments hours late. The Coxes found one visit from Susan and the family after the couple had moved from Washington to Utah particularly worrisome, they recounted to me in their Puyallup home. Josh, running some errands, was to show up at their house to collect Susan and the boys for a ferry outing. Susan dressed the boys warmly to be ready to go at the appointed time because she knew Josh would be irritated if he had to wait for them when he arrived. But he showed up nearly four hours later. Susan seemed largely unconcerned about Josh's behavior, perhaps because of her lack of experience in relationships or an instinctive loyalty to her husband—or her enduring optimistic personality, her parents thought.

More troubling was Josh's behavior during the birth of Charlie. The Coxes traveled to the couple's home in Utah to help before Susan's expected due date. As she went into labor at home, Josh remained stationed were he often was: in front of his computer screen. It was Chuck Cox who had to tell Josh to shut down the computer and take his wife to the hospital. Josh ended up following Susan and her parents in a separate car two hours later because he said he needed time to back up his computer files. He took his laptop along and immediately set it up in the hospital room as Susan's parents ministered to their daughter. Finally, his father-in-law had to grasp him by the shoulders, take the laptop from his hands, and tell him, "Josh, Susan needs you *now.*" Charlie was born in minutes. As Chuck Cox held Susan's hand after her first baby was born, her dad recalled, "She looked at me, and said, 'Dad, did you see how Josh helped me? He really cares. Did you see that?'"

The storm warnings then were developing into a full-blown hurricane in Susan's life in Utah by the time her firstborn boy was three years old. The winning suitor with the big ideas who had wooed Susan had profoundly changed by 2008 to become a nervous, bitter control freak who dominated every aspect of her life in West Valley City. She was expected to run the household with a budget so pared by Josh that it threatened adequate nutrition for her and the boys, who picked at surrounding fruit trees and their own vegetable garden to supplement their diet. Josh had commanded Susan not to buy any meat other than hotdogs and to fill in the amount of each grocery-store purchase she made on an Excel spreadsheet at Josh's basement desk. Josh also ordered Susan not to waste funds on her favorite small treats like makeup and yarn for crocheting, or that "other crap you buy." Nor was he willing to spend the $20 copay required by Susan's health insurance for the psychological counseling his wife so desperately craved to help repair the couple's marriage. From remaining funds Josh allowed Susan, she had to eke out daycare payments so their boys could be looked after while she went to her office because Josh often claimed to be too busy at his basement "work station" in front of his computer—where Susan suspected he actually spent much of his time surfing Internet porn sites. Despite Josh's insistence on total oversight of the family funds, it was Susan who was usually the family's sole breadwinner. She dutifully deposited her paychecks in their joint bank account, and he decided how the funds would be dispensed. For much of their time in Utah, Josh was only sporadically employed and cooking up costly entrepreneurial schemes while staring at his computer screen.

Figure 9.4. Up a tree: A happy Josh Powell mugs with his sons, Charlie (*left*) and Braden, and Susan. *Courtesy of Charles and Judy Cox.*

Still, Susan made the best of it. She was an optimist and had faith that she could fix her marriage. She decorated the Utah home to make a cozy nest for Josh and the boys. She arranged favorite "family day" outings, and quickly made friends with her neighbors, co-workers, and Josh's sister Jennifer, who lived nearby in South Jordan. The high-school grad with a beauty-school degree even studied for and passed a broker's license test to win a promotion as an investment counselor at a local Fidelity Investments, and later moved into a similar post at Wells Fargo. Though Susan might have been young when she fell in love and married Josh, may have been raised to be a good Mormon wife and to believe that marriage lasts forever, she wasn't a pushover. She wasn't happy about what had happened to her marriage, and she was determined to fix it. She was an articulate, insightful young woman who reflected intently on her life in years of journals she kept from the time she was eight years old. She was grappling with her current crisis with her husband in her journal, and making decisions that would forever change her life and her boys' futures.

Those who knew Susan casually in West Valley City that summer were unaware of the pain she was hiding, or that her increasingly fraught relationship with Josh had taken a dark turn. She feared that Josh was spinning dangerously out of control. The conflicts and verbal fights became infused with the threat of violence, and actual physical abuse, Susan confided to her friends, and she hinted that she was afraid for her life and the life of her sons—so frightened that she worried that leaving him could be the death of her. In an e-mail to a friend, Susan wrote about the trip to Washington with Josh and the boys that had so disturbed her parents, and revealed her husband had behaved as he usually did, being "rude, yelling and barking commands at me." When the family returned to their West Valley home, Susan revealed in another e-mail the year before she vanished that Josh's behavior became so disturbing as they argued about the trip, that she considered calling the police:

> We had a huge, hour-long fight (amazed that my voice still works). I even had to threaten calling the police because he was being so irrational and unpredictable. I told him he needs to change, counseling or something. And he said he didn't need counseling because he knows what they'll say, and what to do, and I said, "Do it then."
>
> My friend came over later because Josh was at her house getting help from her hubby for his business, and my friend knows shorthand so she wrote down the crazy stuff he said. I've also written a sort of will in my desk because at this point, I don't know what to think anymore.

TEN

WHAT SUSAN KNEW

As Josh became more dysfunctional, and alienated, Susan grew increasingly afraid. The two had largely stopped having sex, and Josh seemed murderously angry whenever Susan challenged him about his behavior or his treatment of her. Counseling, she believed, was the only way to save the marriage. Over time, she made up her mind that if Josh did not finally agree to counseling, and perhaps some kind of treatment or medication for his behavior, she would leave him. Susan's struggle within her marriage, in her own words in a series of e-mails to friends the summer of 2008, reveal the couple's continuing conflict, her pain and her resolve.

Latest on Josh
From: Susan.Powell
Sent: Sat. 7/05/08

Josh doesn't seem to take responsibility for anything. He got no sleep on 7/03/08 because Charlie wanted to watch fireworks (at the neighbor's, past midnight). And last night, home after midnight, and Charlie saying he's hungry, and I stupidly say, "Stay with him so I can get some sleep" since I actually have to get up at 5 a.m. (but apparently my lack of sleep for a real working day with time schedules is not as important as his, staying at home, on the computer with his schedule . . . ugh!).

    He says I can't take counseling because it will show as employee health history, so I'd be rated poorly there and for life insurance. Oh yeah, PS, when he said I lied because I bought $90 instead of $30 worth of groceries, one of his examples was $.25/ lb. for watermelon as too expensive. I looked at the receipt. It came to $3.35, and just yesterday he bought a watermelon for a flat price of $4 (I remember the one I purchased as larger than his).

133

He says I have "utter contempt" for him specifically because he doesn't work a regular job and therefore isn't a man. I told him I don't mind while he stays home with the boys, and would prefer he not spend the money I earn on another business, but instead work on healing our marriage. His response was that "my actions imply utter contempt, and that he's not a man no matter what my words are."

Figure 10.1. A happy Susan poses for a photo with baby Braden on her lap as Charlie stands next to his mom. *Courtesy of Charles and Judy Cox.*

The only thing I'm holding on to (since I'm denied counseling and he has denied that he needs to fix anything) is one of his lists of things that need to be fixed—so he won't be stressed and our marriage will magically fix itself, according to him—is organizing the paperwork in one central location for ease of access and security. So we got started a little with that, so I guess I've agreed to be strung along with his current excuse.

[Resumed later] Argh! He aggravated me, but at least we spent a family day (bike riding to Wal-Mart and getting donuts at a church flag thing in the a.m., and his family, for the evening), and he wants to hang out with our friends Sunday for dinner.

Also, notes taken with his knowledge on July 2, as follows:

Josh says Susan needs to:

Not spend $ on counseling;

Or anything else (his examples: make-up, yarn, other crap you buy);

Fix missing money (when I asked him to elaborate, he said: "Enter all receipts, quit hiding six or two different filing systems, and no paperwork except in the safe or in the office");

Clean up house (basement, food storage, paperwork in office only), finances, computer;

Josh stated numerous times that Susan has "utter contempt, and acts and has attitude that Josh is worthless."

(He also commented that I "was writing this down to use against him later," and I reminded him I don't know what I need to fix if I never have the specifics written down);

Make photos available.

Every moment I step back and take stock of what I'm dealing with, it feels like a never-ending cycle, but I'm too afraid of the consequences—losing my kids, him kidnapping them, divorce or actions worse on his part—if I take a stand on one of his ultimatums like spending $20 on the counseling co-pay, or cutting off his access to my pay check.

Anyways, thanks for listening!

Susan Powell

————

Latest on Josh

From: Susan Powell

Sent: Mon. 7/07/08

Thanks for the input. Just found out that if I use the counseling services through my employer plan it cannot be reported or used against me as far as being rated for life or health insurance. It's private, confidential. So his only argument left would be forking over the $20 co-pay. I think I might ask the bishop to have the church pay this. That would save them lots more than getting church counseling that doesn't specialize in these areas.

You made me tee up when you said, "If you can't have faith, have hope at least." I want to have hope.

I don't know how you can help except to talk with me and be another individual who would know about the situation if questioned because things went crazy later. Sad that I'm this paranoid.

Sunday was OK, only because I think he's finally realizing that I don't expect him to come to church anymore (less pressure on him). We were with our friends while they did family scripture reading. He looked bored, uninterested, and like he was finding reasons to leave the room.

We've done a little bit of cleaning/organizing around the house, and I realize this is just another one of his stalling-with-excuses tactics, but I always wonder if he's serious about change (i.e., fixing our marriage), if he thinks our problems are not that bad, if he was lying to me at the start when we got married or what.

My huge problem is I don't know what to believe or what to do. I don't want to divorce or separate or take the kids somewhere, and he views it as an act of war if I cut off my paycheck to the joint credit union.

My current tactic is to pretty much not make waves and try to ignore the problems. I'm finding mystery books to check out at the library and be a good mom for the boys. I came home from work on Saturday and felt so depressed that I couldn't make a decent dinner for my boys (the only protein we have is hot dogs, or me making eggs or planning ahead and soaking beans and doing the beans-and-rice thing), so I just kept trying to disguise their food with sour cream and ketchup, etc., and finally lay down in my bed and went to sleep. I only had four hours sleep the night before, so I'm sure Josh just thought I was tired. And then I forgot and ended up fasting from then until about 6 p.m. the next day, so I took another nap (out of depression), but I'm sure he has no clue/doesn't care.

Susan

———

No Subject
From: Susan Powell
Sent: Fri. 7/11/08

Sorry I couldn't go walking with you. I was pouring my heart out to a friend a couple doors down from you until 8:15, and then picking up the blinds at Home Depot while Josh took the kids on the bike ride I wanted to do with them. Then I was talking with someone who he ran into while with the boys (his version of groceries bought is cheap donuts and 10 individual yogurt servings). My appointment to meet the bishop was postponed until Sunday after church.

I plan to ask for help getting counseling for myself for depression and stress in the last three-plus years of our marriage. My expectations are that once Josh sees me getting counseling (confidential, so he can't whine about that), and if the church helps cover the co-pay, then he will have no other excuses, and my bottom line/breaking point is he will go to counseling for himself and/or get meds to deal with his mental issues, and if he refuses, I will not ruin mine and my boys' lives further, and we will divorce, and I hope it's not as ugly as he claims it will be when we've talked about it in the past.

I feel like I'm constantly evolving every time I talk to someone about this. K said as of Sunday I didn't want a divorce and bam, by Thursday I'm declaring my ultimatum of his needing counseling, or else divorce. Funny how I'm pushed and evolving.

I've prayed that I will know what to do and situations will present themselves kind of like a silver platter, and so far, it seems every person I speak to is sharing their own personal experiences or offering advice/guidance on who/how to get counseling, etc. So I guess that part of my prayers seems to be answered.

I don't want to do just marriage/couples counseling, and I don't want to use someone through the church because we've done that before, and I don't think Josh will respect that. I want the psychologist/psychiatrist/masters-level clinician to help me and Josh individually. If he's not willing to do that (obviously, won't improve on his own), then he is officially throwing in the towel. I don't know why he'd think the marriage is worth staying in. I doubt only myself going to counseling would fix all the problems.

Yesterday I helped him organize/clean his office and the loose papers (one of his excuses/stalling tactics to get help), and as I was soundlessly crying myself to sleep last night, I told him kind of desperately, "Now is the time you can say nice things to me," so he said in a tired/bored voice: "Thanks for helping me clean my office and stuff," and that was all. Then he kind of bumped me, and I said as a hopeful suggestion, "Are you trying to hold my hand?" and he muttered something. Then a little bit later I held his hand for a while until he pulled away.

I'm sure he thinks we are making improvements, and he has said I'm the only one who needs counseling. My three-year-old told me for the first time yesterday, "Mommy, I can't; I'm too busy" when I asked him to do something. That's verbatim what his father tells me, and he was stomping around the house acting angry (which we both do), and gives scowls to me and others at church. When I mentioned this to Josh, about seeing both of our bad habits, he didn't care, and I told him it is not acceptable for my three-year-old to tell me he's too busy. If this argument is still legit in Josh's eyes, he needs to be more specific and say, "I've got to do x-y-z," instead of saying: "I'm busy working."

I want him in counseling, on meds. I want my husband, friend, lover back. No more crazy, outrageous, outlandish beliefs/opinions.

Susan

———

Update from yesterday
From: Susan Powell
Sent: Mon. 7/14/08

The Bishop talked with me for an hour, opened with a prayer, and I was already in tears. Managed to ramble out my story. He agreed with me on all points (Josh has mental issues and/or has lost touch with reality, I'm a stressed, overworked, neglected/abused single mother down to her last straw). He repeatedly asked, "What can I do to help?"

I left knowing the church will reimburse the cost of counseling; trying to decide which psychologist or masters-level clinician to choose for myself. Hoping when I get started, Josh will want to get his own counseling. Still have to make appointment with a lawyer for free consultation so I'll know my rights when I give Josh my ultimatum—counseling (at least) or else divorce.

Any advice on a masters-level clinician? I've got a list for each, but location is important—so that I can possibly just bike there, leave kids with friends (Josh can think I'm at the park for the first visit or so).

Josh asked what the bishop appointment was for, and I said: "To see about getting help, food, money for bills and stuff," and he seemed OK with that answer. I did also get approval for one food order [to be paid by the church], so I am being truthful about that.

As always, any advice, opinions, suggestions, experience, insight are welcome and I will not be offended! The more the merrier! Thank you all for your support, help, and me bending your ear.

Susan

Late in the summer of 2008, Josh unexpectedly snagged a computer job working for a West Valley company. The change in his mood was dramatic, according to Susan's e-mails and conversations with friends. He was suddenly chatty, was engaged in his work, and seemed to be enjoying the camaraderie of the office and even workplace gossip. For the first time in months, Josh even initiated sex with Susan. She was touched and pleased, and encouraged by Josh's change, yet she had already begun her own counseling and was talking to a lawyer about divorce. She continued preparations for a divorce—including gathering documentation and filming their possessions ahead of a possible battle over any assets—"just in case" her situation with Josh quickly reverted again. "My gut says he can/wants to change, that I just need to help him create the right environment to change," she wrote hopefully.

Josh update
From: Susan Powell
Sent: Fri. 7/18/08

So while he was doing the job interview on Wednesday, I was setting up a phone consultation with divorce lawyers. I did manage to get hold of one, and feel a lot better about my rights and the process. Spoke to someone who has in-depth experiences with mental illness/bi-polar with family members. It seems that, over all, if someone is bi-polar, you don't want them to feel boxed into a corner or threatened or stressed (or else they'll "swing manic," etc.). I've seen already how much more relaxed/less stressed he is since his job interview—and in a couple of hours they called back and hired him, starting this Monday!

I'm not disillusioned. I realize marriage is always work, and if Josh is willing to get counseling, "getting back to before" still won't be a honeymoon, but I think if he gets help then we can be happily married with regular trials like normal people. The church individuals especially seem to be encouraging divorce if necessary, so I feel an abundance of support for either decision I make. It seems like I keep running into more individuals who have either experienced divorce or bi-polar problems, and have helpful advice/direction to give.

I recognize now that me praying or reading scripture and hoping is not going to cut it anymore. I need help, and so does he. I'm thinking he will be a lot more receptive to my suggestions of counseling for himself once he sees my own improvements. He even initiated some intimate time Wednesday night—right, shocker, I know. Funny, it's been so long it feels like a dream or surreal, and yes I still love him/care about him and think we can have a happy, loving, functional marriage and be a good example for our kids. I'm still documenting all of our belongings and saving info at work or at a friend's house in case this is short-lived, but my gut says he can/wants to change, that I just need to help him create the right environment to change.

    Susan

————

Hello Girlie!
From: Susan Powell
Sent: Sat. 7/26/08

My Wednesday I spent in the yard weeding, raking rocks out the garden, etc. Now exhausted, tired, with some big/raw blisters. Thursday was watching the Pioneer Day parade on TV. Feeling sorry for myself that I wasn't there. Josh had to work but since my friend wasn't around, I couldn't do the videotape of possessions so they can take it off the hard drive digital video camera—just in case—either. I lazed around, doing laundry, cleaning, cooking, trying to nap, and at 5:30 Josh's sis called to let us know we would do the family picture thing a little later—at 7. Whoops, had completely forgotten about that. Washed my hair, did make up, picked clothes for the boys. Cooked dinner that Braden refused to eat and after Charlie woke up from his self-inflicted nap—did eat.

    Josh's sis said it was a red/white/blue theme, and I had just painted my nails orange, about six coats, so I had to paint over them in the car and they got all thick and smudged—but we went to the international peace gardens, and I think I got some really good pictures. Then to Arby's and we all had ice cream cones. And on the way home we watched some fireworks with some neighbors, and didn't get inside until about 11 p.m. So tired we allowed Charlie to go to bed with us.

    My work offered some spontaneous overtime, so I worked Friday 6 a.m. to 7 p.m. (decided to drive to work, not biking at 4 a.m.—5 a.m. is my earliest limit). Was so happy to come home and know that the weeds were gone. Did dinner and took the boys outside. I think Braden is really teething (I can see the teeth) and he's drooling a lot with a runny but clear nose, and he was feverish and falling asleep in my arms. But when I took him inside to clean him up and gave him some baby Tylenol for fever, he seemed to get his second wind.

Then I backed up the garbage disposal so Josh got annoyed with me (no shocker) but all gung-ho with snaking the kitchen and bathtub drains. He did mention his mom suggested he go "out with the boys for lunch on Fridays" to "fit in and be social," and he's already talking about using the little antenna balls from Jack in the Box to "decorate his cubicle." He mentioned there are some "hard core rumors" about a guy with "12 kids" and his boss and another guy they often refer to as their "partner," so I think he is in a very diversified environment. He says they have rubber-band gun-fights and talk politics and they sound like a bunch of computer geeks. He continues to say he needs to "study more" and needs some project done by Monday to prove his worth. They gave him a work-issued laptop and an identity badge so I know he feels special. I pray and hope that his skills will keep his company satisfied and he can stay long term. He did concede, I guess, that he didn't want to do anything final with alternative commuting purchases until he knows this job is permanent. He is still interested in an electric bike and car, but I told him we should seek out the car-pooling field first and do more research.

I set my first shrink appointment—the earliest with my schedule and who I want is September 4, so I'm sad that I have to hold my peace for that long. Josh hasn't made any appointments yet, although I've emailed him the info on how to get it all set up.

That's me in a nutshell. See you in church?

Susan

———

Hello Girlie!
From: Susan Powell
Sent: Mon. 7/28/08

Yeah I think the Relief Society [Mormon charity and education auxiliary] *policy is to only tell one of the partners. K always tells me they only contact me if they can't get hold of her (rarely in the four years I've been here). They've released me from leading music, which was the only RS contact I had on a weekly basis (although they forgot to mention that, and that I'm now "nursery leader" in sacrament, but what-ever). It was a good week because they were speaking about girls camp.*

Josh is with AD, "computer geek for trucking company," contract to hire, which makes me nervous.

His sis is working on the family pics and I want to print and display and post them online. Trust me, I'm excited, too! Funny, I never really thought about the "faith without works is dead" in that concept before. You amaze me sometimes. I know you and everyone else will support me in whatever decisions, even if it means I crash someone's house in the middle of the night with my boys in tow (hope that never happens) or stay with him. But believe me, my bottom line is: he will do counseling at least. I expect by our anniversary next April (eight years) we will both be in counseling, and finally fixing the marriage, or somewhere in mediation/divorce court . . . sad but simple as that.

I'm sure if he fixes himself, you and everyone else will see a much closer version of the guy I married. And it will be easy enough to forget the hell and turmoil he's put me through (this is, of course, assuming things get better permanently). He used to buckle me in and give me a kiss, hold doors open, sincerely worry if I didn't put on a coat, buy groceries and help me cook and clean, or cook and clean for himself—hang out and talk together, watch movies and relaxing TV just for entertainment, and make time for being with friends, group dates, etc., go to church, not be all radical about the latest huge world problems that all his ranting can't fix (although he thinks it can). But when we moved to Utah, and more specifically he got interested in being self-employed, and then we had Charlie, his priorities seemed to change.

I know you'll be my friend no matter what. I just hope, obviously, that this counseling will help Josh, and everyone else can see the guy I fell in love with.

Susan

Josh didn't get help, and his relationship with Susan over the next months continued to deteriorate. As her husband became even more domineering, Susan became more determined to fight his control and flee the marriage—but proceeded cautiously because she feared for her safety. Josh grew more physically violent with Susan, one time pushing her and vowing that she'd "never get out of their marriage alive," she told a friend.

Update on "That Husband"
From: Susan Powell
Sent: Fri. 10/31/08

Sorry for the mass email, but I need all the help I can get.

So about two months back, I told Josh that I'm paying tithing on my income or divorce (I later admitted poor choice of words) and he got angry, and later compromised and said as long as my paycheck goes into the joint account and I pay the tithe out of the joint account it would be OK. I paid it twice, and then, just a few days ago, it comes out that he "never really agreed to pay tithing," and said that it was the only contention in our marriage. He said he would compromise and actually spend money on dates and family fun (like zoos/circus, etc., which has yet to happen) as long as I don't pay tithing in order to "heal our marriage" . . . until we "are millionaires" (yes, you read that right, millionaires). I realize he's once again manipulating me to get what he wants.

So, fast for me this Sunday. I've got family and friends doing that for me. My parents are ready to help pay any lawyer or mediation fees, and if I am supposed to divorce him, I will know with assurance, and somehow the divorce won't be as ugly as I fear (like him kidnapping the kids and taking me for broke). I am planning to go to the temple soon and not leaving until I have my answer. Others fasting for me will help strengthen me to get the answer I need. I'm asking the Lord if it's worth it to stay in this marriage and tolerate his constant manipulation.

Thanks in advance for all your support!

Susan

ELEVEN

GONE

Late in 2009, on a cold day in December, Josh appeared to have a brief, temporary change of heart, and he seemed more like the man Susan had fallen in love with. He agreed to host a meal with a friend in their home, something Susan cherished, and he even offered to make the food.[1] Josh called his dad early Sunday December 6 to "ask for a pancake recipe," Steven Powell later told police. Susan's friend Jovanna Owings came over that afternoon well before the early meal to chat and help Susan untangle yarn for a crochet project the women were working on. Josh cooked and served his pancakes and eggs—and even washed the dishes, something he hadn't done "in years," said Chuck Cox. But shortly after dinner, Susan complained of being tired and not feeling well, and sat, quiet, and unresponsive on the living-room couch. Josh told Owings he was taking his sons out sledding that night, and she left for home.

Susan failed to show up for work the next day, and the boys weren't dropped off at daycare. Neither Susan nor Josh called the child center to say the boys wouldn't be coming, or checked in with their offices. Concerned daycare workers called both parents, but couldn't reach either one. They next reached out to relatives and talked to Josh's sister Jennifer and his mom, who called police when they were unable to reach the couple. By midmorning Monday, police broke into the Powell home. There were no apparent signs of forced entry nor any indication that the home had been ransacked during a robbery or burglary. Later, they would notice two fans plugged in and running next to the sofa and a large wet spot on the living-room carpet. The rug would later be found to contain "stain patterns" of Susan's blood. "Someone was injured and lost blood while on the sofa inside the residence," stated a police affidavit seeking a warrant to collect samples of the carpet and couch. Investigators later also found Susan's purse containing all of her credit cards, cash, ID, and keys in the couple's bedroom "undisturbed."

Owings was the first to eventually reach Josh on his cell phone that afternoon. He told her he was driving around the West Valley City area with the boys and wasn't unaware Susan hadn't shown up for work—which was strange because he drove her to and from work each day; they shared a single car. According to cell-phone tracking later by police, Josh then drove 20 miles south of the city and called Susan's cell phone to leave a message saying that he had just returned with the boys from a camping trip, and asked her if she needed a ride home from work. Jennifer was the next person to reach her brother:

"Where are you?" she demanded.

"I'm at work," he responded.

"You're lying. What have you done?"

"How much do you know?" he asked before the phone suddenly went dead.

Police eventually reached Josh, still tooling around town with his boys, by calling from Jennifer's phone, and he agreed to meet investigators at his West Valley home. Josh explained when he arrived that he hadn't responded to earlier calls from his family and police because he had to preserve his cell-phone battery, which couldn't be recharged in his car. A detective pointed at a cell phone on Josh's console, plugged in to the cigarette lighter, charging. The phone belonged to Susan. Josh "appeared nervous and could not account for the phone being in the vehicle," according to the police report. He was questioned on the scene, then escorted later to the local police station. Josh told investigators that he had decided at the last minute to take the boys camping in Tooele County, a two-hour drive from home, some-time after midnight following dinner, and he had left Susan, safe, sleeping in their bed. Though temperatures were below freezing, and a snowstorm was forecast, he told police he bundled up his young sons for the trip because he wanted to try out his new generator. Pressed about why he would take such a trip just hours before he was due at work, he told investigators he mistakenly believed it was a day earlier instead of early Monday morning when he went camping—and then didn't bother contacting work when he realized his mistake because he assumed he'd been fired for blowing off the day. As for Susan, Josh "didn't know where his wife was, and didn't appear to be concerned about her welfare," noted West Valley police detective David Greco in his report of his encounter with Josh. Police spotted Josh's new generator in his minivan, as well as blankets, a gas can, tarps, a circular saw, a utility knife, latex gloves, a rake, sleds, and a shovel, but no tent or sleeping bags—"not exactly camping equipment," Susan's dad would later remark.

Figure 11.1. A handbill seeks the public's help in locating Susan Cox Powell after she vanished from her home in West Valley City, Utah, before Christmas in 2009. *Courtesy of Charles and Judy Cox.*

The following day, Josh showed up for a second police interview four hours late. He offered the same account of events, and he didn't bother asking if police had made any progress in the search for Susan. He abruptly ended the interview and announced that he planned to speak to an attorney. That evening, Josh drove to the Salt Lake City International Airport to rent a car and made an 800-mile mystery trip over the next two days. His cooperation with police was over.

Charlie, then four years old, told detectives that "his mother went camping" with the family, but "for some reason she stayed at the campsite and didn't come back home with them," according to the police report. A waitress told police that when the family came into her West Valley diner the night Susan went missing, Charlie asked her if she knew where his mom was. Weeks later, he would tell a daycare worker "with no emotion and with no hesitation, 'My mom is dead,'" after the worker threatened to contact his parents because he was misbehaving, Chuck Cox told me. Charlie also explained at one point that "mommy was in the trunk" in a picture of a car he had drawn, a teacher told his grandparents.

Investigators quickly learned about the couple's marital problems. Three co-workers told police that Susan had told them that "if anything were to happen to her, they were to give police a file that she had hidden from her husband." Detectives also found a safe-deposit key in Susan's purse that led them to a letter in a lock box addressed to her family and friends, titled the "Last Will and Testament for Susan Powell," dated in 2008. She asked that whoever opened the note not show it to her husband because she didn't trust him, and that "he has threatened to destroy her if they get divorced and her children will not have a mother and father," said the police case report. She added: "If I die, it may not be an accident, even if it looks like one."

Police quickly suspected Susan's disappearance was a kidnapping and homicide, and Josh looked like their man—but investigators didn't have a body. Josh told a co-worker at a company Christmas party the previous year "that in order to get away with murder, he would hide a body in a mineshaft in the west desert of Utah," stated a search-warrant affidavit. "He believed he could hide this from law enforcement as they would never search an unstable mine." Within days, Josh was making arrangements to pack up his home and get out of Utah. A week after Susan vanished, Josh contacted the head of Charlie and Braden's daycare center to say that the "children would not be coming back," and that the teacher "probably will not ever see them again," according to a police report. The following day, Powell canceled all of his wife's chiropractor appointments. Two days later, he drained Susan's IRA. Police discovered that in the months leading to Susan's disappearance, Josh had taken out a $1 million life-insurance policy on his wife and

$250,000 each on Charlie and Braden. Just weeks after his wife's disappear-
ance, before Christmas, Josh Powell and the boys moved back in with his dad
and adult siblings Alina, John, and Michael in Puyallup.

But Josh wasn't safe from the investigation, as West Valley police continued to search for Susan and investigate his activities. In May, Utah detectives and police from Pierce County in Washington carried out a search of
Steven Powell's home, where Josh was still living with the kids, and discovered a stunning, kinky twist in the case. Investigators discovered a cache of
"multiple images" of Susan Powell, including several of her in her under-
wear, which appeared to have been snapped surreptitiously while she was
in the bathroom during the time Susan and Josh lived in the home with
Josh's dad to save money early in their marriage. Police also found images
of nude women with Susan's face pasted over their heads, and photos of
Steven Powell masturbating in front of images of Susan projected onto a
television screen. Powell admitted to investigators that he took the photos
himself or took copies of photographs from Josh's computer without his
son's knowledge.

Steven told police that he and his daughter-in-law were in love, and that
she was "very sexual" toward him—but that she had emphasized to him that
their "flirtatious relationship could never be in the open due to her Mormon
religion," investigators revealed. He had urged his son and daughter-in-law
to move back in with him in Washington, where Susan could serve as a wife
to both men. "My biggest problem as well as my greatest pleasure lies in
the fact that for over a year I have been madly in love with my daughter-in-
law, Susan," Steven Powell wrote in some 2,000 pages of personal journals
Washington police would later recover in his Puyallup home in a second
search. "What has driven me is primarily lust. I have never lusted for a
woman as I have for Susan," he noted. "I take chances sometimes to take
video clips of her, which I watch regularly. She is an amazing woman. I hope
I am right, that she is in love with me, but of course there is the problem of
her being married to my son." He wrote of taking photos of his daughter-in-
law using mirrors to see her in the bathroom, and admitted many would find
such behavior "sick." It's "what might be considered sociopathic. I mean,
who looks under the bathroom door with a mirror?" he wondered in his

journals. He raged when the couple moved from Washington to Utah. "I am now going crazy with desire for her, but I do not regret any of it," he wrote. He referred often to his son's deteriorating marriage, and how poorly Josh treated Susan. "Theirs is truly a marriage made in hell," he wrote. "It's hard to believe that two people could be so nasty to each other." He didn't believe, however, that they would ever break up because Josh was financially dependent on Susan, and she desperately wanted to save the marriage.

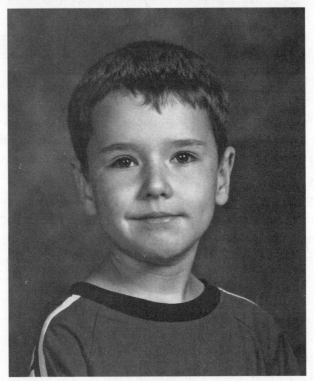

Figure 11.2. Charlie poses for the last school photo of his life. He would later die in a home explosion and fire set off by his dad, Josh Powell. *Courtesy of Charles and Judy Cox.*

Still, he fantasized he had a chance with Susan. "I wasn't going to turn down an opportunity with this beautiful woman, even though she was my son's wife," Powell said in a televised interview.[2] Detectives discovered in pages from Susan's journal that she kept stashed at her Wells Fargo office that she was, in fact, disgusted by Steven Powell. She described him as a "negative influence" on Josh, and a "pedophile," and talked of "how hard it is for her to forgive Steven Powell for what he has said," recounted the police report. "Susan states she does not want Steve Powell involved in her life, her children's life, and how she wishes Josh Powell would eliminate Steven Powell from his life. There were no positive writings about Steven Powell in Susan Powell's journal." Friends said the couple's move to Utah was triggered by Susan's disgust with her father-in-law and her desperation to flee his attention.

As troubling as Susan's photos found in Steven Powell's bedroom were, police also found images of popular cartoon characters having incestuous sex with adults on a laptop belonging to Josh. Despite concerns by social workers, Charlie and Brandon remained in the sole custody of Josh. He zealously guarded the boys from Susan's parents and didn't allow them to visit their grandsons.

As the investigation into Susan's disappearance continued, Steven and Josh forged an ugly new narrative of Susan. It was a skewed, paranoid perspective of his wife that Josh had nurtured in his mind over the years of a flirty, mentally unstable, over-sexed woman with a wandering eye who had "utter contempt" for him. Josh and his dad told reporters that Susan likely ran away with a man from West Valley who had vanished two months before she did and that they married in Brazil. In media interviews, Josh appeared angry and disdainful of his wife. "She's a very sexual person," he said in one TV appearance. He and his dad claimed to have Susan's teenage journals proving she was preoccupied with sex, and they threatened to print them.

As difficult as it was for them to believe, Susan's parents soon became convinced that their daughter had been murdered by Josh with the knowledge, if not the help or instigation, of Steven Powell. Like Josh, Steven had failed to show up for work the day Susan vanished and the following day. The Coxes were horrified that Josh, the prime suspect in Susan's disappearance, retained sole custody of their grandsons. They spoke out in the media against the situation and challenged Josh's custody of the boys as West Valley police continued to investigate Susan's disappearance.

In August 2011, investigators executed another search warrant in Steven Powell's home, seeking "love songs" he had boasted to the press he had written to his daughter-in-law, as well as the diaries written by Susan he claimed to have. That's when they uncovered his own journals stretching back ten years, and an additional thousands of photos, not only of Susan, but also of women whose pictures were snapped surreptitiously and filed under topics such as "skirts," "through the bathroom" and "breasts." Among the photos were pictures taken from Steven Powell's bedroom of two sisters next door, ages eight and nine, through their window into their bathroom as the girl took baths, changed, and sat on the toilet. Within days, Washington's Pierce County sheriff's deputies arrested Steven Powell, and he was charged with voyeurism and child pornography.

After their paternal grandfather was busted, Braden and Charlie were removed from his house to a foster home, then placed with Susan's parents. A psychological evaluation was ordered for Josh, though the findings underscored that "Joshua Powell has not been charged with any crime related to either his wife's disappearance or related to the charges with which his father is currently in custody." However, the assessment noted, Powell "is currently the only person of interest in his wife's murder." Officials were further troubled by the fact that Steven Powell had spoken publicly about his sexual obsession with his daughter-in-law, yet Josh stayed with his sons in his father's home. "When asked if he would have turned in his father if he did have knowledge of child pornography, Joshua Powell hesitantly replied: 'Only if it were a threat to children,'" the evaluation noted. Josh instead seemed "fixated on his in-laws and what he perceives as their unjust vendetta again him." The report also touched on a disturbing drawing by Charlie Powell showing a child stick figure bending over as an apparent adult figure stands behind him, evocative of a sexual assault. The image is crossed over with a large X and the words: "Don't play with me." Charlie was reluctant to discuss the drawing in therapy and insisted neither of the figures in the drawing was him. "Charlie continues to state he doesn't have friends, doesn't want friends, likes to do stuff alone when he is at school," the psychologist's report stated.

The social-service department was also "concerned" by various statements made by the boys and their dad. "Charles and Braden have been heard, during the short time they were in foster care, making statements about 'Mormons trying to steal them,' 'Mormons trying to harm them,' and that they 'hate Jesus.' Given the children's age, it would seem that these ideas were not generated of their own mind/opinion," the report stated. Charlie also "told school personnel how to kill an animal and cover it up so that it couldn't be discovered."

Figure 11.3. Braden horses around with grandpop Charles Cox as Charlie smiles at the piano in the living room of their grandparents' Washington home in Puyallup. *Courtesy of Charles and Judy Cox.*

As for Josh, a psychologist noted that he "cannot stay on topic, has rapid speech," and veers into "verbal rants about the Cox family." He also described his wife as troubled and suicidal, and he mentioned that after Susan visited a therapist several times, he agreed to a few months of marital counseling. Despite the concerns, however, the assessment determined that Josh had "excellent parenting skills." He was observed on one occasion making quesadillas and brownies for the boys in his dad's home. He was upbeat while also being "very organized and very much in control," though he sometimes used a "loud, raised, hardened tone," noted the evaluation. But he was clearly at ease cooking and taking care of the boys, and they were relaxed with him, according to the report. He was able to "redirect" misbehavior and diffuse conflict between the boys, encouraged them to share, and praised them when they did something that pleased him. "He appeared to be practiced and fairly patient," though the report also warned that the interactions could have been "staged." He was also observed playing with helicopter toys with his sons in a new, "sparsely furnished" three-bedroom house he had rented so he could win back custody of his boys since he was no longer living with his father. The report concluded that while Josh seemed to be a good parent, and there was no indication or history of abuse, he did speak inappropriately in front of the children about his perceived persecution at the hands of his in-laws. The evaluator was also concerned about the "potential for future conflict between father and sons when they become more independent thinkers. If Mr. Powell maintains his present parenting style, this may lead to strong disagreements and alienation about things contrary to Mr. Powell's wishes, as they have with some of this family members." The report nevertheless supported continued supervised visits by Josh with his boys until the courts made some final determination.

At his next court hearing concerning custody, Josh, his voice breaking, described himself as an excellent parent who provided a stable, loving home for his children. "I had no knowledge of any wrongdoing or any indication that there could be wrongdoing on my father's part, nor did anyone else in our house," he said. But while Josh was optimistic that his sons would be back with him soon because he had his own home, his hopes were dashed by the judge's ruling ordering Josh to undergo detailed, diagnostic psychosexual tests, which would have included a polygraph test, and might have involved use of a penile plethysmograph, which is attached to a subject's penis to measure response to certain images to ascertain if Josh was aroused by children or by images of incest. The supervised visits would continue, and the boys would remain in their grandparents' custody.

The Coxes could have been relieved by the ruling, but they weren't. They were more frightened than ever. Chuck and Judy were stunned Josh would continue to have supervised visits with the boys at his home. They wanted the visits held at a neutral third location or at social-services offices where there would be more control. "We kept warning social workers that there was no telling what Josh might do when he felt cornered," said Chuck Cox. "We were afraid he'd kill himself and take the boys with him out of spite."

The final chapter of Susan and Josh Powell's small family was written in fire February 5, 2012, just days after Josh's custody hearing. The boys were reluctant to leave their grandparents' home to visit their dad that day, but the Coxes had little choice; it was a court order that Josh be granted visitation. Judy Cox recalls with tears in her eyes how she talked her grandsons into the trip. "You'll have fun," which they usually did, she told them, and "you'll be back here soon."

Child Protective Services worker Elizabeth Griffin-Hall drove the boys from the Coxes' home to Josh's home, as she usually did. She was fond of the brothers, and found them charming and funny. She parked her Prius and was walking the boys up the front walkway when an excited Josh opened the door and shouted, "Charlie! Braden! I've got a surprise for you!" The boys broke away from Griffin-Hall and ran inside, and Josh slammed and locked the door with a sheepish look of apology in his eyes, she would later tell police. Griffin-Hall quickly backed away from the house as she was struck by a strong smell of gasoline, and she nervously called 911.

> *Griffin-Hall: I'm on a supervised visitation for a court-ordered visit and something really weird has happened. The kids went in the house and the biological parent, Josh Powell, will not let me in the door. What should I do?*
>
> *Dispatcher: What's the address?*
>
> *Griffin-Hall: I don't know . . . let me get in the car. Nothing like this has happened before. I'm shocked, and I could hear one of the kids crying, and he still won't let me in. He's on a very short leash with social services. He looked right at me and closed the door. It's 8119 189th Street East Puyallup. I'd like to pull out of the driveway because I smell gasoline, and he won't let me in.*

Dispatcher: He won't let you out of the driveway?

Griffin-Hall: He won't let me in the house!

Dispatcher: Whose house is it?

Griffin-Hall: Josh Powell.

Dispatcher: You don't live there?

Griffin-Hall: No, I'm contracted by the state to provide supervised visitation. He's the husband of Susan Powell. This is a high-profile case. I was one step behind them . . .

Dispatcher: So they went in the house and locked you out?

Griffin-Hall: Yes, he shut the door in my face. The kids have been in there by now approximately ten minutes, and he knows it's a supervised visit. Braden is 5 and Charlie is 7. He won't let me in! I rang the doorbell and everything. I begged him to let me in!

Dispatcher: OK, we'll have someone look for you there.

Griffin-Hall: Do you know how long it will be?

Dispatcher: They have to respond to emergencies, life-threatening situations first.

Griffin-Hall: This could be life-threatening! He was in court on Wednesday and he didn't get his kids back and this is really . . . I'm afraid for their lives!

As Griffin-Hall waited nervously outside the home, the house suddenly erupted in a ground-shaking explosion and fireball, sending orange tongues of flame and a curling plume of oily smoke into the sky. The engulfed house burned with a roar and a rush of hot wind. Panicked, Griffin-Hall desperately called 911 again:

Dispatcher: Hello. Were you calling about the fire on 189th street?

Griffin-Hall: Yes, he exploded the house! He exploded the house!

Dispatcher: Ma'am, do you know the exact address?

Griffin-Hall: It's 8119 189th East in Puyallup!

Dispatcher: What are you calling about?

Griffin-Hall: It exploded, the house!

Dispatcher: Do you know if there's anyone in the house?

Griffin-Hall: Yes! There was a man and two children. I just dropped off the children and he wouldn't let me in the door.

Dispatcher: Stay on the line with me. I'm going to get the fire department. Hang on. Don't hang up. Stay on the phone here with me, Ma'am.

Griffin-Hall: I can hear the fire trucks, but they're not here yet.

Dispatcher: We have an engine there.

Griffin-Hall: There are boys there, 5 and 7; he has supervised visitation and he blew up the house and the kids!

Dispatcher: The kids and the father were in the house?

Griffin-Hall: Yes! He slammed the door in my face so I kept knocking. I thought it was a mistake, I kept knocking and then I called 911.

Dispatcher: You saw him go back in the house?

Griffin-Hall: He never left the house, he just opened the door, the kids were one step ahead of me, they are 5 and 7, they were one step ahead of me and he slammed the door in my face.

Dispatcher: Do you think he might have done this intentionally?

Griffin-Hall: Yes! (Crying.)

Minutes later, after a sheriff arrived on the scene, a dispatcher received a 911 call from Josh's sister, Alina Powell.

Alina Powell (sobbing): I think my brother might be in trouble or something.

Dispatcher: What's going on with your brother?

Powell: He's sending weird e-mails and stuff.

Dispatcher: What's his last name?

Powell: Powell.

Dispatcher: And his first name?

Powell: Josh.

Dispatcher: What makes you think there's a problem with Josh?

Powell (crying): There's been a lot of abuse against him and he's really upset. There are e-mails and stuff, and he left me a voicemail. He said something like he can't live without his sons and goodbye.

Dispatcher: Does he live at 189th Street East?

Powell: I think that's the house, I don't know.

Dispatcher: Was he going to have supervised visits today?

Powell: I think so. He normally does.

Dispatcher: This is the Josh that has been in the media?

Powell: Yes, the one who has been abused by everyone. (Crying.) The boys are 5 and 7.

Dispatcher: Did he say he'd harm himself?

Powell: No, he was just saying goodbye. (Crying.)

Dispatcher: How long has he lived there for?

Powell: A few months, four or five months. I know it's been hard on him; the abuse has been extremely difficult.

Dispatcher: What else did the e-mail say?

Powell: He sent several e-mails about how to handle his property and his utilities. They started a while ago; I didn't think anything of it. They started early this morning. They were just weird e-mails.

Dispatcher: Is he home by himself?

Powell: I don't know. He might be. [She offers to drive over to his house to confirm the exact address, but says she's afraid. The dispatcher says he can have an officer meet her.]

Powell: I'm not afraid of him, he'd never hurt me, I'm afraid of what I'll find. (Sobbing.)

By the time firefighters arrived 22 minutes after Griffin-Hall's first call, Josh and both boys were dead. The home and car outside were transformed into blackened shells in the inferno, fueled by four five-gallon drums of gasoline that Powell had used to rig his home for the explosion. Police would discover that Josh Powell's home was little more than a "stage" rigged to go up in flames. He had already emptied it of its few furnishings and had given the boys' toys and books to charity. Father and sons died of carbon-monoxide poisoning, though Josh had attacked the boys before their death with an ax that was found near his body. Both boys suffered "chop marks" on their necks and head, according to the autopsy.

Almost a year later, a Child Fatality Review[3] by the Children's Administration of the Washington Department of Health and Human Services concluded that "better communication" between Washington's Department of Social and Health Service and the West Valley City Police Department might have saved the boys' lives. A Washington intake worker answered "no" when asked on a form in the boys' files if anyone had used or threatened to use physical force against an adult in the home—even though officers told social workers that they believed Josh had killed his wife. The report concluded that "the lack of training on best practices regarding domestic violence . . . may have contributed to the lack of further exploration of domestic violence in this case." But the report also found that social workers performed "all their duties above and beyond the expected requirements by the state, and no one could predict that Josh would murder his own children."

Steven Powell went on trial for voyeurism and child pornography for the photos he took of the neighbor girls. The Coxes were hoping he would trade information on their missing daughter as part of possible plea deal. But if he had any information, he kept his mouth shut. "He's had a pornography problem for as long as I can remember," his daughter Jennifer Graves testified. "And with pornography, you don't sit on the fence. You either get worse or you get better. You take steps to improve and get that out of your life or you go down the other path and you end up doing worse and worse things. It's not a surprise at all to me he's ended up where he's at now." A detective testified that Steven Powell had written in his journal that he "likes taking video shots of pretty girls in shorts and skirts, beautiful women of every age," and wrote, "I sometimes use these images for self-stimulation."

The mother of the girls Powell photographed from his bedroom window testified in court about the fear she felt when a detective, who called her outside away from her daughters, told her what had been going on. One of her daughters was afraid to be in the bathroom with the door closed, so it was left open, and the mother never imaged that someone would take advantage of the situation to satisfy a kinky quirk. Powell was convicted of 14 counts of voyeurism and sentenced to 30 months in in prison. The girls' mother has filed a civil suit against Powell.

The Susan Powell case remains active, though West Valley police have significantly scaled back their search for her and their investigation. The department continues to offer a $10,000 reward for information leading to her whereabouts.

In one more toll of the case, Josh Powell's youngest brother, Michael, 30, a graduate student at the University of Minnesota, leaped to his death from the upper level of a parking garage in Minneapolis in early 2013. He had recently lost a court battle with Susan's parents over a $1.5 million life-insurance policy left by Josh. Just months before he killed himself, Josh changed the policy to list Michael and a family trust as beneficiaries, rather than Susan.

The Coxes, steady, determined people, continue to seek closure for their daughter. They're comforted by their religious faith and the belief that Susan has been reunited with Braden and Charlie, but they're angry with the West Valley police, Washington social services, and Steven Powell. They continue to battle for all remaining information in all police files not yet released by investigators. They hope that some overlooked detail might help the search for their daughter's body. They've established the Susan Cox Powell Foundation to assist and support families whose loved ones are missing, and they are raising awareness about the Christmas Box House, a Utah facility that provides shelter for abused children. The Coxes marked the third anniversary of Susan's disappearance in late 2012 by unveiling an angel memorial statue installed near Charlie and Braden's grave in Woodbine Cemetery in Puyallup. It's been a long, painful road. "Something positive has developed out of this," Chuck said of the foundation the Coxes have established. "But we need to find Susan."

TWELVE

THIS MODERN LIFE

William Beadle thought about killing his wife and children for three years.[1] He had been a proud, successful Connecticut retailer, wealthier than most, according to one reporter. But business went south, and he made an investment in currency that failed badly, and he was so shaken by his plunging fortune that he considered suicide—and taking his family with him. Increasingly preoccupied with the idea, as the bloody day approached, he began to place a carving knife and an ax along his bedside each evening, apparently prepared to take action in the middle of the night if it came to that. Usually a loving husband and indulgent dad, Beadle was forced to adopt the "most rigid family economy" while attempting to maintain an outward appearance of normalcy, according to friend Stephen Mix Mitchell, who wrote an account of what was soon to be Beadle's notorious activities.[2] It didn't work. "I am in such a situation" that I can't provide food, clothing, nor fuel for myself and family, the 52-year-old dad wrote to his friend John Chester in a letter found among a collection of writings by Beadle that may be the most complete personal account ever of the thought processes leading to a family annihilation.[3] "Is it not time to die?"

Besides, he felt rotten. A man could become "meaner than meanness itself" if he fell "by unavoidable accident into poverty, and then submits to be laughed at and despised and trampled upon by a set of wretches as far below him as the moon is below the sun," explained Beadle in one of his letters.

But he struggled with his conscience before he attacked his family. He decided to murder his children relatively easily. He believed he was in charge of their fate, and opted to kill his three young daughters and son—ages 6 to 11—to "consign them over to better hands" in an afterlife.

He had a more difficult time deciding the future of his wife, Lydia. Beadle had doubts as to whether it was his duty to "destroy my wife, as I had no hand in bringing her into the world." But he weighed that against her inability to earn a living or to find another partner after his suicide, particularly in the wake of what he knew would be considered the "shocking disaster" of his murder of their children. In addition, losing her babies in such a massacre would be a disturbing "distraction" for his wife, to say the least, and might even cause a "state of mind that would be worse," Beadle admitted. He eventually decided that he and his wife should "take our leave together." As for suicide, he boasted to his friend: "It's the act of a hero."

One nagging doubt remained: Would he suffer in hell for his actions? Beadle fell back on his religion to find peace of mind. He believed in Deism, a quirky faith that included the beliefs that natural phenomenon, as opposed to miracles or divine revelation, was sufficient to determine the existence of God, and that each individual could know God in his own way without an intermediary or interpretation by organized religion or a religious authority. The Deist also believed that nature runs its course following scientific laws determined by God.

His faith provided him with immunity, Beadle concluded. "I mean to die a proper Deist; I . . . believe that all is right, that we are all impelled to say and act all that we do say and act. That a tyrant king deluging three quarters of the world in blood, that my killing my family, that a man destroying a nest of wasps . . . is as much directed by the hand of heaven as the making this whole world was. And if this is the case, there is no such thing as sin," he wrote, adding later, "I really believe that the true God supports me." He imagined when the day came, "I shall do it as deliberately and steadily as I would go to bed." In his will, he declared: "I and my family shall go off this state martyrs to that cause that I fondly believed to be the cause of justice, virtue and freedom."

Shortly before Beadle massacred his family, he "rehearsed the murders" in his mind, gazing at his family as they slept, clutching the "means of death" in his hand, he wrote to his friend Chester. His wife was bothered during this time by premonitions of death that came to her in dreams. She saw in her dreams her husband's many papers "spotted with blood," and her children lying dead. In another dream, she was seized with a dreadful confusion but then was "free and happy," wrote Beadle in a letter. He took the vision as a sign that the "hand of heaven is really with us." Just weeks later, in early December, he killed the family, the morning after a Christmas party. The day before the massacre, he was almost giddy. "Thank heaven, for I believe the day is now come," he wrote. "This is a glorious one, and providence seems to smile on the deed." He likely drugged his wife and children and attacked them as they slept. He struck Lydia, and then each of his children, in the head with an ax, then cut their throats. He hung his wife and son's heads over the side of their beds so their blood would not stain the sheets. He arranged his three daughters side by side on the floor of their bedroom, "like lambs," noted a witness, and covered them with a blanket. Finally, when his family lay dead in his house, Beadle raised two pistols to his head, one in each hand, pressed the muzzle of each into the opposite temples of his head, and fired.

The maid, told that her mistress was ill, had been sent earlier by Beadle with a letter to fetch Dr. Jonas Farnsworth. Troubled by what Beadle had written in the note delivered to him, Farnsworth rushed with another man and Beadle's friend Mitchell to the home. When the maid returned with the three men and opened the door of the children's bedroom, her "horror was so great"[4] that she fainted and tumbled backwards down the stairs before the doctor caught her. "Surely a more distressing sight never agonized the human feelings than now present itself," Mitchell wrote in his book, recalling the shock as the men entered the room. What they saw was "clearly an act of horror no man could have done. It was so disturbing to see these children in such a state of mangled flesh. The floor was swimming in blood."

The case triggered widespread horror and outrage in the young American republic at the time it occurred, 1783. Beadle's community was so incensed that residents were desperate to punish him, even after his death. His body was shoved through a window of his home, and the bloody knife he used in the murders was tied to his chest. His corpse was pulled, roughly, exposed, on a horse-drawn sled through town and the winter country-side, and dumped in a hole by the Connecticut River. Visitors to the open gravesite continued to desecrate the body.

Beadle's suicidal family annihilation was the second in America in three years, and among a rash of seven in the same time period. The earlier massacre also involved an ax and a religious fervor. James Yates was considered by his neighbors a "sane and pedestrian cottager" until he fatally bludgeoned his wife and four children, and used an ax to hack to death his dog, two horses, and two cows at his Chester County home in Pennsylvania, in an attack similar to Christopher Foster's rampage in Britain some 240 years later.[5] Yates told authorities he was following orders from on high, and said aloud in a prayer to God, "My father, for thy glory I have done this deed."

Another "barbarous" family annihilation 30 years earlier in Pennsylvania by farmer John Myrack in 1750, who bashed his wife, two children, and an infant nursing there, failed to rivet the attention of the community in quite the same way the Beadle murders did. It was written off by the *London Intelligencer* as likely caused by "excessive abuse of mad-making liquor."[6]

But the two more "modern" murders sparked painful self-reflection and concerns that something about modern life, or perhaps, modern American life, was linked to the bloodshed. The Beadle and Yates killings followed decades of a troubling increase in criminal violence in the colonies, and a violence that was leaking into the home. Citizens grasped at some explanation for the profoundly disturbing murders. Beadle's "free-thinking" avant-garde religion was held accountable by at least one angry minister, who warned his flock about such an outcome from a "monster Deist" who had turned his back on the Bible and religious authority.

But it couldn't be so simple. A strange miasma continued to infect Americans' sense of themselves in the wake of the child murders so unfathomable that they shook the soul. "Something strange and horrible happened in a number of American households of the early republic," writes researcher Daniel Cohen.[7] "In a series of curiously clustered incidents, spaced over a period of six decades, a handful of men, loving husbands and affectionate fathers, took axes from under their beds and slaughtered their wives and children." The killings occurred in a variety of regions and involved men from their mid-20s to mid-50s, in various occupations from farmer to craftsman to merchant, in what seems to have "constituted a representative cross-section of American men of the early republic," Cohen notes. "What set them apart from their neighbors were a series of appalling crimes."

This rash of family-annihilation cases after the Revolutionary War marks America as the "birthplace" of modern familicide, believes family-annihilation expert Neil Websdale, a professor at Northern Arizona University. Such murders occurred earlier, according to medieval accounts, but extremely rarely. The face of violent crime centuries ago was largely male-on-male murder, as it is today, and murders within a family constituted a far smaller proportion of total murders than they did in early modern times, according to Websdale. The peculiar and disturbing crime of family annihilation was forged in the last few centuries in the crucible of modern stresses, he's convinced, and it was born in the American republic.

Websdale has conducted the most detailed study of the widest range of family annihilations in in his book *Familicidal Hearts: The Emotional Styles of 211 Killers.* He studied the circumstances of each case, examined the background of the killers, and pored over official and media accounts. In a number of the rare cases in which the killer was still alive, he interviewed him (or her). Websdale takes as one of his research launching points Martin Daly and Margo Wilson's views of domestic murder and family annihilation. He acknowledges drawing on their insights, including their view that domestic violence is steeped in the evolutionary drives behind man's sometimes-violent "sexual proprietariness" concerning women, forged by natural selection. "Daly and Wilson's point that biological forces have a major role to play in explaining intimate partner homicide and familicide is an important touchstone," Websdale notes.[8] But he also believes that such theories are inadequate to fully understand the complexity of murderous domestic violence in modern times. "My point is not that these perspectives are incorrect as much as it is that they do not take us far enough," he writes. While men may be primed for violence in certain situations by evolution, the theory isn't fine-tuned enough to help discern which of the vast population of human males are likely to be the few who kill their wives, children, or their entire family, notes Websdale. He believes researchers must seek out patterns of behavior to more clearly define which kind of men kill families in an effort to develop predictive theories that could be used to prevent future bloodshed.

The cases he studied were complicated. It was apparent that "male per-petrators were powerful in some ways and not in others, and that the relationship between this power and their violence/tyranny was complex," he writes.[9] He concluded that it was not so much male power that led to murderous violence but, rather, fading, or a sense of diminishing, power or the fear of a loss of power that triggered violence.

Websdale argues that a killer's anxiety about his tenuous hold on control in his life is the result of a modern phenomenon of stresses that exacts a particular toll on men. The modern male must respond to a mind-blowing array of mixed signals of behavior and comportment expectations within the demands of a modern economy shaped by history, society, and culture. Today's *Homo sapiens* male is expected to be an aggressive, competitive go-getter, successful at work with an enviable lifestyle. But he must also be a romantic partner and caring father, and always calm and dependable. Few men can find a comfortable spot on a bar set so high, and so are left frustrated and ashamed when they can't deliver what they believe they're expected to do, Websdale believes. Though he studies killers in his book, Websdale says the work is not so much about murder but about "familicidal hearts" in society. He believes the extreme cases of murder-suicide reveal dark pressures of what many people struggle with and their link to the ugliness of family violence. Familicides "tell us a lot about the way we live our lives. The book isn't really about people who kill; it's about the emotional life that informs that tendency to kill," he explained to me in an interview. "There are a lot more familicidal hearts out there than people who will commit familicide. It never ceases to amaze me how many men are depressed, how many have fantasies about killing their families. That says something profound about the way we live."

Other family-violence experts also recognize that males play a key role in child homicides. Michael Petit of Every Child Matters told me that he views the critical danger in most abuses cases as the "isolated, alienated, immature male," sometimes the father, but also a mother's lover who comes into a household angry, impatient, and perhaps competitive with a mother's baby or child for her attention. Richard Gelles, too, noted in an interview with me that some males have so few tools to deal with their economic or social pressures that they have only the physicality of their "masculinity to fall back on."

Like Daly and Wilson, Websdale recognizes radically different types of family annihilators in his book. He labels familicides carried out in a rage—those triggered by a "grievance" against a wife who seeks to leave a marriage or whom her husband suspects of cheating in Daly and Wilson's research scenario—cases of "livid coercive hearts."[10] Those driven by what the killer might consider an altruistic reason to spare the family pain, like William Parente—which Daly and Wilson see as revolving around a "depressed and brooding" father—Websdale calls murders by "civil reputable hearts."[11]

In his study detailing the livid coercive heart, he focuses in particular on eight cases, one involving a killer mother (92.6 percent of his 211 cases involved killer fathers, further supporting the view that family annihilations are almost always committed by dads). Three of the male killers did not commit suicide, but it wasn't for lack of trying. In one case "Ben" (Websdale uses aliases in the crimes) drove his car off a 150-foot cliff as he was traveling with his four-year-old daughter and pregnant wife, "Laurie," 34. Ben, 37, was the only one in the car to survive. Laurie had planned to leave Ben and return to her father's home with their daughter once her baby was born. Jealous Ben suspected Laurie's pregnancy wasn't thanks to him. It was. In another case, "Oscar" killed his longtime lover and his two stepchildren and fled with his two biological kids before he was captured eight years later.

Websdale discovered that each of the men in the cases had extremely troubled childhoods and tended to be from working-class backgrounds. They entered into their own adult relationships desperate to create what they lacked in childhood—a loving, normal family that would provide them not only a warm, intimate home life, but also a place in respectable society whose price of admission is being part of an upstanding family. Websdale found that men in the livid coercive cases were almost too eager to fall in love. Their attraction to their partner often outweighed their mate's attachment to them and bordered on the obsessive. Family killer Oscar recalled the face of the woman he would later murder as being transformed as they dated. He took it as a "supernatural sign" that she was "for me."[12] He also saw her as a "passport" to a "respectable life," even though he discovered later that she had worked for a time as a prostitute, Websdale recounts.

But it was exactly their desperate hunger for normalcy, and their constant anxiety about losing it, that almost immediately created friction in their new families. Their grasping fear of losing what they saw as their only hold on respectability and status had the opposite result of what they sought: Instead of drawing family members closer, it drove them farther away.

"The nuclear family provided a vehicle for legitimately incorporating themselves into various social networks; in other words, the nuclear family offered a means of belonging," writes Websdale.[13] "The developing familicidal hearts often entered these relationships with alacrity, at the same time guarding lovers nervously, like a hungry predator protects its food." Not content with the ebb and flow of love and attention common in many families, the angry husbands quickly moved to "force the hearts of their loved ones toward them," writes Websdale. "As they forced, their loved ones resisted." In fact, their "interpersonal domination slowly and paradoxically corrodes the love, affection and romance that the livid coercive heart initially tasted or thought they experienced and longed to retain."[14]

The livid coercive men tended to resort to physical force to keep their partners and children in line with their vision of the dutiful love and respect they were convinced they deserved. The women victims in the livid coercive cases studied by Websdale stated while they were alive that they feared their husbands might kill them. Yet very few victims ever resigned themselves to that fate. They attempted to escape their relationships, or strategized within them in a bid to save their marriages while also protecting themselves.

Josh Powell met most of Websdale's markers for a "livid coercive" killer. He had a troubled childhood, likely suffered from some kind of personality disorder, and was singled out in a strange, often-abusive relationship by his father, according to family members. He appeared to be determined to marry, and marry quickly, and successfully wooed Susan Cox. But he was a dysfunctional provider, fired repeatedly from work, and furious when he imagined his wife had nothing but "utter contempt" for him because of his own shortcomings of which he was excruciatingly aware.

Josh also fit the evolutionary model of control of the female in his life. He was clearly focused on dominating Susan, even though she was the more capable parent and provider in their home. He worried about what she thought of him, and, after her disappearance, clearly harbored a simmering fury about a wife he described as flirtatious and "highly sexual," and feared was restless. Susan, like other victims of familicide cases examined by Websdale, worried about the violence her husband was capable of, yet had a strategy to change the situation—and leave Josh if she was unsuccessful.

But while Powell's murders and suicide are consistent with many aspects of most cases of familicides, his crime was also extremely unusual because it occurred in stages. First Susan vanished, then Powell killed his sons and committed suicide. The individual characteristics of Powell's crime is a testament to the complex challenges of understanding family annihilations and other types of fatal domestic violence because they often combine several key factors from biological forces to societal pressures, to mental illness, even while they exhibit startlingly similar patterns.

Powell's killing of his two young sons is more typical among dads who murder their children to punish an unfaithful wife or a mate who is leaving or about to leave. Such a "reprisal murder" was suspected in the Michigan case of John Skelton, whose three young sons, Andrew, Alexander, and Tanner, disappeared while he had custody of them over Thanksgiving in 2010 after his wife had divorced him. He was sentenced to up to 15 years in prison after pleading no contest to an unlawful imprisonment charges. The prosecution case was hurt because the boys' bodies were never found. Skelton claimed he had given his sons to some unidentified organization to protect them from his ex-wife.

But Susan Cox Powell was already dead when Braden and Charlie were killed, so there was no errant wife to "punish." Josh Powell was enraged with several other people, however, whom he wanted to "show"—his in-laws, his own estranged family members, civil authorities who were barring Powell from his children. Powell also faced intrusive court-ordered tests to determine if he was capable of incest or sexually attracted to children. Powell may have been so humiliated by the prospect that he would have to submit to the tests—or, perhaps, that he would be exposed as a pedophile or incestuous father—that he opted for murder-suicide. He was likely also infuriated by the thought that he would be denied access to his own kids. The fact that he not only killed himself and his kids, but also used a gas-fueled explosion to do so added a special emphasis to his deadly "message," the kind of "overkill" that police were struck by at Chris Foster's estate.

Bill Parente was far more typical among his "genre" of family annihilators, and he shared several aspects of familicidal "civil reputable hearts" studied by Websdale. Interestingly, there are more mothers who commit this type of family annihilation than in the livid coercive cases (though they don't kill their spouses). Websdale argues that in either situation, a parent appears to be "overwhelmed by their gender calling"—in the case of a male, a sense of failure at being a good provider, while women may be ashamed— or angry—because a husband is leaving her.

"The vast majority of familicidal hearts experienced acute shame at failing to live up to the imperatives of their gendered callings as providers, lovers, fathers, husbands, wives, mothers or partners," the author writes.

Parente was regarded as a good provider, a solid citizen, a devoted dad and husband, and a religious man. If anything, he was too "enmeshed" with his family and seemed to have little life beyond his work and wife and daughters. He also suffered a devastating turnaround in his fortunes and was about to face major ignominy and community revulsion with what had to be imminent arrest to be followed by the hurt, shock, and humiliation of his family. He may have truly wanted to spare them the shame of his actions, or perhaps he couldn't bear to imagine them angry and disgusted by him after his suicide. Or, as Gelles has noted, he simply regarded the family as a single entity, and that his suicide inevitably in his mind involved a "family suicide."

Parente, as other similar killers, was clearly not as stable as he might have appeared to be to many. "Civil reputable" killers are affected, as are the livid coercive murderers, by a sense of alienation, anomie, and alienation, Websdale has concluded. These "perpetrators appear conformist, proper, respectable, almost emotionally constipated or tightly constrained," noted Websdale.[15] "By virtue of their social locations, upbringings, physiologies and temperaments, civil reputable hearts subdue extreme emotions such as rage, or perhaps experience them much less than the livid coercive heart." Yet evidence suggests that many "lived lives full of tension and apprehension about the future, often quietly worrying about their days," he adds. Unlike livid coercive killers, the Parente genre of family annihilators tend to live in "well-to-do or at least upwardly mobile or economically aspiring families," and are "well thought of in their communities, sometimes pillars of them," notes Websdale. "They have much farther to fall than their livid coercive peers. Indeed, the prospect of losing face, of falling from grace, looms large" in their lives.[16]

Their murder-suicides are particularly shocking to the community and friends and acquaintances, whose very concepts of relationships and human behavior are profoundly shaken by the attacks, says Websdale. "When men and women of honor and respectability commit familicide it raises the possibility that other like-situated persons have the same potential, and it makes us doubt the genuineness of manifestations of honor, civility, caring and nurturing," he points out in his book.[17]

One of the most famous cases of a family annihilation was New Jersey accountant John List's murder of his wife, his mother, and his two sons and a daughter in 1971. He fled, assumed a new name, and wasn't apprehended for 18 years. By then he had a new family. Like Parente, he was the only son of a devoted mom. He was a loner whose social life hinged on his family. When he lost his job, he didn't tell his wife, pretended to go to work each day, and sank deeper and deeper into debt. "My professional career had reached a dead end, but I was too proud—or ashamed—to admit it, even to myself," he said in an interview after he was busted.[18] When he shot his family, he arranged their bodies under blankets, and left classical music playing for them on the radio. Like William Parente, he planned his attack, and, as Websdale notes, "killed with care."

It's not only modern society that may have some link to family anni-hilations, but, Websdale fears, something in particular about relationships forged in America, the birthplace of familicides, that fuels the murderous intent. He suspects the problem may be more pronounced in this country, though no international evidence has yet been gathered to support that view. The "don't tread on me" and "rugged individualist" aspects of US culture may be particularly demanding for families under stress. A culture formed in the "white heat of individual responsibility" sees "less willingness to recognize the importance of community and caring for others," argues Websdale.[19] "Rather, we see enormous expenditures on the criminal justice juggernaut and incarcerations, and an abject failure to connect individual malevolence and pathology to social, economic and political arrangements."

THIRTEEN

MASKED

THAT'S WHEN I REALIZED. SCOTT SAID THAT SHE WAS "MISSING." AND I JUST, I JUST KNEW, I KNEW SHE WAS MISSING.

—Sharon Rocha, mother of Laci Peterson,
in testimony at the 2004 murder trial
of her son-in-law Scott Peterson

He was a strikingly handsome salesman from Modesto with a wrestler's build and smoldering dark eyes, a pretty, loquacious wife, a swimming pool in a comfortable California neighborhood, and a baby boy on the way.[1] But Scott Peterson, who was close to turning 30, wasn't happy. He was once a restaurateur in Southern California, glad-handing the customers and flirting with the women. The restaurant wasn't a roaring financial success, and his determined wife, Laci, wanted to be closer to her mom in her hometown of Modesto, especially once she planned to have a baby. So there was Scott: a charismatic head-turner with the women, but, essentially, now a pedestrian family man selling fertilizer, and not very effectively, in a dusty middle-class cow town in the landlocked Central Valley of California—"just a normal, every-day town, not anything unusual or different than any other city," is how his mother-in-law would describe it later in court. That's the kind of mediocrity Scott was struggling with as he floated in his pool on a hot, dry summer afternoon in 2002, his heels cooling in the water that collected in the bottom of his air mattress. He was talking, quietly, to his brother-in-law, Brent Rocha, who had become good friends with Scott since he married Laci five years earlier. Laci, along with Brent's wife, Rose, and the Rochas' toddler son were in one section of the pool, and "me and Scott were on the other end, and we were just kind of talking about life," Brent would later testify in court. "We were just talking about, you know, not only about him being a parent, but in general how he wasn't doing good at his job, and kind of had a lot going on: He's turning 30, and he was going to be a father. He was down, kind of quiet. He was talking about how he was trying to interview new associates at his business, and hoping they would be better sales people than he would be." Scott wasn't thrilled about having a baby, Brent's wife would later recall, pointing to a chat with Scott about starting a family. "We were talking about pregnancy or having a family, and I believe I said something to the effect of, to Scott, 'Are you ready for this?' and he looked at me and said, 'I was kind of hoping for infertility,'" she would testify. "He wasn't laughing, he wasn't smiling, so when I heard that I was kind of surprised, I was kind of shocked by what he said, and I didn't know how to read him."

On Christmas Eve that year, Laci Peterson, eight months pregnant with the couple's first child, vanished. Later in spring, a couple walking their dog would find her fetus entangled in seaweed on the shore of San Francisco Bay. A day later, Laci's torso was found nearby.

Scott Peterson was the man who launched me on this book. I covered his 2004 trial for the capital crime murder of his wife and unborn son for the *New York Daily News*. When I walked into the courtroom, I was already suspicious he was guilty. For one thing, statistics were on my side. Any time a family member is missing or murdered, the most likely suspect is the spouse, or, in the case of a child, a parent, so Scott was doubly suspect. And Scott's early concern for his missing wife looked canned. He cried too easily, talked too articulately when TV cameras were on him, casually skipped at least one community vigil for Laci, and started to store furniture in the nursery he and Laci had prepared for the boy. He knew his baby wouldn't be returning to use it. In the cynicism of the newsrooms of places like the *New York Daily News* or *New York Post*, reporters and editors alike watching dads and moms like Scott cry so easily at pleas for lost children, quickly scoff "guilty" when they're clustered around TV monitors or looking up from their desks at televised press conferences, before turning back to news of the next dead body. The innocent who have lost loved ones are often paralyzed by sorrow; they have a difficult time even communicating, so wracked by fear and worry are they. The anguish of Laci's mom, Sharon Rocha, was palpably painful to witness.

Figure 13.1. Laci flashes a smile and rests her hands on her pregnant belly. Though Laci grew increasingly uncomfortable as the months progressed, she was thrilled to be pregnant. *Presented in evidence at Scott Peterson's murder trial.*

A relaxed Scott smiled lazily, and often, at the defense table in the Redwood City courtroom where he was tried, but I could see death row in the faces of the jury, and he'd have no glad-handing as a restaurateur, not even a life in Modesto, nor a baby boy on the way—a son he and Laci had already named Conner. The son-about-to-be had a nursery waiting for him in the couple's Covena Avenue home in Modesto, decorated in a nautical theme with a plaid life preserver over his crib that said "Welcome Aboard" when Laci's body was found.

I didn't get it. Every day, squeezing past knees to my courtroom seat, I wondered, again, what could drive a man to kill the only offspring he'd ever have? There'd be no chance for Scott to father a child in San Quentin. It seemed to be against every human instinct to kill a pregnant wife. Did Scott have some profound biological defect in his brain wiring that created a lethal personality? Was he turned into a killer by an abusive childhood? Or was something in him so twisted by social forces that it overrode a primeval human drive to procreate? Were we creating a culture that somehow helped unleash a twisted machismo that destroyed its own spawn? Mothers killing their children are as profoundly upsetting. But, as a woman, I could more easily understand many cases in which a mother was clearly mentally unstable (killing a child to exorcise "demons," for example) or in the throes of a vicious postpartum depression. An apparently cold, calculated decision to eliminate a pregnant wife and son so close to birth, simply—as it appeared to be in Scott's case—to exchange one woman and one life for another without the bother of divorce court, the expense of alimony and child support, and the tarnish of a failed relationship, I found completely incomprehensible.

Absolutely nothing in Scott Peterson's background indicated he would become a killer of his wife and unborn son—he had no known history of violence, no arrest record. "Scott does not have the genetics of a cold-blooded, premeditated killer," his attorney Mark Geragos told *People* magazine just as the trial was about to begin.[2] Laci never complained of abuse; in fact, she seemed to have a near-perfect marriage. There wasn't a whisper of trouble to her friends, nor did she ever confide that anything was wrong to her mom, Sharon Rocha, who was described by Sharon's longtime companion as Laci's "best friend."

Scott was the much-loved last child of Lee and Jackie Peterson, who merged their earlier families in a kind of Brady Bunch before Scott's birth. Jackie had given up two babies for adoption before she met Lee—and nearly a third one until her doctor talked her out of it—because she feared she couldn't adequately care for them as a single mom. It was clear at the trial from Jackie's fiercely defensive behavior with the press and Laci's family that she had desperately tried to make up with her son for the children she had left behind. When Jackie was asked on the witness stand if she was Scott's mother, she responded: "Proudly so, yes." At the penalty phase of the trial, she pleaded with the jury "not to take my son away." He's an "exceptional young man and he's my son," she said. "I know he's not perfect. But he is genuinely a loving, caring, nurturing, kind, gentle person."

Figure 13.2. Laci and Scott pose happily for a snapshot long before there was another woman in Scott's life. *Presented in evidence at Scott Peterson's murder trial.*

Scott was a popular student, a sought-after date, a star golfer in high school. He met Laci while the two were students at California Polytechnic in San Luis Obispo. Laci majored in decorative horticulture, and Scott in agricultural business. As he attended school, he worked at a packaging company owned by his parents, who had given him an investment stake in it, but he later cashed it out to combine funds with money from Laci to launch a burger restaurant called The Shack. Laci gushed to her mom about Scott, who was tender and attentive, and wooed her with thoughtful, romantic flourishes. The first time Sharon Rocha traveled to San Luis Obispo to meet Scott at Laci's insistence in 1994, he had a special table waiting for them at a restaurant where he worked at the time. There were a dozen red roses on the table for Laci, and a dozen white roses for Sharon. Scott and Laci married three years later, shortly after Laci graduated. She found a job as a wine distributor in the Monterey area, so she lived in Prunedale while Scott finished up his degree the following year and continued working at The Shack. They bought their Modesto home with financial help from the Petersons. Laci eventually settled into regular work as a substitute teacher. Scott found a job selling fertilizer for agricultural supplier Tradecorp, and joined the nearby expensive Del Rio Country Club to pursue his passion for golf. He barbecued, the couple put in a swimming pool in the backyard, he called his mother-in-law "Mom." "You thought the world of him" before the day Laci vanished, "is that a fair statement?" Scott's attorney Mark Geragos asked Sharon Rocha on the witness stand.

Rocha: Yes, it is.

Geragos: He called you Mom?

Rocha: Yes.

Geragos: He would talk to you, and you had no qualms about the way he treated your daughter whatsoever; isn't that correct?

Rocha: Yes.

Geragos: You never saw him ever get violent with her, did you?

Rocha: No.

Geragos: You never saw him even get angry in the sense where he would yell at her or raise his voice at her, did you?

Rocha: No, not that I ever recall.

There were even times, Geragos pressed Rocha, "when he probably should have been mad at Laci, and did not get mad at her, would just say, 'Oh, honey, that's okay.' Is that an accurate characterization of the relationship?" To which Laci's mom conceded: "Possibly."

Sharon Rocha's common-law husband, Ron Grantski, the man who helped raise Laci from the time she was two, sometimes found Scott unnaturally patient with the occasionally pushy Laci, whom Grantski had nicknamed "JJ" for "Jabberjaws." Laci "got basically anything she wanted because Scott tried to give it to her, isn't that correct?" Geragos asked Grantski when he was on the witness stand, and Grantski agreed.

But despite every appearance, the relationship was crumbling, and Sharon and Laci didn't have a clue. Scott had an intense, secret life he kept well hidden from his friends, his wife, and his mother-in-law, which he launched just months before his son was about to be born. Scott was wooing another woman just as Laci was struggling with the increasing discomforts of her advancing pregnancy. "She was complaining about her feet swelling, having a hard time standing up for any length of time or walking, her back was aching and she seemed to be tired all the time," her mom testified. Scott's brand-new secret mistress was everything Laci was not at that moment—petite, blonde, fragile, and painfully shy.

Scott had set up a blind dinner date with 27-year-old massage therapist and single mom Amber Frey just two months before Conner's due date. A flirtatious Scott had struck out first with Shawn Sibley, a brunette saleswoman whom he had met at a conference of the California Association of Pest Control Advisors six months earlier. Shawn told him she was already engaged to her "soul mate." Scott "told me that that at one point in his life he had found a woman that he thought was his soul mate—but then he lost her," Sibley would testify. "He asked me, did that mean that this was going to mean that he was going the to spend the rest of his life alone? I told him, I said, 'No, I don't believe that. I believe there are a thousand people out there in this world who can be your soul mate, but because of circumstances, or whatever, you are not going to meet all thousand of those people.'" So Scott pressed Shawn to help him find one of the "other" thousand he was meant to be with, and to set him up with an appropriate single friend of hers. Sibley thought of her pal Amber, but recalled telling Scott that "she's been through a lot of bad relationships, so if you're not serious about having a long-term, meaningful relationship, then I don't want to hook you up with her. But if you are, then I would be willing to introduce you. He was very interested in meeting her," Sibley testified. "His first question was, 'Is she intelligent?' And I said, 'You know, there are different levels of intelligence. I think she is intelligent.'" He asked if she was pretty. "I said, 'I think she's pretty. Some people think she is too thin.' He said, 'I like thin women.'" Scott and Shawn e-mailed after the conference, and Scott continued to press for a meeting with Amber, signing his e-mails "HB" for "Horny Bastard."

Figure 13.3. Scott and Amber Frey get up close and personal in a car on their way to a night out on the town while a pregnant Laci spends the evening home alone. *Presented in evidence at Scott Peterson's murder trial.*

Amber and Scott finally talked on the phone after Shawn helped arrange the conversation for "HB." Scott used the same tender manner and careful attention to romantic, thoughtful detail that he had used to woo Laci. He joked about himself over the phone setting up the date, saying he was "not very tall, overweight, belly, long greasy hair, kind of jokingly telling me about himself," recalled Amber in her courtroom testimony, which elicited a laugh from the easily spooked, relationship-shy woman. He was thrilled to see her the evening they met at the Elephant Bar in in her hometown of Fresno before having dinner at a nearby Japanese restaurant. He arranged for them to dine in a small private room, where they exchanged a litany of personal information. Scott presented an imaginary alter ego. He worked in Modesto, but lived in Sacramento, and had a condo in San Diego, he told Amber. He was spending the Thanksgiving holiday fly-fishing with his dad, brother, and uncle in Alaska, and would be spending Christmas with his parents at their compound in Kennebunkport, Maine. "He was easygoing," Amber testified. "He was easy to talk to. He made me feel comfortable." He pulled out a bottle of champagne and strawberries later in a Fresno hotel room. He poured the champagne, and dropped a single strawberry into each of their glasses—though Amber would testify that her strawberry was a "little bit sour." They slept together that night. Scott continued to see Amber when he could, but there were so many demands on his time, he explained, like his adventure travels in Alaska, a sales trip to Paris—none of which actually occurred. He sent fake photos and pretended to be calling from far-off locales to support his tall tales.

In early December, Scott and Amber planned to hike Squaw's Leap in the mountains of Auberry with Amber's two-year-old daughter, Ayiana. Scott arrived at Amber's home with a potted amaryllis plant and a bag of groceries so he could prepare dinner. First they hiked to the peak, where Scott pulled out a blanket and baby carrots, almonds, cookies, drinks, Frey testified.

> *Frey: He lay back, we talked. We were all munching a little bit, watching a helicopter that kept flying by overhead.*
> *Prosecutor David Harris: Was that a nice afternoon?*
> *Frey: It was chilly.*

As it became colder, the three headed back down the hill, Scott carrying Ayiana, and they sat in his truck.

Figure 13.4. A dressed-up Scott and Amber pose together at a Christmas party just weeks before Laci was due to give birth to Scott's son. Amber had no idea Scott was married or that he had a baby on the way. *Presented in evidence at Scott Peterson's murder trial.*

Frey: We sat on the back of his truck bed, and we're looking at stars.

Harris: It was dark at this point in time? Sitting in the back of the pickup truck, and you are looking at the stars, did you have some kind of contest at that time?

Frey: Who could find the first star. Seeing who could find the first star.

Harris: Who found the first star?

Frey: Scott.

The three returned home, where Scott cooked seafood lasagna and spent the night. The following afternoon, Scott picked up Ayiana from daycare, and Amber came home from work that day to find her daughter happily ensconced in her high chair, eating, and Scott fixing lasagna leftovers and pouring wine. The three traveled after dinner to buy a Christmas tree, which they set up and decorated. During pillow talk that night, Amber asked Scott if "he had any children, or if he ever was close to having children. And he said no," she testified. Then the issue of trust came up.

Frey: I was talking about, I don't recall how the conversation was brought up, but about trust and how I felt about trust and lies and how for me, it's easier to handle the truth, no matter what it is, versus a lie, and that knowing that a person could come to you with the truth is easier to handle than it later coming out that it was a lie. And, basically, just being truthful and how I responded to that.

Harris: Did the defendant make any comments or agree or disagree during this part of the conversation?

Frey: Yes.

Harris: What did he say?

Frey: He complimented me on my way of thinking about other people or how to handle situations that we were talking about.

Despite the conversation, Scott continued to spin a secret life for Amber. His lies were overblown, grandiose, and served to portray him as a wealthy jetsetter rather than a Modesto fertilizer salesman. He kept up the subterfuge even as rescuers were searching for Laci's body. On New Year's

Eve, Scott pretended he was calling Amber from Paris during a fireworks celebration, and acted as he were having a difficult time hearing her because of a scratchy phone connection from way across the sea, revealed in a tape of the call played at his murder trial:

Frey: Hello.
Peterson: (loud music playing) Amber?
Frey: Hi.
Peterson: Amber?
Frey: I can hear you.
Peterson: (loud static) Amber?
Frey: l can hear you.
Peterson: Amber, if you can hear me it's New Year's.
Frey: I know. I can hear you.
Peterson: (static) Amber? Amber it's News Year's! Are you there?
Frey: Yes. Are you having a good time?
Peterson: Amber? Hey, Happy New Years!
Frey: Happy New Year.
Peterson: I wanted to call you.
Frey: Thank you.
Peterson: Amber, are you there?
Frey: I'm here.
Peterson: Amber?
Frey: I wish you could hear me.
Peterson: I'm on the, uh ... I think that you're there. I'm uh near the Eiffel
    Tower and the New Year's celebration is unreal. The crowd is huge.
Frey: The crowd's huge?
Peterson: Amber?
Frey: Yeah, I'm here.
Peterson: Amber, if you're there I can't hear you right now, but I'll call you on
    your New Year's.
Frey: Okay. I'll hear from you then.
Peterson: Amber? Amber, I miss ya. I'll see you soon.

Figure 13.5. Scott clowns around in a Santa hat with his mistress, Amber, before a Christmas party. Laci vanished a short time after this photo was taken, and Scott was arrested for her murder a few months later when her body washed up on shore in San Francisco Bay. *Presented in evidence at Scott Peterson's murder trial.*

Scott kept up the Europe tale for a number of days. He next "traveled" to Brussels, and told his lover he did a face-plant while jogging on the slippery cobblestones. "Can you hear the light-rail train?" he asks her at one point, and gushes about the "neat big churches," and the "clean" European capitals where people get up in the morning at 9 or 10 and enjoy "two months off a year." His "French has gotten a lot better in the last week," he tells her. Then, it's off to Madrid, where his company's production headquarters are located (Brussels is the firm's "financial headquarters," he tells Amber). He tries to explain the time differences between California and Europe, and peppers his conversations with: "Amber, are you there?"—pretending to be having trouble with his international phone connection. These lengthy, affectionate calls in which Scott professes his love and calls Amber "Sweetie" occur when volunteers are hunting for Laci, divers are searching the park canal, and members of the public are reporting sighting women who look like her. Scott asks Amber, "Can I tell you how wonderful you are?" and cites poetry to her: "*We huddle under a large tree round with ivy with the storm raging around us. The only thing keeping me grounded are my hands on your waist.*"

The last time Peterson saw Amber in person was December 14, and he used several stories—other than traveling to Europe—to explain his absence, including the distance to her home from his "in Sacramento," Detective Allen Brocchini testified. Their last night together, he told Amber he was going back to Sacramento, then flying out from San Francisco to Maine or Arizona, Brocchini testified. Frey "also said that she spoke to him twice on Christmas day, correct?" prosecutor Rick Distaso asked Brocchini.

Brocchini: Yes.
Distaso: Before that, she said he called two days later from Sacramento, and said that he was getting ready to go to Kennebunkport in Maine, to stay with his parents for Christmas, right?
Brocchini: Yes.
Distaso: And did you later find out that that information was not true?
Brocchini: Yes.
Distaso: Where was he?
Brocchini: At the police station.
Distaso: Okay. So he wasn't in Kennebunkport, Maine?
Brocchini: No.

Chillingly, Scott told Amber that December that he'd be able to spend more time with her in January. He also told her that he intended to get a vasectomy because he didn't want children. He then mentioned an interesting book he had read: Jack Kerouac's *On the Road*. It was "mentally interesting to me simply because I never had a prolonged period of freedom like that from responsibility, you know, and interesting to me and something that you could incorporate into life," Scott said in his taped phone conversation played for jurors. He also named his favorite movie, *The Shining*, about a psychopathic killer dad, played by Jack Nicholson, who tries to murder his wife and young son.

Just weeks before Laci went missing, Shawn Sibley learned from a mutual business associate that Scott was married. She was furious, and she confronted him, but Scott again insisted he was single. Later, he left a voice message on her cell phone. "He's sobbing on my voicemail saying, 'I'm sorry I lied to you earlier. I had been married. It's just too painful for me to talk about. Call me,'" Sibley testified. When she called him, "Scott's just sobbing hysterically," she recalled. "He says, 'I'm so sorry I lied to you earlier. I had been married. I lost my wife. It's too painful for me to talk about. Please just give me the opportunity to tell Amber in person. Please don't tell her. He's begging me this whole time. And I said, 'Scott, I don't care if you are widowed, or you're divorced. All I care about is are you currently married right now?' And he said, 'No, absolutely not.'"

A week later Scott arranged over the phone to meet with Amber at her house because he had something important to tell her.

> Harris: And what did the defendant say to you?
> Frey (so softly the judge had to tell her repeatedly to speak up): He said that he had lied to me about ever being married, and he stated that sometimes for himself, it was easier for him to say that he was not or never had been married.
> Harris: Did he tell you why he had lied about being married?
> Frey: That it was painful for him.
> Harris: Did you ask him or did he explain why it was painful for him to say he had been married?
> Frey: [He said] he had lost his wife. I asked him, as far as the time frame is, had it been long. And he stated that this was the first holidays that he would be spending without her. I thanked him for sharing that with me, it being so painful for him, and understanding that it was hard for him to do so.

Harris: What did he say?

Frey: He said that I was amazing, and that he was intrigued by me and by my response. After he stated it was the first holidays without her, I asked if he was ready for a relationship with me.

Harris: What did he say?

Frey: He said absolutely.

Figure 13.6. A boat mobile and tiny life preserver decorate a nursery awaiting Baby Conner in the Petersons' Modesto home. Shortly after Laci's disappearance, Scott would begin to use the room for storage. *Presented in evidence at Scott Peterson's murder trial.*

Laci Peterson disappeared the day of Christmas Eve 2002 on what was supposed to be the couple's last holiday time together before they became parents. They were going to dinner that night at Sharon Rocha's house, and Laci planned to have her mom and family at her home the following day. She had already set up candles, glasses, and Christmas crackers on their pine dining-room table in preparation for the guests. She intended to cook that day, and hopefully have time to pick up some quick extra gifts for family members. She might walk the Petersons' golden retriever, McKenzie, in the nearby park or the neighborhood, but she was doing that less and less because of her discomfort and occasional dizziness from her advancing pregnancy. Scott had offered to pick up a large fruit basket for Laci's grandfather. When Scott was getting a haircut at a local salon from Laci's half sister, Amy, the previous day, she had mentioned the basket that she had ordered. He said he could swing by the fruit stand preparing the basket, which was close to the Del Rio Country Club, because he planned to play golf there before Christmas Eve dinner.

Exactly what happened that day remains a mystery. Scott told Amy and Grantski that he was going golfing that day, but instead drove almost 200 miles in his truck, telling police it was too cold to golf so he decided instead to drive from Modesto 90 miles to the Berkeley Marina to fish, using a new boat he kept at his company warehouse, that neither Laci nor his in-laws knew he owned, according to the prosecution. A surprised Amy received a late-afternoon call from the Vella fruit stand informing her that no one had come to collect the fruit.

Later that day, Sharon Rocha was about to get dressed for her Christmas Eve dinner, and she told Grantski to call Laci to tell her to bring whipping cream for apple pie that Sharon had made. No one picked up Laci's cell, so Grantski left a message. Shortly after, Sharon got a call from Scott.

Rocha: I remember looking at the clock on my stove in the kitchen and it was 5:15, and I remember thinking that I needed to get myself together because everybody was supposed to be there at 6 o'clock. So it was another minute or so when I walked down the hall to my bedroom. And then when I get into the bedroom the phone rang. He said, "Hi, Mom." He said, "Is Laci there with you?" I said, "No." And he said that her car is there in the driveway, and the dog was in the backyard with the leash on and Laci was missing. I remember telling him to call her friends to see if anybody had seen or talked to her that day. I just thought that maybe she was with one of her friends, but I remember hanging up the phone and walking back toward the door of the bedroom to walk down the hall. I was going to

*tell Ron, and that's when I realized he said that she was "missing." And
I just, I just knew. I knew she was missing. He wouldn't have used the
word "missing." I remember changing my clothes that time. I was already
dressing warmer because I felt I knew something was wrong, and I knew
that I needed to go to the park because he said the dog has his leash on so
my first thought is she would have been walking the dog.*

Rocha told Grantski to call 911, and she communicated again with Scott,
arranging to meet him in the park. Her friend, Sandy Rikart, came with her.

*Rocha: Sandy and I drove down into the park. I got out of the car and I
was running all around through that area and I was screaming her
name, and I just kept yelling her name. The lights were on in the park
in that area, the outer areas weren't lit, but I was running all through
that area that I could. I was looking in, I remember looking in trash
cans, and then Laci's neighbors came to the park. The police arrived,
and I remember seeing Scott at one point. He was walking alone, closer
to the river, looking toward the river to the left and he had McKenzie on
a leash in his right hand. I kept calling out his name, and he never did
turn to acknowledge that I was calling out to him. I was yelling his name.
I was yelling out to let him know here we are. "We're over here."*
Distaso: And how would you say your demeanor was at that time?
*Rocha: I was very upset. I was anxious. I was looking for Laci. Scott never did
acknowledge that I was yelling his name.*
Distaso: Did you ask him anything else down in the park?
Rocha: I'm thinking that's when I asked him, "Where do you think she is?"
Distaso: And did he say?
Rocha: No.

When they returned to the house, Rocha testified, she walked over to
give Scott "a hug because I felt that, you know, we were all upset, and I knew
his family wasn't here and we'd always been close so I wanted to console
him—and myself, for that matter. And as I walked up to him I was never
able to do that because he kept kind of angling, like, away from me so that

we never had eye contact. I wanted to ask him some questions," she added. "And finally I did. I asked him what Laci was doing, or what her plans were for the day. And he told me that she had planned on going to the store, and then coming home to make gingerbread and walking the dog. I asked where he had been. He told me that he had been fishing."

Figure 13.7. Laci and mom, Sharon Rocha, show off mother-daughter grins. Many considered the two women best friends. *Presented in evidence at Scott Peterson's murder trial.*

As the days wound on, Rocha testified, she would try to schedule times to get together with Scott to discuss the situation, and he "would always cancel, and I felt that he was trying to avoid being alone with me. And, of course, that made me a little suspicious." Soon after, she learned of Scott's affair with Amber Frey. She finally got Scott on the phone, and returned to the day her daughter vanished. A tape of the recorded conversation bares Sharon's frustration in trying to pin Scott down on details:

> *Rocha: How come you didn't notice when you walked in the door that she hadn't been baking or the lights were off or anything?*
> *Peterson: 'Cause I was late and I was rushing.*

Rocha: I mean, surely, McKenzie came up to you when you walked in the back gate with his leash on.

Peterson: Yeah . . . I took it off of him and I didn't—it didn't even register.

Rocha: It didn't register that Laci wasn't in the house when you walked in—it was a dark house, didn't smell like she'd been cooking, everything was cleaned up and neat and tidy—and nothing even registered to you?

Peterson: No I, ah, grabbed a piece of pizza out of the fridge and jumped into the shower immediately and when I got out then I looked at the messages. I assumed she was over, you know, at your place.

Rocha: I mean we've never even had this conversation all this time.

Peterson: True. I know. And it wasn't until you asked about the McKenzie thing—he had his leash on.

Rocha: I didn't mention it—you told me he had his leash.

Peterson: Right, well you asked about McKenzie if he was in the yard.

Rocha: No you told me he was.

Peterson: Okay, I mean, either way.

The day Laci disappeared, Ron Grantski innocently pointed out Scott's alibi contradictions as he stood with police officers outside Laci and Scott's home, trying not to interfere, but staying close by so he could help if needed. When he spotted Scott on the Petersons' lawn, Grantski greeted him with small talk, trying to diffuse some of the tension of the situation. "We were standing out in the front under a tree, and I was talking with a couple officers and Scott came walking up. And I said, 'Hi, Scott. How was your golf today?'" Grantski testified. "He said, 'No, I didn't play golf, I went fishing. And I, being the smart behind I am, I said, 'Well, what time did you go fishing?' He said, 'Oh, about 9:30.' I said: '9:30? That's when I come home from fishing, that's not when I go.' And he turned around and walked away. I was just kidding, but I felt bad that I had said that," he added, worried that he may have made Scott appear suspicious in front of the police.

But investigators were already suspicious of Scott, largely because of his mercurial golf and fishing alibis. And they were quickly concerned about Laci when they found her purse—cell phone, credit cards, and wallet inside—still hanging from a hook in her closet where she usually left it. They also noted that Scott had already washed the clothes that he had worn that day. But Scott's first colossal blunder was not thinking through his fishing alibi carefully. He looked stunned, like a deer caught in headlights, when a police officer on the scene pressed him for a minor detail: *What* was he fishing *for?* He appeared to be completely stumped when Officer Matthew Spurlock posed the question—and marched out the house furious with himself and muttering under his breath.

> *Spurlock: I asked Mr. Peterson if, if he could tell me roughly what time he went fishing. He really didn't give me a responsive time. Just kind of shuffled off the question, didn't really answer.*
>
> *Distaso: What happened next?*
>
> *Spurlock: I asked Mr. Peterson what kind of fishing he was doing, what kind of fish he was fishing for today. And at that point there was a pause. He hesitated in answering me. He had this blank look on his face for a second or so, his eyes shifted a little bit and he kind of mumbled some stuff, but again blew off my question, didn't really give me an answer. I then asked Mr. Peterson if he could maybe describe what he was using as far as bait or lure, and again I got the same type of response: kind of the blank stare, shifting-of-the-eye kind of thing. And then something clicked, and he said, "I was using a silver lure," and he gave me a hand gesture of about seven to eight inches in length.*
>
> *Distaso: And did you, did you ask him anything else?*
>
> *Spurlock: I did. He was wearing some clothing that was pretty light, and I knew it was cold outside. And I asked him if these were the clothes, which he was wearing when he went fishing, and he stated no, that he had changed. Assuming he changed, I thought, well, maybe he just put his clothes in the clothes hamper. So I asked him, "Did you place your clothes in the clothes hamper?" And he stated, "No, I washed them."*
>
> *Spurlock: I loosely followed him at a distance, went to the front door. As he was stepping out of the front door and onto that sidewalk area, I heard what sounded like a cuss word, and, if you want, I can say it in court.*
>
> *Distaso: Go ahead.*
>
> *Spurlock: Sounded like the word "fuck," and it came through what sounded like gritted teeth.*

Police Officer Derrick Letsinger witnessed the same behavior. As Peterson was "leaving through the front door, I could see out, and Mr. Peterson threw his flashlight down on the ground," Letsinger testified. "And then I heard something under his breath, like a curse word."

Peterson's ultimate nemesis would be short, black-haired Allen Brocchini, a persistent, no-nonsense Modesto detective with a body like a truck and face like a pugilist. He was called into the case almost immediately because it was quickly determined to be a "suspicious missing person" situation. He finished his Christmas Eve dinner with his family and headed over to Covena Avenue, and walked through the Peterson house one more time with Scott. Like Spurlock, he spotted the dirty rags on top of the washing machine, and inside, a pair of blue jeans, a blue t-shirt, and a green pull-over, already washed but still wet. Scott explained that he had taken out the dirty rags that the cleaning woman had placed in the machine, and instead washed his clothes because they were wet from fishing.

Brocchini then walked with Scott to the driveway, where Laci's Land Rover and Scott's pickup were parked. Brocchini noticed a cell phone plugged into a dashboard charger of Laci's car, and spotted a toolbox, two large tarps, and a number of large patio umbrellas in the bed of the pickup, along with up to 100 feet of orange nylon rope. When police returned the day after Christmas with a search warrant, the rope had vanished, and the blue tarp was discovered in a tool shed on the property, under a lawn mower leaking gas. There was also a gun in the glove compartment of Scott's truck. He told the detective he had two guns, but that one had been stolen. There was a Big 5 Sporting Goods bag inside the truck with two new fishing lures still in their packaging and a fishing pole with a receipt dated four days before Laci disappeared—and in the back seat, a dry camouflage jacket that Scott said he had worn in the boat, Brocchini testified. A pair of pliers with a strand of black hair would later be found on Scott's boat.

Close to midnight, Brocchini accompanied Scott to the police department for an interview to, he explained, "go over what we had been talking about." Scott was "calm, cool, relaxed," the detective testified. Brocchini said he was already "suspicious of a lot of things," but that he tried to keep their interaction "friendly." Brocchini videotaped Peterson as he answered basic questions about his whereabouts that day.

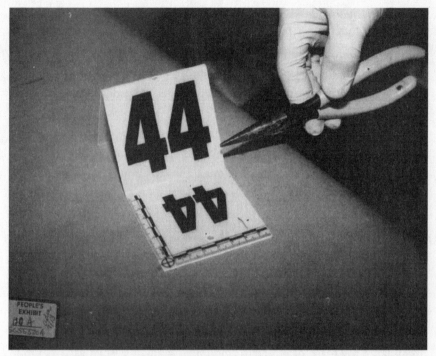

Figure 13.8. This police evidence photo shows needle-nosed pliers holding two black hairs that were found in Scott's boat, which police believe Peterson used to transport Laci's body to the bay. *Presented in evidence at Scott Peterson's murder trial.*

The case looked far worse for Scott when Amber, who learned of the news reports about Laci and Scott, called the Modesto police tip line to tell detectives about their affair. Police began recording Scott's conversations with her. In one of the conversations, he tells her that his wife is missing, and warns her to "protect" herself from "the media." Frey, who knew what had happened by that point, acts stunned to hear the news about Laci from Scott, and accuses him of "lying about lying," and demands an explanation, which he says he can't give yet. "You deserve so much better," says Scott. "There's no question you deserve so much better." Frey responds: "Yeah and I deserve to understand an explanation of why you told me you lost your wife and this was the first holidays you'd spend without her. That was December 9 you told me this, and now all of sudden your wife's missing? Are you kidding me?" She says in another conversation: "Isn't is so ironic that she goes missing before the first holidays? Are you following me, Scott?" He admits, "That sounds pretty sinister." She also confronts him about referring to her daughter, Ayiana, as the "only child" in his life. "But you had a child on the way that whole time in that conversation," she adds. Scott responds, "I understand your confusion, definitely."

When Brocchini later parked near a vigil for Laci, Scott walked over to his car to thank him for discussing the case on *America's Most Wanted* and for answering the tip line. "You got some explaining to do," Brocchini responded. Scott told him: "You don't know. I just stop on the side of the road and break down for no apparent reason." Brocchini said he wasn't acting like "somebody that missed is his pregnant wife." When Brocchini was asked in court what Scott's demeanor was at that point, the detective answered: "Emotionless, matter of fact. Calm."

Months later, in mid-April, a couple walking their dog discovered the body of a late-term male fetus among a wash of seaweed and garbage on the shore of San Francisco Bay at a Richmond Point park north of Berkeley. A day later, the torso of a recently pregnant woman washed ashore a mile away from where the baby's body was found. The body was missing the head, the forearms, the right foot and lower left leg. Two cracked ribs apparently occurred at the time of death. The bodies were identified as Conner and Laci. Because of the state of Laci's body it was impossible to determine cause of death.

Five days after the first body was found, Scott Peterson was arrested in La Jolla near the Mexican border. He was carrying his mother's driver's license, $15,000 in cash, camping equipment, four cell phones, a gun, and a map to Amber Frey's home. He was sporting a new goatee, and his hair and beard were suddenly blond, though he insisted the color change was caused by swimming in a chlorinated pool.

The jury convicted Peterson after two days of deliberation and sentenced him to death in the penalty phase of the trial. The prosecution made a case that Peterson had likely smothered or strangled Laci the morning she disappeared or the night before, and he transported her body to San Francisco Bay wrapped in a tarp, and tossed her overboard, weighted down with missing cement anchors of the five that investigators believe he made at his shop. After months, rope used to lash her to an anchor likely ate through her neck and limbs, finally allowing her torso to float free.

Figure 13.9. This is how Scott appeared when he was picked up by police near the Mexican border with camping supplies, $15,000 in cash, and blond hair. He insisted his hair changed color because he had been in a chlorinated pool. *Presented in evidence at Scott Peterson's murder trial.*

During the victim impact statement of the penalty phase of the trial, Laci's mom described long days lying in bed, so depressed by the murder of her daughter that she couldn't face the day. "I miss her. I wanted to know my grandson. I wanted Laci to be a mother. I wanted to hear her called 'Mom,'" said Rocha. She said she still sometimes reached for the phone, thinking it was her daughter. "There's been several times, but I remember the first time it happened I was on my way outside. I already locked the door. I heard the phone ring and then I unlocked the door and went back in. I, I was thinking it was Laci. I hadn't heard from her in a long time," said Rocha. "And then I realized it wasn't. It will never be her. I remember another time walking into the house. I opened the door and walked into the entryway and I had to stop, and she turned around and said, 'Hi, Mom.' It was as though she was right there. I saw her. A lot of times I think when I have a question about something that's been going on, I'll just ask her and she'll tell me. But I can't. Laci didn't deserve to die."

––––––

Scott Peterson's murder of his pregnant wife was exceptionally coldhearted. In my search for "types" of killer dads (or, in Scott's case, killer dads-to-be)—from murderous stepfathers to family annihilators driven either by rage or a twisted devotion to their loved ones to furious fathers who kill their children to punish wives who have left them—Peterson's crime stood alone as chillingly emotionless. He showed no signs of anger with Laci that anyone could see; in fact, he seemed at times too-perfectly patient or tolerant in his relationship, beyond the norm of engaging in even minor conflicts or arguments married couples typically experience. And he wasn't suddenly, unexpectedly swept off his feet by a lover so captivating that he had to possess after getting his wife out of the picture. He didn't spot Amber Frey across a crowded room and become smitten. He discovered her as part of a determined hunt for "another soul mate" just months before his wife was due to give birth to his son. His prime motivation seemed to be that he had grown bored with his life and was in the mood for a change. He wanted his wife "lost," and he set out to make it a reality. "Divorce is always an option," Laci's heartsick mom said in her victim impact statement. He dodged divorce court, alimony, and child support—and at the same time won "poor Scott" sympathy for his tragic "loss." When Amber heard from her friend Shawn that Scott might, in fact, be a married man, he broke down in tears to confess that he had lost his wife, eliciting tenderhearted sympathy from Amber and turning Laci's disappearance into a kind of macabre pick-up line to solidify his relationship with his lover.

Even for a murderer (and far more so for an innocent man), Scott's repeated lengthy, fawning, jocular phone conversations with Amber Frey while cadaver dogs were searching for his wife's body and police cars were parked outside his door are stupefying. He called Amber nearly 200 times after Laci vanished, and most of the conversations were recorded because Amber was secretly cooperating with police. He appeared to be an attentive, thoughtful, empathetic lover—with Amber just as he had been in wooing Laci years earlier. Scott said the right things, made all the right sounds, had all the moves, but apparently had no real heart. Even after Amber tells him she knows that police are searching for Laci, he begs her to let him come to her home—or to a house on California's Lake Arrowhead—to see her. "I just never felt such a strong desire as I do," he says, sniffling. "I think it would be good for us." Frey defers, telling him at one point that she feels like a magnet "to wolves in sheep's clothing." He promises to "explain everything" at some point in the future.

With a man like Scott Peterson, the "observer is confronted with a convincing mask of sanity" . . . complete with "verbal and facial expressions, tones of voice, and all the other signs we have come to regard as implying conviction and emotion and the normal experiencing of life as we know it ourselves and as we assume it to be in others," wrote Hervey Cleckley in his 1941 book *The Mask of Sanity*, which is still today a kind of bible on psychopathic or sociopathic personalities.[3] "Only very slowly and by a complex estimation or judgment based on multitudinous small impressions does the conviction come upon us that . . . we are dealing not with a complete man at all but with something that suggests a subtly constructed reflex machine which can mimic the human personality perfectly. We know that reality, in the sense of a full, healthy experiencing of life, is not there."

Peterson's crime is similar to only a handful of other killer-father cases, most notably the crimes of Jeffrey MacDonald and Neil Entwistle. All three insist they're innocent.

MacDonald claimed a murderous band of Charles Mason–like hippies stormed his North Carolina home in Fort Bragg in 1970 and brutally bludgeoned and stabbed his pregnant wife, Collette, and two young daughters to death. Collette and the younger daughter, two-year-old Kristen, were stabbed with a knife and an ice pick more than 37 times. MacDonald suffered relatively minor injuries while "fighting for his life," he testified in court. The handsome, athletic Green Beret surgeon was sentenced to life in prison. The gripping case of the man-with-everything turned murderer is detailed in author Joe McGinness's book *Fatal Vision*. But the killer's cause was recently taken up by Errol Morris, whose book *A Wilderness of Error: The Trials of Jeffrey Macdonald*, argues that he's innocent, attacks the case against him, and points to Helena Stoeckley, a troubled drug user who at various times confessed to the crime, then claimed to have no memory of it (and no evidence was found to charge her). McGinness has convincingly refuted each point in Morris's book, and has noted that falling into MacDonald's sway is part of the power of the charismatic psychopath that MacDonald is. The killer dad's latest appeal was shot down, and McGinness has published a short new digital book, *Final Vision*, updating the case 42 years after the murders.[4]

Similarities of MacDonald's personality to Peterson's are striking. Both men were "golden boys" (MacDonald's Long Island high school in Patchogue not only voted him Most Popular but also Most Likely to Succeed), appeared to all to be loving, upstanding family men and husbands, and lied with particular aplomb. Especially intriguing in McGinness's book are chapters in MacDonald's own words, based on tape recordings the surgeon made after his murder conviction and describing his life and his relationship with his wife and children. He talks of some tough times raising a family amid training and work, and recognizes his wife's difficulty being in charge of two young daughters, sometimes living with his parents, during his long work hours and army assignments. Yet he focused largely on his own work and a future that would bring him the most excitement and satisfaction with little concern for his family. He decided after medical school to join the army, noting he and Colette were cranky and "we didn't have sex as much."[5] He looked at joining the military as an "adventure," whereas Colette saw it as an "abandonment of the family and a chance for me getting killed," he noted. "At the time, this didn't bother me at all." He also presents himself as a steadfast, loyal husband and father, yet witnesses and women stepped forward after his crime to reveal that he had serial casual affairs. He alludes vaguely to it himself when he noted at one point that he and Collette were "really recommitting ourselves to each other" and that there "weren't other contributing things. . . . I wasn't dating any nurses, I wasn't seeing people on the side."[6] As an alibi, MacDonald's tale of murderous hippies stands out as particularly over-the-top, much like Peterson's over-heated, recklessly exaggerated lies to Amber. In fact, Peterson came off in his trial as a pathological liar, who, as Amber said in the taped phone conversation with him played in court, "lied about lying." Peterson seemed to lie simply as default mode. Once police began tracking his locations via cell-phone towers and calls, it was clear he often lied about his location with no clear reason why. Tracking showed him close to the Berkeley Marina when police were searching for Laci's body, but he told his family he was hundreds of miles away. "Where are you?" his mom asked at one point. "West Fresno," he told her. Hours later he called Sharon Rocha, who asked him, "Where are you headed now?" "Well, I'm actually in Bakersfield now," he told her, but he was actually 220 miles away from there. He later also told his dad he was in Bakersfield, and two pals that he was in the town of Buttonwood. And his lies to Amber were so grandiose that it seemed impossible to maintain the subterfuge for any length of time. While he appeared to be cultivating a long-term relationship with his mistress, how would Peterson ever reconcile his lies about his parents' Kennebunkport compound, fly-fishing stints with his dad and brothers, and trips to Europe? Yet he seemed to maintain a blind faith in his lies. When police confronted him with a photo of himself at a Christmas party with Amber, he told his family that it was "amazing" how much the "stranger" in the photo resembled him. Both Peterson and MacDonald seemed to have a preening arrogance when it came to their crimes. They were both overly confident that they could outsmart police and forensic evidence with very little effort. Peterson was so lackadaisical about his alibi that he couldn't quite decide which one he was using—golf or fishing—and hadn't bothered to work out the details of his fishing story.

Neil Entwistle, another killer dad who shares similarities with MacDonald and Peterson, shot his wife, Rachel, and baby daughter, Lillian, as they cuddled in bed in the family home in Massachusetts in 2006. Entwistle, from England, met his bride while she was studying abroad. They appeared to have an ideal marriage, and Entwistle was an affectionate, engaging husband who looked to be remarkably successful in his work as a computer-programmer whiz. The young couple rented a spacious, expensive home close to Rachel's parents, Joe and Priscilla Matterazzo, who were crazy about their son-in-law and new granddaughter.

Police were contacted by Rachel's worried parents when they were unable to reach their daughter. By the time an officer discovered Rachel and Lilly shot dead in the master bedroom, Entwistle had already fled home to England. Phoned there by Massachusetts State Trooper Robert Manning, Entwistle sounds eerily calm in an audiotape of the call that was played at his murder trial. He responds quietly, "Oh, yes, yes," when the trooper asks if he'll answer some questions. He tells of walking into his home to find his wife in bed looking "very pale." When he pulls down the covers, he sees blood. "Lilly was a mess," he adds, and says he realized instantly the two were dead. He offers no theory about the murders. "I don't remember seeing the house disturbed," he notes helpfully. Entwistle claims he had "no way of contacting" Rachel's parents to alert them—"I didn't know their numbers"—so he drove to their empty home, took a knife from the kitchen drawer and thought briefly of suicide (police said he had actually taken a long-barreled .22-caliber Colt revolver from the Matterazzo's Carver home and was returning it after shooting his wife and daughter). Then he drove around aimlessly . . . "I'm not sure what was going on in my mind at that time," he says on the tape, and "ended up at Logan Airport." He sat for a time in the parking lot. "I wanted to kind of let the emotions out but nothing would come out," he recalls to the trooper on the phone. "It just didn't seem right what had just happened. I haven't even cried yet," adding, "I don't know what I'm thinking at the moment. It doesn't even seem real." The trooper snaps, "Let me tell you, it is real," and "something happened over here. I have a hard time understanding why you didn't call 911." Entwistle responds, "Yeah, I can see that." He later asked if Rachel and Lilly could be buried together because "that's the way I left them—I mean, that's the way I found them."

Investigators discovered he was deeply in debt and had no job in Massachusetts. He spent long hours on the Internet selling what he could on Ebay and running a porn business pushing things like "penis pumps"— and searching for new sex partners for himself. Detectives found extensive escort-service searches on his computer, apparently on his own behalf, before the killings, as well as searches on "euthanasia" and "smothering." Entwistle agreed to return to the United States and was tried and sentenced to life imprisonment without parole. Several press reports remarked on his preternatural calm at his trial. At one point, while crime-scene photos of his dead wife and daughter were shown in court, the *Boston Herald* reported that he "broke down," but in fact seemed to be giggling, and covered his mouth and lowered his head to hide his facial expression. Several newspapers reported that he was "laughing" or "smirking," comments that drew a sharp rebuke from the defense. "Some of you were reporting our client, Neil Entwistle, was smiling or laughing," said attorney Elliot Weinstein. "We are offended by that kind of reporting." His co-counsel Stephanie Page added, "There is no way Neil would be laughing. He's grieving. He lost his wife. He lost his baby."

Judge Diane Kottmeyer spoke to the pure shock of Entwistle's crimes when she sentenced him in 2008. "These crimes are incomprehensible," she said. "They defy comprehension because they involve the planned and deliberate murders of the defendant's wife and nine-month-old child in violation of bonds that we recognize as central to our identity as human beings, those of husband and wife, and parent and child."

Entwistle and his parents still insist he's innocent of the murders, and claim that Rachel murdered her baby before committing suicide. In the summer of 2012, Entwistle lost an appeal of his conviction, arguing that police had conducted an illegal search of his home.

FOURTEEN

CLASH

O n Saturdays the parking lot outside the mosque at the Islamic Center is a sea of black suits and colorful hijabs. Wendy Wasinski is sometimes among the crowd. She prefers a pale, purple veil (though she also wears light green) because it's one of her favorite colors. Each morning, she first carefully tucks in her hair beneath an under scarf that keeps wisps from straying outside her hijab. She says her prayers in the mosque like millions of other Muslims around the world. But worshipers at the Islamic Center also have very particular characteristics that set them apart. Some of the families will head to Country Kitchen for scrambled eggs and hash browns after services, a few of the kids will leave their parents to skateboard. Almost every one of them speaks English, and most talk with the flat *A*'s, rounded *O*'s, and the twang of an American Midwestern accent. The Islamic Center of America in Dearborn, Michigan, was the first and remains the biggest mosque in North America, and it's in the heart of the largest concentration of Muslims in the United States. Nearly a third of Dearborn's 100,000 residents are Muslim, and it's not unusual to see signs in Arabic in the city or in nearby communities, like Warren, where Wendy lives. Most of the original Muslim families initially immigrated largely from Lebanon, but also from Yemen and Iraq. The new Americans, like earlier Americans, were drawn to the region by the promise of good jobs in the automobile industry.

The region is so concentrated with Muslims that it has become an unfortunate target in the Islamic-Christian cultural clashes in the United States, and a focus of Americans furious over a Muslim influence in the country. Right-wing evangelical preacher Terry Jones came to Dearborn to burn a copy of the Koran while the faithful raged in protests nearby. The YouTube anti-Islam video "The Innocence of Muslims" that sparked violent protests across North Africa and the Middle East in 2012 was particularly offensive to local Muslims, and hundreds took to the streets to protest—and were quickly accused online by conservative blogs like *Atlas Shrugged* and *Jihad Watch* of protests against the First Amendment.

One sign of assimilation, an indication that the community may have truly "arrived" in the United States, at least in the world of American pop-culturedom, was having its very own reality series—TLC's *All-American Muslim*. The series focused on members of five Lebanese-American families in Dearborn, featuring a high-school football coach, a Dearborn cop, a young married couple, two sisters with very different attitudes about their religion and culture, and a young mom who married an Irish-American Catholic who planned to convert to Islam (and struggled fiercely with fasting during the holy month of Ramadan). Despite portrayals that made the families appear most strikingly like average Americans, the series instantly triggered controversy, and at least two advertisers withdrew their support after they were contacted by the Florida Family Association, a born-again Christian group opposed to featuring Muslims on national TV, arguing that it provided a conduit for "Muslim propaganda." Lowe's was the first advertiser to bail, though executives insisted it wasn't because of pressure from any one particular group. While Lowe's apologized for upsetting people with its action and emphasized that it was "committed" to religious and cultural diversity, a company statement released December 10, 2011, explained: "Individuals and groups have strong political and societal views on this topic, and this program became a lightning rod for many of those views. As a result we did pull our advertising on this program. We believe it is best to respectfully defer to communities, individuals and groups to discuss and consider such issues of importance." The action triggered calls in turn by civil-rights groups, celebrities, and politicians to boycott Lowe's. The Florida Family Association claimed other advertisers were fleeing the program. TLC stood by *All-American Muslim*, but the program was cancelled in 2012 after its initial season of eight episodes.

Beneath the headline-grabbing, glitzy reality-program battle that year was a far more gruesome culture clash that involved a murder—initially labeled by officials as one of a small new crop of North American "honor killings." It involved a conflict between a Muslim man and his stepdaughter, arguments about wearing the hijab, and a rape. Wendy Wasinski's 20-year-old daughter, Jessica Mokdad, was in her grandmother's home where she had been staying in Warren, when the murder occurred the afternoon of April 30, 2011.[1] She had just placed a box of her things on her bed. As the young woman stood there, ear buds playing music into her ears, her stepdad, Rahim Alfetlawi, 46, walked up behind her and shot her in the head. "I don't know how you do that," Macomb County Assistant Prosecutor William Cataldo told the judge at Alfetlawi's sentencing a year later. "He walked up behind her, put a gun to her head, and blew her away."

Figure 14.1. Jessica poses for a photo in a hijab and the modest clothing that her stepdad preferred. *Courtesy of Wendy Wasinski, in memory of her loving daughter and best friend, Jessica Amanda Mohamad Mokdad.*

The murder made national news because the media quickly labeled it as an honor killing in which Jessica was murdered to save her stepfather's "honor." He thought she was becoming "too Westernized," said Cataldo after Alfetlawi was busted. "I think this was a very nice young lady wanting to experiment with Western culture without control and without abuse."

But the "honor killing" label was immediately contentious. The brand angered many in the local Muslim community, who emphasized that the homicide had nothing to do with them, with their religion, or with their cultural beliefs. Jessica's biological father, Mohamed Mokdad, and his wife complained to the press and went on TV to denounce the label, calling Alfetlawi a sick man obsessed with Jessica whose attack had absolutely no connection to Islam. County officials quickly responded to and removed the "honor" issue from the killings. This "has little or nothing to do with Arabic culture," Cataldo clarified. "It has everything to do with male domination of women, something that transcends cultures."

The case was complicated. Details emerged that Alfetlawi was obsessed with managing every aspect of Jessica's life, to such an extent that he arranged to have spyware installed on her computer and phone, and he hid recording devices in their home and in family cars in which she traveled so he could track her every move. A frightened Jessica confided to a passenger she met on a train shortly before her death that she fought with Alfetlawi over her decision to go out without her hijab—and that she feared he would kill her one day.

Americans were on the alert for any hint of honor killings. There had already been a handful of the notorious honor murders of daughters by their dads in the United States. But as the circumstances of Jessica's murder became clearer, it defied easy categorization as an honor killing. Even though he had raised her and treated her like his own daughter, Alfetlawi was Jessica's stepdad, which raised issues about the sometimes-fraught relationships between fathers and stepchildren and the increased potential for violence uncovered by researchers Martin Daly and Margo Wilson. Other information emerged that Alfetlawi's relationship was hardly a typical father-daughter interaction, and that the murder may have been the furious violence of a male losing control over a young woman he considered not a daughter, but a sex partner. In a particularly disturbing development, prosecutors revealed in court that Alfetlawi had raped Jessica at least once. Jessica told her mother of the attack the night before she was killed, Wendy told me in an interview. "He said that if I tell you, he would kill you, Mom," Wasinski quoted Jessica as saying. Investigators believe Alfetlawi decided to kill Jessica in part to stop her from reporting the rape to police. "That's what put him over the edge," said Cataldo at Alfetlawi's trial, though the prosecutor also pointed out that Rahim would be "embarrassed" if information about his rape became known, which could also represent a threat to his honor.

The crime became a locus of heated debate in the culture wars. Many argued that officials were too quick to brand Jessica's murder an honor killing, while others then criticized law enforcement authorities for a "whitewash" after too hastily backing off the label because they were too concerned about "political correctness" in the face of anger by the Dearborn Muslim community. Some argued that branding the case an honor killing was a distraction from the serious problem of domestic violence and child abuse throughout the country, while others argued that it was one more nuance in a range of domestic murder that demanded a thorough examination. Jessica's murder—yet another iteration of the murder of a child by her stepfather—did involve unique cultural aspects of Alfetlawi's background, but it also concerned the more common domestic-violence ingredients of American-style paternalism, access to guns, and sex abuse.

Jessica's mom, Wendy Wasinski, was born in Hamtranck, Michigan, to a Polish-American Catholic family in Michigan, but grew up with Muslim friends. She met and fell in love with Mohamed Mokdad. They married and had a baby, Jessica, a "girlie girl," as her mom described her daughter to me, who loved to wear dresses and play with dolls. "She was a compassionate, thoughtful girl. Jessica was always the kind of kid who would hold doors open for people, or get a shopping cart for an elderly woman at the grocery store," said her mom. Wendy worked for a time at a daycare facility for elderly people and often took Jessica with her. "She had a blast with the old people, and they loved her," said Wendy. Wendy and Mohamed divorced, but she then met Rahim Alfetlawi when Jessica was seven years old. Rahim raised Jessica like his own daughter, and the girl eventually donned the head-covering hijab veil of her faith in heartland America. "He cared for her, he watched after, he protected her," recalled Wendy, who had converted to Islam just months before she met Rahim and quickly donned the hijab herself. Islam intrigued Wendy. She was impressed by the families of her Muslim friends. "Ironically, I especially appreciated how close their families were," she told me. "They helped one another. You didn't have to leave the home at 18. They were always there for each other."

Figure 14.2. Jessica snuggles up to her mom, Wendy. Her mother, born in Michigan, converted to Islam before she married Jessica's stepdad. *Courtesy of Wendy Wasinski, in memory of her loving daughter and best friend, Jessica Amanda Mohamad Mokdad.*

But Wendy's husband eventually turned out to be the very antithesis of that image. Initially, he demanded Jessica be respectful and obedient, do well in her studies, remain chaste until marriage, and follow the tenets of Islam, including not drinking, and wearing the hair-covering hijab any time she was outside of her home. But his control took a dark twist as she became a teenager, and his attention became an obsession, said Wendy. "There was a point when he wouldn't let her do what her friends were doing, and they were Muslim girls," she said. "He wouldn't let her go to the mall with them.

So I went around him. I would drive her to the mall myself, telling him we were going shopping, but I would arrange for her to meet her friends there. That was the start of a lot of things I did for her behind his back."

Figure 14.3. Jessica lets her hair down and mugs in her "other life" as a typical Michigan teenager with pal Kayla Chuba. *Courtesy of Wendy Wasinski, in memory of her loving daughter and best friend, Jessica Amanda Mohamad Mokdad.*

In a bizarre development, Rahim pressured Jessica at 18 to marry a boyfriend in a religious ceremony that wasn't legally binding. The two lived for time in the family home. But even though they were "married," Rahim tried to strictly control their interaction, at times even stopping them from touching one another or even sitting next to each other on the couch, Wendy noted. Jessica eventually left the family's home in Minnesota and attended Macomb Community College in Michigan, where she pursued different interests, including her passion for art that eventually evolved into photography. She lived for a time with her biological dad, but his second wife was only three years older than Jessica, which sometimes caused tension, according to Wasinski. Jessica eventually moved in with her maternal grandmother. Her "husband" joined her for a time, but their relationship soon waned and they broke up.

Throughout it all, Jessica fretted about Alfetlawi. "I hate him with a passion," Jessica wrote of her stepdad to a friend in texts obtained by police. "He's in love with me. He's obsessed with me. He would punish me and make me cry every day. I'd like to see his ass beat like he's done to me all these years." In one text, she talked of Alfetlawi making a surprise visit to her grandmother's home where she was staying at the time, and discovering "I don't wear a scarf."

Wasinski says Alfetlawi was never physically abusive, but "you could say he was verbally and psychologically abusive" to Jessica. When her daughter was a little girl, Wendy was glad Alfetlawi cared enough to help raise her and set rules for her, even though he began to slip off the rails as she became older. But she never saw him physically violent. "That's why it blew my mind when he shot Jessica," said Wendy.

Jessica's biological dad stood by to help as she grew up, but his relationship with his daughter waned because Alfetlawi was jealous of it, according to Wasinski. After Alfetlawi was arrested, he initially told police he had taken a gun to Warren to shoot Mohammed Mokdad, but accidentally shot Jessica instead.

Jessica was living in Michigan when Alfetlawi "abducted" her and "forced" her to return to the family's home in Minnesota, she said in texts, just weeks before her murder. She remained there until her mom took her to the train station while Alfetlawi slept so Jessica could return to her grandmother's home. That was the last time Wendy would see Jessica alive. "I hugged her and I kissed her and told her I loved her, and let her go," Wasinski recalled. She usually kept in daily phone contact with her daughter while she lived in Michigan, but always called from work to conceal her conversations from Alfetlawi.

On the train, a distraught, shaken Jessica poured out her heart to a lawyer she met on the trip. She revealed to him that her stepfather had a long history of control and abuse, he later testified at Alfetlawi's trial. Alfetlawi was temperamental and would often "lose it," she said, and used "fear, intimidation and violence to get his way," Jessica told him. Alfetlawi had threatened to harm her and her mother if she attempted to run away again, added Jessica, who described a pattern of multiple forms of abuse against her and her mother, adding that her most recent dispute with her stepdad concerned her decision to not wear the hijab. Jessica used Marlowe's phone to text her friends while she was traveling because she feared Alfetlawi was tracking her calls. The texts recovered from his cell phone, coupled with his testimony, was key in the decision to file first-degree murder charges against Alfetlawi. Jessica was clearly terrified of her stalking stepdad and was fleeing from him.

Figure 14.4. Jessica flashes a smile in a hijab she often wore. She argued with her stepfather when she opted not to wear a veil, and texted a friend about her conflicts with Alfetlawi shortly before he murdered her. *Courtesy of Wendy Wasinski, in memory of her loving daughter and best friend, Jessica Amanda Mohamad Mokdad.*

The day Jessica arrived back in Warren, she helped her grandmother sort through her late great-grandmother's things. Alfetlawi drove from his Minnesota home to help, he said, and carried boxes of belongings to his mother-in-law's house where Jessica was staying. "He wanted me to come along, but I had to work, and it would be a long drive to have to turn around again," said Wasinski. "He told me he loved me when he left."

Later that day, after Alfetlawi shot Jessica, he phoned Wendy. "He told me he was going to turn himself in to the police. I said, 'What's going on? Why are you going to the police?'" Wasinski recalled. "He said, 'I smacked Jessica. You're probably going to hear about it.' He told me he loved me, then hung up. So I'm in a panic and I call my mom to ask her where Jessica is. She doesn't really know, so she goes to Jessica's room and sees her lying on the floor. But she doesn't see blood, so she thinks Jessica might just be unconscious, and goes outside for help." Jessica's grandmother called out to a neighbor passing by, and he rushed in to help, checked Jessica, and he realized "right away she's dead," said Wasinski.

The first thing Wasinski thought of was to kill herself, she told me, but the image of a woman from her mosque came into her head, and she phoned her instead. The woman arrived to calm her down, sat with her, and helped arrange for payment for a trip to Warren for Wendy. "I saw Rahim in jail and demanded to know what happened. He had said he couldn't tell me on the phone because he knew I would freak out. He told me to my face that it was an accident, and acted like it was big surprise she was dead," recalled Wasinski. "I said, 'Shut up, quit acting.'" Alfetlawi tried various stories on the police. First, he insisted he was out to get Mohamed Mokdad and accidentally shot Jessica, then he said a gun he carried for protection accidentally went off when Jessica hugged him. He later claimed he was suffering from post-traumatic stress disorder from years of torture in Saddam Hussein's jails. It took a jury 30 minutes to convict him, and he was sentenced to life in prison without the possibility of parole.

Judge David Viviano made it a point to stress that Jessica's murder was not an honor killing but stemmed largely from Alfetlawi's "bizarre obsession" with Jessica's "every move." There is "no religion which sanctions your actions," Viviano said to Alfetlawi. "This was not an honor killing. There is no code of honor that supports a coward and a hypocrite." Alfetlawi was driven to dictate every aspect of Jessica's behavior, and "in his last act of control, he took her life," said the judge.

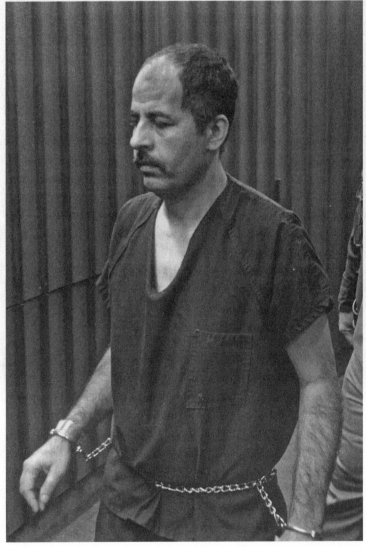

Figure 14.5. Jessica's stepdad, Rahim Alfetlawi, is led away in handcuffs following his sentencing. He apologized to the court for murdering Jessica, the girl he had raised from the age of eight. *Reprinted by permission from David Posavetz.*

Figure 14.6. Jessica Mokdad's mom, Wendy Wasinski, listens to the judge in a Michigan courtroom send ex-husband Rahim Alfetlawi to life in prison for murdering her daughter. *Reprinted by permission from David Posavetz.*

Rahim apologized to the court before he was sentenced, "but not to me, which really pissed me off," said Wendy. In her victim impact statement before Alfetlawi's sentencing, the bitter mom addressed him: "You said before that Allah, God, the prophet Muhammad, and his family were with you. And now, as you can see after all the prayers you made during the trial, they are not with you. Allah, God, will not forgive you for what you've done, and neither will I. You took my daughter from me, my only child. You are a coldhearted killer and deserve to spend all your life in prison. She spent her life taking orders from you. Now you will spend the rest of your life taking orders from prison guards, and you can see how that feels. I hope every day in prison feels like a year, and every year feels like ten."

Wasinski is still stunned by the murder of her daughter by a man she lived with and trusted for 12 years. She believes it was largely triggered by the fury of Rahim at Jessica's refusal to follow his orders and her efforts to break free from him. Wendy now knows that Rahim likely considered Jessica a kind of wife to him, and that her independence represented a sort of divorce that infuriated him. "He was obsessed with her, I realize now," she said in our interview. "He was sexually attracted to her, and it's something I didn't see at the time, but when I look back now, everything is much clearer. There was a point he would try to hug and kiss Jessica, and she would push him away, saying she was too old for that. I only realized in hindsight what was happening." The catalyst for the murder may have been Jessica's revelation to her mom that Rahim had raped her. Her daughter told her of the assault the night before her murder, in a cellphone call to Wendy as her mom was driving. "'I need to tell you that Rahim raped me before,'" Wasinski quoted her daughter as telling her. "She said it was a couple of years ago," after she was with Mike, the teen Rahim made Jessica marry. Rahim "had bugged my car, so he could have figured out what Jessica was telling me by listening to my side of the conversation," said Wasinski. He likely feared prosecution for the rape, she believes, but may have also been concerned about how revelation of the attack would damage his honor in her eyes and in the view of his friends and the public. It's possible, Wasinski believes, that he could have blamed Jessica for his sexual attraction to her. But another key component in the murder were likely "mental problems" related to his imprisonment and torture in Iraq, she's convinced, which appeared to be more of a problem as he grew older. He suffered from anxiety and night terrors, for which he was being treated, said Wasinski. He had been prescribed medicine as part of his treatment, but he took the drugs only sporadically, she added.

As prosecutors prepared their case against Rahim Alfetlawi, others were battling the latest culture clash provoked by Jessica's murder, a conflict with implications for concerns about and understanding of violence against women and children. A conservative faction fearing the "talibanization" of the country by American Muslims hosted a controversial "Jessica Mokdad Human Rights Conference" at the Dearborn Hyatt a year after her death. The conference logo was a drawing of Jessica wearing a hijab with a tear trailing down her cheek, crying out "help" in a cartoon bubble over her head. It was hosted by Pamela Geller, author of *Atlas Shrugged*, and famous for spearheading the opposition against establishing a mosque at Ground Zero in Manhattan, and who referred to herself in a 2010 *New York Times* interview as a "racist-Islamophobic-anti-Muslim-bigot."[2]

"Thank you for coming and being brave," and withstanding the "Islamaphobic narrative that we get smeared with all the time," Geller said as she opened the videotaped April 29, 2011, conference. It's "important that we're here today, it's very important that we increase awareness of honor killing," she said, and asked why the local Muslim community isn't "speaking out against honor killings. This girl, Jessica Mokdad, who was honor-murdered, lived in abject fear of her life, she feared being honor-killed" because she resisted "Islamic tradition," Geller added. "These girls deserve the same freedoms, the same rights to choose as every other American." Geller criticized local officials for backing off their "honor killing" label in the murder. Assistant Prosecutor William Cataldo has said Alfetlawi "wanted her sexually—well, FYI, that's part of honor killing," said Geller. A friend of Jessica's, Darwin Jiles, also spoke at the conference, calling her a "beautiful person inside and out. She was definitely someone who really wanted to discover God for herself."

Interestingly, one of the speakers made a point to emphasize that Jessica's murder was not domestic violence. It was a "final act of control because she shamed his family," said conservative journalist Michael Coren of Toronto's Sun TV. "This wasn't domestic violence. This was an honor killing. It's different."

Figure 14.7. Jessica poses with a rose, without her hijab. She was becoming increasingly skilled in photography before her death. *Courtesy of Wendy Wasinski, in memory of her loving daughter and best friend, Jessica Amanda Mohamad Mokdad.*

The same day, the Arab American Society and other organizations hosted a counter conference, "Rejecting Islamophobia: A Community Stand against Hate," in another hotel a few miles away. It featured religious and community leaders and politicians, who decried discrimination against Muslims in America, discussed funding for hate groups, and talked about political exploitation of cultural conflicts. Democratic Rep. Hansen Clarke, who represents the Detroit area and is on the committee for Homeland Security, talked of being singled out by security even on government business because he's not Caucasian. He's the son of an African-American mom and a Muslim dad from India, now Bangladesh (though Clarke himself is a Catholic). He called an attack on Muslim immigrants an "attack on us all" and on the Constitution, asking at one point, "How dare people undermine our faith in God?" Neither honor killings, nor Jessica's murder, were mentioned in a tape of the conference.

FIFTEEN
INFIDEL

Vincent Van Gogh's 47-year-old great grandnephew, Theo, was riding his bike in Amsterdam when he was struck by bullets that catapulted him through the air to land on the cobblestone intersection of Linnaeusstraat and Tweede Oosterparkstraat. As the wounded Van Gogh pleaded for his life, Dutch-Moroccan gunman Mohammed Bouyeri shot him four more times, then opened his neck with a knife and nailed a five-page letter to Van Gogh's chest with a second knife.

The 2004 killing was punishment, and the letter was addressed to Ayaan Hirsi Ali, Somali-born member of Dutch parliament, and a Muslim turned atheist. Hirsi Ali and Van Gogh had collaborated on a controversial film, *Submission*, a ten-minute movie in English about oppression of Muslim women. "Theo and I knew it was a dangerous film to make," Hirsi Ali, now 41, writes in her book *Infidel*.[1] "However, some things must be said, and there are times when silence becomes an accomplice to injustice."

Hirsi Ali is now involved in the debate about American honor killings. She knows what it's like to be Muslim living in a Western country, and realizes that attitudes and customs she had hoped to escape can continue to stalk a girl in a new culture.

In 2007, Hirsi Ali and supporters launched the AHA Foundation headquartered in New York to "protect and defend the rights of women and girls in the West from oppression justified by religion and culture," according to the organization's website.[2] The group tracks and members speak out about honor killings and assaults, forced marriages, and genital mutilation. Though the issues are far more significant in some other Western nations, American "honor killings" have occurred. Though the killings in North

221

America—all victims have been female—are rare, the loss of a single life is unacceptable, AHA spokeswoman Amanda Parker told me in a phone interview. And while the public is aware of only a handful of cases, AHA is convinced that there have, in fact, been "dozens," said Parker. The killings also point to an underlying world of behaviors such as forced marriage and nonfatal child abuse linked to expectations about daughters and concepts of honor and punishment.

For every honor killing in the United States "there are hundreds of other cases of honor abuse, from the mild to the extreme, that are often brought on by things like dating, drinking, dressing 'immodestly' or rejecting Islam," cardiologist Zuhdi Jasser, president of the American Islamic Forum for Democracy, and a commissioner on the US Commission on International Religious Freedom, wrote in a 2012 opinion piece in *USA Today*.[3] Jasser, like the AHA, is attempting to walk a political tightrope between the shrill Pamela Geller, who used Jessica Mokdad's killing to Islam-bash, and officials of some Arab activist organizations who are reluctant to admit that any honor killings have occurred in America.

Girls at home in America who may feel threatened because of perceived issues of honor are often faced with more difficulty in obtaining help from civil authorities because so few officials have any experience dealing with their situations or recognizing legitimate danger signs. A girl may tell a social worker or a teacher or a cop, "'My dad's going to kill me because I'm wearing too much makeup,' and the cop thinks, 'Yeah, I just told my daughter that last week,'" Parker explained to me. But in a rare instance, it "can actually be a life-or-death situation," she said. AHA last year helped a 17-year-old girl who first learned she was pregnant sitting in her pediatrician's examining room with her mother. "Dad's going to kill me," she said. Again, the comment wasn't the kind of typical hyperbolic response many American teens might give in such a situation. "She really and truly believed her father was going to take her life," said Parker. "Her mother told her, 'I can't protect you from your father. I'm disowning you,' and stood up and walked out." The pediatrician attempted to hospitalize the girl to protect her until some arrangements could be made, but the hospital refused because the girl wasn't ill. AHA, contacted by the pediatrician, reached out for help to a local child-protection agency, which couldn't take action, officials explained, because there was no history of abuse and no physical harm. Finally, a detective who had investigated an Arizona honor killing of two teenage daughters in his precinct contacted local police to explain the danger the girl might be in and urged them to check on her at home. When police arrived, they found the teen covered with bruises, and she was removed to a shelter, said Parker. She lives apart from her family now and is raising her baby daughter. To help officials spot danger zones, AHA offers training to police and social workers who may encounter honor threats in a home or receive pleas of help from a frightened child.

Honor killings are an intriguing inverse of the William Parente brand of family annihilation. In a familicide, the father presumably doesn't want to leave his family alive to suffer his shame after his death. In an honor killing, the perceived shame reflection is reversed: The father regards his daughter as casting dishonor on him and the rest of the family. In both cases, it's the child who suffers the worst consequences. Honor killings don't occur only among Muslim families, and some may argue that other kinds of male killings of an intimate partner represent a kind of "honor killing" to a man because he may feel his masculinity or honor is tarnished when a wife leaves or cheats on him. Honor killings, in other words, may be one more iteration of the sometimes-murderous evolutionary-based relationship between the sexes and a male's drive to control a female. The killing may be far less about "honor" than essentially about zealously guarding a female's sexual fidelity so an intimate partner isn't duped into expending resources on a child not his own. But in the case of many honor killings, chastity is guarded not by the intimate partner but by a father (and sometimes by a young woman's brothers), almost as if he's a proxy husband until a daughter (or sister) marries.

In Hirsi Ali's characterization of honor killings, acts of honor "are rewarded and those acts perceived as shameful are severely punished," she noted at a videotaped symposium on honor killing and forced marriage June 6, 2011, at John Jay College of Criminal Justice in Manhattan. These "shameful" acts are "unique to women in certain cultures. It has to do with their sexuality—virginity, chastity, fidelity, and purity are emblems of honor.

Sex before marriage is considered infidelity. These are sources of shame for the family or tribe. The women in these cultures don't own their bodies. Their sexuality is a commodity and it's of high value, which is owned by their families. These sexual commodities are seen to lose value once they're believed to be tainted." She complained at the conference about pressure groups that insist that "there is no violence" and that any attribution of violence to these cultures "they claim is racism or anti-Islam."

Domestic violence and child abuse beyond the scope of honor killings are already serious problems in the United States, Hirsi Ali believes. The difference between an honor killer and the more typical killer father in the United States is that most abusers in a case of domestic violence know that "when he hits his wife or child, he's doing something wrong, and the wife knows she should not be taking the abuse," she said at the symposium. "Domestic violence, even though it occurs a lot in the West, is morally unacceptable and socially wrong. Things are different in cultures governed in shame, however."

Jasser has spoken out strongly against honor killings in America—at the same time, he defends Islam. The religion does not sanction murder of a child, he emphasizes, but he acknowledges that the religion has been "hijacked" by "pre-Islamic, tribal and medieval," even "Neanderthal" cultures by those who use Islam to mask other murderous motivations or sanction killings, he noted in his *USA Today* article. Honor killings are "completely wrong and immoral," and it's up to moderate Muslims to address this issue and set up family processes to protect women and daughters in danger, he wrote.

The motivations behind Jessica's murder were complex, but AHA believes the crime had several aspects of an honor killing—the extreme control, battles over the hijab, Jessica's marriage to a boyfriend at her stepfather's insistence. Marriages may be forced or quickly arranged by a father if he fears his daughter is, or is about to become, sexually active. The marriage is a way to "legitimize" the sex and therefore not bring dishonor to the family, Parker explained to me. The perceived support of a family or a community marks the difference between other kinds of domestic violence and an honor killing, Parker emphasized. Amnesty International has defined "so-called honor killings" as "part of a community mentality. Large sections of society share traditional conceptions of family honor and approve of the killings to preserve that honor. Even mothers whose daughters have been killed in the name of honor often condone such violent acts."[4] However, no one in Alfetlawi's community or family supported the killing of Jessica Mokdad or aided Alfetlawi after he was arrested—though he may have imagined some kind of cultural justification for his actions.

Though Jessica's case continues to be controversial, other murders in North America were clearly considered honor killings by murderous dads who took their daughters' lives, and by authorities who prosecuted them. The murderers represent a distinct form of killer dads, whose motivations present more clues into what drives a father to kill his own child.

In the first widely covered honor-killing case in 1989, naturalized American citizen and Palestinian immigrant Zein Isa stabbed to death his screaming 16-year-old daughter, Tina, while his wife held her down in their St. Louis, Missouri, home, as Zein shouted in Arabic: "Die! Die quickly! Die, my daughter, die." The murder was recorded on electronic bugs planted by the FBI, whose agents were tracking Zein's participation in a possible American terror plot at the time. The jury concluded that Zein killed his daughter because he believed she had shamed the family by becoming too rebellious and Westernized, listening to American music and dating a non-Muslim boy. Zein was sentenced to death (he later died of complications from diabetes while in prison).

In 2009, unemployed Arizona trucker Faleh Hassan Almaleki ran down his 20-year-old year-old daughter, Noor, and the mother of her boyfriend while they walked in a parking lot outside a welfare office in the Phoenix suburb of Peoria. Noor died thirteen days later, her spine crushed. Her boyfriend's mom, Amal Khalaf, with whom Noor was living, survived with several broken bones and had difficulty walking for months. She saw Almaleki's "angry face" through the car window just as he struck her, Amal later testified at his murder trial, throwing her some 30 feet and shattering her femur and several vertebrae. He then made a beeline for Noor, and the impact of her body cracked the grill of his Jeep Laredo in half, a police investigation revealed. He ran over his daughter, snagging her body on the undercarriage as he drove across the parking lot, and Noor tumbled from beneath the car at a curb. The "weapon was a motor vehicle, a 4,000-pound piece of metal," said Detective Chris Boughey, the key investigator in the case.

Minutes before she was struck, Noor had spotted her dad walking into the welfare office where she was applying for benefits. "Dude, I'm so scared," she texted a friend, according to evidence presented at Almaleki's trial. "At the welfare place, and guess who walks in? My dad! I'm so shaky!" She added: "I've never known a person with so much evil."

The eldest of seven children, Noor, at the age of four, had moved from Iraq with her parents in 1998 to escape Saddam Hussein's regime. She straddled two cultures, quickly absorbing her new American culture at school but remaining true to her religion. She traveled to Iraq at the age of 18 to wed a man chosen for her in an arranged marriage, but she fled just months later to move back to America, the jury learned at Almaleki's murder trial.

After Almaleki mowed down his daughter, he fled across the border to Mexico, then flew to England, with the help of money from a relative, police learned. As police hunted for the missing father, his eldest son explained in a news interview that his sister had "triggered my dad's anger" and went "out of her way to be disrespectful to the family," adding, "I don't like Noor's boyfriend," and "there are different values in different cultures."[5]

Police tracked Almaleki to London, where immigration officials allowed Peoria investigators to question him. "The interview was long. It was frustrating. It was a cat-and-mouse game for several hours," Chris Boughey explained at the 2011 AHA-sponsored Manhattan seminar on honor killings. "He was not very forthcoming. He changed his story several times. It went from being an accident. He lost control and lost his mind. Then, he said he wanted to scare them. He was always blaming her boyfriends for 'being out of their culture' and being bad people because of that. He never took responsibility for anything he did. He said if he wanted to kill them, he would use a gun or knife. Then, finally, he admitted he did mean to hurt them. During the interview, he made an analogy, saying that if you have a little fire, you have to put it out or that small fire will burn the whole house down. Noor was the fire. The whole house was the family."

Boughey added that while Noor clung to life, "not once" did Almaleki "ask how his daughter was. We had a five-and-a-half-hour plane ride back to Phoenix. He never asked how his daughter was doing."

In phone calls from prison secretly taped by police, Almaleki told a cousin to ask the Iraqi consulate to intervene with the American government on his behalf. "Connect it to honor and dishonor and, I don't know, whatever," he said in a transcript of the call. "An Iraqi is worth nothing without honor." He later told his wife on the phone, "No one hates his daughter, but honor is precious, and nothing is better than honor, and we are a tribal society that can't change." He told her to write "'honor' on signs" in a demonstration outside the embassy. "I'm not a criminal. I didn't kill someone off the street. I tried to give her a chance, but no result." At one point, he says, referring to Amal, "What can you do about these bitches who are burning us?" and "No one messed up our life except Noor." His wife, who appears to fluctuate from support to anger over the killing, at one point suggests, "We can say that you have . . . a psychological problem. You have to tell them, 'I am suffering because of the war.'" He agrees it's a good idea. "Tell them I am tired and feel nervous," he says. "Tell them I got sick in Iraq. OK?"

Prosecutor Laura Reckart told jurors in her closing arguments that Faleh Almaleki believed his "own law was above all others." It's "chilling that you could mow down your own flesh and blood with your car because it suits your culture. It's just cold," said Reckart. Defense attorney Jeffrey Kirchler argued that Almaleki cared deeply about his daughter, showing a blown-up photo of the newborn Noor gripping her father's finger with her tiny hand on the day "everything changed for him." As a father, "you want your child to be good, to have manners, to have values," Kirchler said. Before he was sentenced to 34 years in prison, Almaleki told Maricopa County Superior Court Judge Roland Steinle, "I wish I was dead and not her." As Steinle sentenced Almaleki, he called the case "the most difficult in my six years on the bench." He said the "press moniker" labeling the case an "honor killing bothered me. I cannot believe that a religion would allow" the killing of "other human beings." He concluded that the case had nothing to do with religion and that, more accurately, it was about a defendant who apparently believed, "'I brought Noor into the world, she's my property, and I will take her out of the world," adding: "To me, he became Saddam Hussein in Phoenix. He became the man he fled from."

The case particularly rattled Reckart and Boughey, Reckart revealed at the AHA seminar. "This case affected us like no other. It really got to us. Why did this case have such a profound effect on us? We decided it's about entitlement. This makes you go crazy. He believed he was entitled to this, and that's what made a difference," she said.

The detective agreed, pointing out that the Maricopa County town just west of Phoenix is a common bedroom community like countless others where an honor killing was something he never expected to encounter. "This case threw us both," he said. "This is going on in the US. It happened in Peoria, Arizona, so I'm guessing it's happening in New York City and elsewhere," he added, offering to help other law enforcement officers dealing with any similar situations. "Contact us. We're not experts, but we hopefully can be a resource," he added at the conference. "Do we know about everything? No. This is new ground for us as investigators and prosecutors. I think we need to remember that murder is murder. Wrong is wrong. That's what we do," find the criminals. "That's our job. That is what you entrusted us to do, regardless of where you come from, where you live, what religion you are, what color you are, what preferences you have. You call us, we show up and do our jobs. I think it's important that we do a better job of making it easier for these victims, for these women, to feel comfortable reporting problems."

The year before the Almaleki case, Texas cab driver and Egyptian immigrant Yaser Abdel Said allegedly shot to death his daughters Amina, 18, and Sarah, 17, because he was furious they had become "too Westernized" and had non-Muslim boyfriends, officials say. Sarah Said, shot nine times, managed to phone the Irving Police Department's 911 call center as she lay mortally wounded. "My dad shot me and my sister," she said, "I'm dying," police records show. Said is a fugitive and has made the FBI's "most wanted" list. He's believed to be in Egypt or possibly behind the wheel of a cab in New York City.

Across the border in Montreal, an Afghan father and his wife—along with their son—were found guilty in 2011 of killing their three teenage daughters and a "co-wife" in what the judge described in court as "cold-blooded, shameful murders" committed because of a "twisted concept of honor."[6] Mohammad Shafia, 58, his wife Tooba Yahya, 42, and their son Hamed, 21, killed the three teenage sisters because they dishonored the family by defying Shafia's strict rules on dress, dating, and using the Internet. Prosecutors said the defendants drowned their victims Zainab, 19, Sahar, 17, and Geeti, 13, and Rona Mohammad Amir, 50. They were all found in the family's newly purchased used Nissan, at the bottom of a lock on the Rideau Canal in the summer of 2009. The sisters were all Tooba's biological children, though Shafia's first wife (Rona) had helped raise them as her own. The parents and son were charged with killing the women elsewhere, then placing their bodies in the car and pushing it into the canal. They insisted the Nissan had accidentally plunged into the canal after the eldest daughter, Zainab, took it for a joy ride with her sisters and Rona. Hamed said he watched the accident, although he didn't call police from the scene.

The family had left Afghanistan in 1992 and lived in Pakistan, Australia, and Dubai before settling in Canada in 2007. Shafia, a prosperous businessman, owned commercial property in the Montreal area and ran a business buying used cars in North America and shipping them overseas. He took a second wife because his first wife could not have children. Shafia was a strict disciplinarian, and his son acted in his stead when he was away on business, the jury heard. The months leading up to the deaths were increasingly tense in the Shafia household, according to evidence presented at trial. Zainab, the oldest daughter, was forbidden to attend school for a year because she had a young Pakistani-Canadian boyfriend. She fled, terrified of her father, to a battered woman's shelter, but was eventually sent back home. The prosecution said her dad became livid after finding condoms in Sahar's room along with photos of her wearing short skirts and hugging her Christian boyfriend, a relationship she had kept secret. Both Zainab and Sahar wore fashionable clothes and resisted pressure from their parents and eldest brother to wear the hijab. They also both reported incidents or threats of violence from their father and brother to authorities. Geeti was becoming almost impossible to control, her parents believed, skipping school, failing classes, being sent home for wearing revealing clothes and stealing, while declaring to teachers that she wanted to be placed in foster care, according to the prosecution.

Wiretaps of Shafia's phone conversations, which were revealed in court, captured him spewing vitriol about his dead daughters, calling them treacherous whores, and invoking the devil to shit on their graves. "There can be no betrayal, no treachery, no violation more than this," Shafia said on one recording. "Even if they hoist me up onto the gallows . . . nothing is more dear to me than my honor."

As Judge Robert Maranger of the Ontario Superior Court of Justice sentenced each of them to life in prison without the possibility of parole, he declared: "It's difficult to conceive of a more despicable, more heinous crime. The apparent reason behind these cold-blooded, shameful murders was that the four completely innocent victims offended your completely twisted concept of honor, a notion of honor that is founded upon the domination and control of women, a sick notion of honor that has absolutely no place in any civilized society."

The murders sparked a debate in the public and in the media about the wisdom of singling out the attacks as honor killings, with some community spokesmen emphasizing that intolerance of violence against women is not just a Canadian value but a universal value, and that Afghans, like any other people, condemn such acts. "Calling the murders 'honor killings' accomplishes two goals: First, it makes it seem as if femicide is a highly unusual event. Second, it makes it seem as if femicide is confined to specific populations within Canada and specific national cultures or religions in the world at large," said an editorial in the *Montreal Gazette*.[7] "But Canadian statistics prove otherwise. From 2000 to 2009, an average of 58 women a year were killed in this country as a result of spousal violence. In that same period, 67 children and young people aged 12 to 17 were murdered by family members. In contrast, recent estimates tell us that there have been 12 or 13 so-called honor killings in Canada in the last decade. It does not take a genius to see that comparing 12 or 13 against the hundreds of women and children who were victims of familial violence serves only to frame 'honor killing' as peculiar, when in reality it is part of a larger pattern of violence against women."

SIXTEEN
WHAT TO DO

When pediatrician Dr. Kaija Hartiala came to work at her practice in Turku, Finland, one day in 2011, she was looking forward to meeting a new patient scheduled that morning. Something about the face of the young mother, who was bringing in her newborn to be checked out, rang a distant bell, but the doctor didn't waste much time puzzling over it. As she usually did with new patients, Kaija sat down with the mom first to introduce herself and explain some of her background and what kind of care to expect. The pediatrician typically introduces herself as a mom of four children, a former member of the local city council, and a deputy mayor in Turku, and notes that she has spent years working at the main hospital in town. "'Oh,'" responded the surprised patient, Kaija recently told me over dinner in California, "'you must know about me in that case. That's where I was bought after my father tried to kill me.'" In fact, Kaija had been working in the emergency room some 20 years earlier when the young mother now before her, then a little girl of nine, was rushed in with a bullet in her brain. Her father, despondent over the family's failing business, had waited until his wife left on an errand, then methodically shot his three children before turning the gun on himself. The older daughter and son died instantly; the third made it to an examining table before Kaija. Two decades later, that same girl, now a young woman, sat before her.

"The bullet's path was quite remarkable," recalled Hartiala. "It damaged very little." The girl was treated for brain swelling and was watched carefully, but the bullet, too dangerous to remove, was left where it was. The girl went back home in time to live with her mother, but not for long because of continuing problems at home, she told Kaija as they talked that day. She was

231

raised instead by an "'amazing'" aunt, the survivor said. "'It's just so horrible to think about,'" said the young mom, referring to her dad's murder-suicide. "'But what can you do? You go on to live your life.'" The encounter triggered very mixed emotions for Hartiala. It was "so tragic and shocking when I saw that girl shot by her father so many years ago, but also amazing to see her so long after sitting in front of me, looking healthy and happy, and with a little baby of her own now," she told me.

Finland, with a strikingly low crime rate, especially by American standards, has suffered in the past from a disturbing incidence of family annihilations and child homicides by parents. More than 60 percent of all child homicides in a 24-year period from 1970 to 1994 were committed by parents, either by fatal battering, or shooting, drowning, suffocating, burning, stabbing, or intentionally killing their children in car accidents, according to a study on filicides and intrafamilial child homicides in Finland.[1] The study found that the victims' greatest risk was the day of their birth, though danger remained particularly high for the first four months of life. Of the 200 homicides by parents over that period, 60 percent were committed by moms, but 71 percent of the 75 murder-suicides were committed by fathers. Most of the murder-suicides involved a firearm. Mothers in 74 percent of the cases reported "mental health distress," noted the study, while killer dads abused alcohol and/or were violent to other family members in 45 percent of the cases. Psychosis or "psychotic depression" was diagnosed for 51 percent of killer moms, and a personality disorder was diagnosed for 67 percent of killer dads and 4 percent of moms. The years of the study, the homicide rates of children under the age of one were over five times greater in Finland than the rates in Sweden and Italy, which had the lowest rates. The United States and New Zealand had the highest homicide rates for children ages one to four in the same period.

The study recommended that special attention be paid by healthcare providers to new moms suffering from postpartum depression, who typically have very clear symptoms, from insomnia to suicidal thoughts. "Intensive and rapid support is needed, especially in the care of the baby," noted the study. In addition, "clinicians should pay attention to depressed, anxious and even psychotic parents.... Support and treatment should be given without delay because the crisis in the family may exacerbate within days. Parents with personality disorders and substance abuse need early intervention, even during the pregnancy, in order to be able to attach to the child and learn better skills in reading the child's mind and intentions," the report urged.

Finland was also losing children to injuries and accidents at home. "At one point, we decided this was something we had to focus on," recalled Kaija. "In the case of accidents at home, we reached out to families and established educational campaigns to teach parents how better to protect their children, things like locking up household cleaning products. We turned things around," she told me. (The outreach, of course, wasn't fail-safe. In one case, a conscientious mom thought her kids would benefit from her idea to place a large plant at the bottom of a stairway railing to keep her sons from sliding down, only to have one of her boys impale himself on the plant stake when he shot down the railing, Kaija recalled during our talk. Fortunately, the stake went through his body without damaging any major organs. The mom was mortified; the son recovered.)

Though the nation is still struggling to save more children from accidents and violence, from 1990 to 2010, Finland cut its under-five child mortality rate in half, and its child and adolescent death rates were also slashed by 50 percent, according to a Child Safety Country Profile conducted annually with the Eurozone.[2]

"I think there's a sense in Finland that we're all in this together, and if we don't fix our problems, no one else will," said Kaija. "And many people believe they need to put some of their efforts into improving life in our communities. We're also a much smaller nation than US, so I think it's easier for us to decide the kinds of issues we want to focus on, come up with a plan, and institute it. That kind of agreement and unified intention and action, I suspect, is much more difficult in a nation the size of America," added Kaija, who lived for several years with her family in California.

———

America is definitely not Finland. It's not only a sprawling, bumptious nation with 310 million people, but those residents are divided into starkly different political factions and lifestyles with radically at-odds attitudes about families, child-rearing, gender roles, criminal justice, and the role of the government.

I assumed when I got to the end of my book, some solutions to the problem of fathers killing children would be obvious. They weren't. I set out to gather all the facts I could on the killings, assuming the information would unlock the key to motivations and mechanisms toward murder. They didn't. In some cases I was convinced I got to "the bottom" of a crime, but, just as I did during the lonely night I spent in the hotel room where William Parente killed his family, I found nothing but emptiness.

The problem is tremendously complicated, as complex as the human heart, shaped by eons of our evolutionary past as well as by the politics and economics and social pressures and our own child-rearing that brought us to this time and this place. Families struggle on their own to deal with crushing economic or health issues, and friends and relatives help if they're capable, and if they're aware a problem exists. Communities across the nation work to institute innovative public programs or bolster tried-and-true methods, all the while grappling with budgetary constraints. But much of the answer has to do with our attention to the issue of child abuse and homicide by their parents, and our intention to do something about it. Family-violence expert Richard Gelles believes we're confused as a society about how far to go to fix dysfunctional families, which is also complicated by a market-driven economy, finite resources, and attitudes about rewards and punishment.

"The real issue is that as a society we're really ambivalent about if we really want to help, and who we want to help," he explained in a 2012 Big Think video interview. "So we set up programs that are safety net programs that almost always have a means test. For welfare, the means test is, well, just how poor are you? Housing, the means test is, how much housing do you need? For domestic violence, unfortunately, the means test is, are you the victim of a form of violence? For child abuse, the means test is, are their caregivers inadequate in terms of neglect or medical neglect or physical abuse or sexual abuse? Almost every government program has this test, which means there's an enormous bureaucracy hired to decide when the gate gets opened and when the gate gets closed. And that diverts monetary resources and energy that would otherwise be spent on the program itself.

"The second ambivalence is in fact that bright line: Who gets the services? And in a market economy, we're really reluctant to help everyone because we think, well, you don't want to reward behavior that we think is inappropriate. So why would you have a Welfare benefit increase with the second out-of-wedlock child, when we don't want children born out of wedlock to folks who aren't able to support them?"

Gelles isn't a big fan of government programs, many of which he considers "terribly ineffective" and incapable of delivering the kind of help needed, intended, and expected. The title of his latest book, *The Third Lie*, is "based on an old and not very good joke that there are three lies," he notes.[3] "The first one—this is the older part of the joke, of course—is 'I'll respect you in the morning'; the second is, 'The check is in the mail,' and the third lie is: 'I'm from the government and I'm here to help you.'" He blames government program failures in dealing with family violence in part to a "disconnect between research and government social policy." He accuses policymakers of using research "like a drunk uses a lamppost—much more for support than for illumination."

The results are frustrating. "I cannot bear to be involved in more fatality reviews of little babies," Gelles wrote in his 1996 book *The Book of David: How Preserving Families Can Cost Children's Lives*.[4] "I cannot bear the frustration of devoting a lifetime of research and practice to the ideal of protecting children only to find that current policies ignore the research results. We must change the system."

Gelles has long been a critic of the policy push by US social-service agencies to "make all reasonable efforts" to keep families together, despite all signs that it may be the worst strategy for a child. "Most families, 98 percent of them, can be helped, but some are hopeless," he told me recently. "In those cases the child must be removed from the home." Many experts view the strategy to keep a child with a family at nearly any cost not only forced by official policy but necessitated by budgetary constraints because there are few other options for abused children and not enough funds to establish or support them. In Gelles's view, the policy is also part of a "larger ideology"—the "sacrosanct belief that children always (or nearly always) are better off with the biological parents," he told me.

In *The Book of David*, Gelles examines the case of a boy he calls "David Edwards." Despite repeated abuse at the hands of his mother, "Darlene," who had severely abused David's older sister, the boy was returned to his home. He was eventually suffocated by his mom. "I became convinced that the system was just as responsible for his death as the actual perpetrator. While we may not be able to change people like Darlene, we could and should have prevented the death of her little boy," he writes.[5]

The abuse and murder of children are "major social problems, public health threats to children, and crimes that require strong and effective response," he added. "The child welfare system, which was instituted to protect children, continues to fail them. The problem is not simply that resources are lacking, but that the central mission of child welfare agencies, preserving families, does not work, and places many children at significant risk of continued injury and death."[6]

Michael Petit of Every Child Matters points out a key difference in focus when civil authorities deal with violence against a wife and mother. As Gelles has also pointed out, domestic violence against a wife is dealt with by law enforcement, while almost all child-abuse cases are addressed by social-welfare agencies. When a wife is assaulted, the attacker is removed from the home by police; yet in the case of an abused child, it's the child who's removed from the home by a social worker, and the attacker is allowed to stay. While the family may also desperately require the aid of a social-service agency, a social worker is not usually the best person to deal with a violent male in the household, notes Petit. "He's not going to be deterred in that situation," he explained to me in an interview. "It's no longer effective to sit down with that guy and say, 'Let's talk. What's bothering you?' The most violent cases, whether against a woman or a child, must be handled in the criminal justice system."

Gelles is often quoted for his shocking comments about the violence of families and the dangers they represent to children. He has called the family the "most violent social institution" and the "most violence prone," and he believes the family is at least as often a locus of violence as of love. He attributes dangers to a child within a family to a variety of causes, from the amount of time spent in a family (increasing chances of victimization) to the range of ages and gender-role expectations that can trigger conflict. He says he hasn't moderated his harsh view of the family over decades of research, except to note that evidence indicates that women gain somewhat greater protections from violence from their mates as wives, rather than as lovers.

Despite Gelles's criticism of child-protection services in the United States, he does not believe they should be gutted, but that strategies should change, and services be strengthened. The problem of child abuse and child homicides by their parents demands more attention and funding to address the problem. He notes in *The Book of David* that a heavily subsidized convention center within miles of the home where David was suffocated still lies vacant. "A society that can subsidize a convention center and hotel, airport and shopping mall can subsidize the physical and emotional well-being of children. Not all programs will work and not every program is effective for every family and child," he writes.[7] "Yet this is an investment we must make, because the costs of not making it, the cost in dollars, suffering, and lives, is simply too high to pay."

Neil Websdale agrees that the nation must expend more effort, attention, and funds on protecting children at home. "We need to intervene more effectively and we must begin with more social services and a better safety net to keep families from imploding," he told me. "We must establish a process that pumps money into creating more caring communities to battle the isolation many families experience."

Another key strategy in the battle to save kids at home is to gather as much information as possible on the problem. There's a hunger among academics, child-protection advocates, as well as professionals in child-protection agencies, law enforcement, and healthcare for more, and more accurate, data. Petit believes the persistent statistical undercount of child fatalities at the hands of their parents dampens public interest and engagement in battling the problem, but it also hinders effective preventive strategies not to have accurate information.

One way to glean the most complete information possible from fatal situations is the use of child-fatality review panels, which involve experts, advocates, social workers, law enforcement and healthcare professionals, as well as relatives and family members of a victim, in order to conduct a kind of "social autopsy" of a child's death that involves examination of official reports of the deaths, investigations of public agencies that may have touched the victim's life, risk factors, and possible alternative actions that may have prevented the death. The aim is to find clues in one death to devise strategies to prevent another. Several different kinds of fatality-review systems exist to analyze a range of situations, from elder-abuse deaths, to infant mortality, to the domestic-violence death of an intimate partner and child fatalities. "The unifying feature of these different types of fatality reviews is that they are wide-angle, multidisciplinary case studies conducted in a climate that promotes open discovery of information," noted a conference report by the National Center for Child Death Review.[8] As the report states, "review teams obtain information on deaths from multiple sources for their discussions on the often extremely complex death events. The teams examine records, discuss the events leading up to and causing the death, and work to identify what could be done differently to prevent other deaths. They make recommendations to agencies and other decision makers for prevention activities and/or changes to service systems. The ultimate purpose is catalyzing action for prevention, rather than merely counting and calculating death rates."

An increasing number of states have expanded use of the review panels and are now routinely exchanging information with other states in an attempt to create as broad an examination as possible of the deaths. The hope is to learn from one another and to develop a "best practices" approach to deal with children at risk. Neil Websdale first talked to some of the killers discussed at length in his book *Familicidal Hearts* through his work as former director of the National Domestic Fatality Review, which focuses on homicides of both intimate partners and children.

A kind of an über–fatality commission was being created in early 2013 under the "Protect Our Kids Act" (HR 6655) passed by Congress. The national commission will examine the issue of child-abuse fatalities and come up with recommendations to stem the tide of domestic child fatalities. Getting the law passed was a key focus of Coalition to End Child Abuse, which includes the Every Child Matters Education Fund, the National Association of Social Workers, the National District Attorneys Association, the National Center for the Review and Prevention of Child Deaths, and the National Children's Alliance.

Many child advocates immediately mention gun control as an obvious way to save children's lives. Guns are particularly a factor in family annihilations. Firearms were used in vast majority of the murder-suicides tracked by the Violence Policy Center. David Adams, who has studied men who murder their intimate partners, pointed out at the 2012 conference on domestic violence, held by the National Institute of Justice, that guns are the "low-hanging fruit" that could be easily picked off to help stem the problem.

But there's also an interesting debate, particularly internationally, about what role physical punishment in the home might play in child abuse, abuse fatalities, and child homicides by parents. Gelles believes we must reconsider our tolerance of corporal punishment at home to make inroads against child abuse. "There's something troubling when a child experiences his first violence at the hands of someone he loves," he told me. But he's not optimistic things will change soon in the United States. "I think you have to start with ending capital punishment," he explained. "You can't arrest someone for spanking their kid when we're putting people to death." Studies have found conflicting evidence linking corporal punishment at home to child abuse. But it's interesting that after Rahim Alfetlawi shot his stepdaughter in the head, he told his wife that he had "smacked her."

In its latest report on child-abuse fatalities in industrialized nations, UNICEF authors weave a careful argument supporting the suppression of corporal punishment of children by their parents. Strictures against such treatment of kids at home is a logical part of a strategy to develop a "culture of peace" within societies that will be safer for children, they argue. Though poverty and substance abuse has been linked to child abuse, it's "unlikely that such problems will be fixed soon," the report concedes.[9] But it's important for adults to realize in the interim that regardless of the pressures of their own lives, they should not take it for granted that they can "take it out on the kids."

The "challenge of ending child abuse is the challenge of breaking the link between adults' problems and children's pain. It ought not to be part of family culture, or of our societies' culture, for the psychological, social or economic stresses of adults to be vented on children, or for problems and frustrations to be so easily translated into abuse of the defenseless," states the UNICEF report. "The task is therefore one of creating a culture of non-violence toward children, of building a barrier of social and individual conscience which says that it is totally unacceptable in any circumstances for adults to express either their will or their frustrations in the language of violence towards the young."

Nordic countries have been the first to take the lead in criminalizing corporal punishment in the home. The movement has also involved campaigning against the "promotion of 'violence-as-normal' in everything from toys to television programming," with its centerpiece a drive to end the "most common violence of all—the hitting of children by parents or care-givers for the purposes of chastisement and discipline," notes the UNICEF report.[10] Many countries would consider cracking down on spanking by parents a "radical idea," the report acknowledges. "Probably a large majority of the world's children are subjected to some degree of physical violence at the hands of their parents or care-givers, and it may be that there are very few societies, past or present, in which this has not been the case." The report cites a survey in Britain that found that 97 percent of four-year-olds were subject to physical punishment at home, almost half of them more often than once a week. Research in the United States found that 94 percent of three- and four-year -old kids are "smacked, spanked or beaten," notes the UNICEF report. Such punishment often begins at a very early age. Two-thirds of moms in a sample survey in the United Kingdom cited in the report admitted to "smacking" their children before the child's first birthday. The same study in the United Kingdom found that about 25 percent of children were hit regularly with straps or canes. The use of physical punishment at home usually declines with age, but a 1995 Gallup poll found that 40 percent of American thirteen-year-old children were regularly hit, and a quarter of kids ages fifteen and older were struck. "In short, the hitting of children by parents or care-givers is, by a significant margin, the most common form of violence in the industrialized world," states the UNICEF report. "Is there then a case for attempting to end a practice which is widely accepted as normal in almost every society, past and present, and is today practiced by a clear majority of adults, most of whom regard occasional physical punishment of children as not only normal but necessary?"

The report presents an argument that hitting a child at home is a violation of fundamental human rights. Physical violence against another person is recognized as illegal in all nations, the report notes, yet it's acceptable against the "most vulnerable members of society." If it's illegal to slap a stranger in a grocery store, why is it not illegal for a parent to do the same to a child? A number of European nations have now begun to reconcile that inconsistency. The first to do so was Sweden, which in 1957 deleted a legal provision exempting from the definition of "common assault" parents whose use of physical punishment caused minor injuries to their children. Similar amendments became part of the law in Finland in 1969, Norway in 1972, and Austria 1977. By 1979, Sweden banned corporal punishment outright in the home, declaring in law that "children are to be treated with respect for their person and individuality, and may not be subjected to physical punishment or other injurious or humiliating treatment." The groundbreaking "anti-smacking" legislation stunned many and triggered debates about overly intrusive "nanny states." But it was generally viewed in Sweden as a logical step in increasing strictures against violence at home and was supported by a "clear majority" of the population, notes the UNICEF report. It was passed in the Riksdag 259 to 6. Within years, Finland passed a law that a child "shall not be subdued, corporally punished, or otherwise humiliated," and Austria passed family legislation stating that "using violence and inflicting physical or mental suffering is unlawful." In 1994, the government of Cyprus declared illegal "the exercise of violence on behalf of any member of the family against another member of the family." Similar restrictions were passed in Latvia, Croatia, and Germany, which declared that "children have a right to a non-violent upbringing," and prohibited corporal punishment, psychological injuries, and other "humiliating measures." In 2003, Iceland joined the list by passing a new Children's Act outlawing physical punishment of children. Among those nations, only Austria, Denmark, Finland, Germany, Iceland, Norway, and Sweden currently have laws that *explicitly prohibit* physical punishment. "They are persuaded, and are persuading others, that legalized violence toward children is a breach of human rights even when it takes place within the home. They are convinced that removing the bottom rungs will make the ladder of serious child abuse more difficult to climb," the UNICEF report notes. Far from regarding physical punishment as a "socializing discipline," the laws recognize it as a model of "bad behavior," and challenge the "legitimacy of violence as a means of resolving conflicts and asserting will."

Several nations have vastly increased protections of children not in legislation but through court decisions. In a landmark case in Italy, which the UNICEF report refers to as creating "Ippolito's law," a father was brought to court for repeatedly hitting and kicking his child for lying and doing poorly at school. His lawyer argued that because his intent—to correct and discipline his child—was good, and because he had caused no significant physical harm, he committed no crime. Judge Francesco Ippolito eventually ruled in Italy's Supreme Court in 1996 that physical punishment, regardless of intent, could not be used. He later called the case an "opportunity to establish the legal principal that parents in Italy are absolutely forbidden from using any violence or corporal punishment to correct their children's conduct."[11] Decades after the end of Fascism in Italy, it was time to drop the concept of the authoritarian father, he argued.

In the United States, laws relating to physical punishment are up to each state, and as of 2003 only Minnesota had a law that bars corporal punishment at home, according to the report. Several states allow corporal punishment in schools, which is permitted worldwide only in laws in the United States, Australia, Canada, and Mexico, notes the UNICEF report.

Strictures against corporal punishment of children at home is part of the UN Convention on the Rights of the Child, which has been ratified by every member nation except Somalia and the United States. Article 19 of the human-rights treaty requires all countries to protect children against "all forms of physical and mental violence . . . while in the care of parents, legal guardians or any other person who has the care of the child." The Convention recognizes the rights of children to express their opinions, to participate in decisions when they are able, and to grow toward maturity in an atmosphere of "mutual trust and respect—rights which are unlikely to flourish in a climate that is constantly darkened by the threat of physical punishment," stress the authors of the UNICEF report. Rights of children to be protected from physical violence at home is increasingly being recognized, notes the report, which cites a ruling by the European Court of Human Rights that found that the beating of a British child by his stepfather was a breach of the boy's human rights.

Such social change is likely slow in coming to the United States, where parents tend to zealously guard their rights to raise their children the way they want without interference from a Big Brother government, and where "spare the rod, spoil the child" is a principle still followed by many Americans. The American belief that physical punishment has a social benefit is clear in our continuing use of the death penalty, many believe. Michael Petit is convinced a key reason that the United States will not ratify the UN Convention on the Rights of Children is because of its clause banning the death penalty for children.

Beyond banning corporal punishment at home, laws against such action have the added effect of elevating the recognized "personhood" of children. Laws that protect children from the same kinds of assaults that adults are shielded from defines a status in society for children separate from their "minor" roles within a family. As Britain has struggled with issues such as forced marriage, a key strategy has been to equip children to bypass parental control and go directly to the courts for protection. Its groundbreaking Forced Marriage Act was passed in 2007 and allows children to obtain a Forced Marriage Protection Order against their own parents, protecting them from being forced to marry someone against their will. The protection orders can require a variety of actions, including being removed from a home, or passport confiscation to stop daughters from being sent overseas to a forced marriage. In changes to the law expected in 2013, a forced marriage would be a crime, and parents, friends, and relatives responsible for arranging such a marriage could face prison, though potential victims could still opt to use civil, rather than criminal, orders and penalties. Opponents of such changes fear that criminalization of the problem will force the practice deeper underground, where victims may be more difficult to protect. Britain's Forced Marriage Unit, established to deal with the problem, gave advice or support in 1,468 instances related to possible forced marriages in 2012. Of those, 78 percent involved females and 22 percent males.

———

How far have we come from the langurs—and how far can we go? Are we still buying in to the idea of the legitimacy of an alpha male in our troops, no matter how violent? Maybe we're all "drinking daddy's Kool-Aid," concocted in our evolutionary past, whether daddy is an intimidating patriarch at home or a patriarchal Congress or police department reluctant to adequately challenge violent fathers. But that leaves thousands of children unprotected. "When people ask me the best way for kids to be safe, I tell them, 'be born to the right parents,'" Michael Petit told me. "If you don't have the right parents, pray you're in a culture that will look out for you." We can make this culture one that looks out for kids and saves a little girl from being beaten to death before her fifth birthday.

Even one life saved would be a tremendous victory.

NOTES

INTRODUCTION

1. *Fiscal Year 2012 Historical Tables, Budget of the United States Government, Office of Management and Budget, Executive Office of the President of the United States* (Washington, DC: US Government Printing Office, 2012): 53, 55, 90.

2. *Fiscal Year 2012 Budget in Brief, US Department of Homeland Security* (Washington, DC: US Government Printing Office, 2012): 12.

3. "America's Child Death Shame," *BBC News Magazine,* October 17, 2011.

4. Wood, Joanne N., et al., "Local Macroeconomic Trends and Hospital Admissions for Child Abuse, 2000–2009," *Pediatrics* 130, no. 2 (Aug. 2012): 358; "Poor Economy Leaves More Children at Risk," *New York Times,* December 2, 2011, sec. 1, A25.

5. Violence Policy Center, "American Roulette: Murder-Suicide in the United States," 4th ed. (Washington, DC: Violence Policy Center, May 2012): 8.

CHAPTER 1: RAGE

1. CBC News, "B.C. Man Admits Killing Girl, 5: Police," June 28, 2010.

2. "Mother of Murdered B.C. Girl Speaks Out," CTV News, October 23, 2010.

3. Ibid.

4. "Tragedy Unfolds for Abby Family," *Abbotsford-Mission Times,* January 4, 2011, sec. 1, A3.

5. "Mother of Murdered B.C. Girls Speaks Out," CTV News.

CHAPTER 3: MUG'S GAME

1. Hrdy, Sarah Blaffer, *The Langurs of Abu: Female and Male Strategies of Reproduction* (Cambridge, MA: Harvard University Press, 1977), 242–266.

2. Ibid., 242.

3. Jay, Phyllis C., "The Social Behavior of the Langur Monkey" (PhD diss., University of Chicago, 1963), 8.

4. Calhoun, John B., "Population Density and Social Pathology," *Scientific American* 206 (1962).

5. Hrdy, *Langurs of Abu*, vii.

6. Ibid., 76.

7. Ibid., 243.

8. Ibid., 68.

9. Ibid., 11.

10. Hrdy, Sarah Blaffer, *Mother Nature: Maternal Instincts and How They Shape the Human Species* (New York: Ballantine Books, 1999), 232.

11. Hrdy, *Langurs of Abu*, 11.

12. Ibid., 308.

13. Fossey, Dian, "Infanticide in Mountain Gorillas with Comparative Notes on Chimpanzees," in *Infanticide*, eds. Glenn Hausfater and Sarah Blaffer Hrdy (New York: Aldine, 1984), 217.

14. Goodall, Jane, "Life and Death at Gombe: Violence Never Seen before Erupts among Africa's Chimpanzees in the Continuing Chronicle of Their Behavior by a Pioneer Observer," *National Geographic* (May 1979).

15. Goodall, Jane, *Reason for Hope: A Spiritual Journey* (New York: Grand Central Publishing, 2000), 117.

16. Ibid., 118.

17. Hrdy, *Langurs of Abu*, 289–290.

18. Ibid., 1.

19. Hausfater, Glenn, and Sarah Blaffer Hrdy, eds., *Infanticide: Comparative and Evolutionary Perspectives* (New Brunswick, NJ: Aldine Transaction, 1984/2008), xi.

20. Hrdy, *Mother Nature*, 25.

21. Ibid., 251.

22. Ibid., 228.

23. Ibid., 236.

24. Hrdy, Sarah Blaffer, *Mothers and Others: The Evolutionary Origins of Mutual Understanding* (Cambridge, MA: Belknap Press, 2009), 3.

25. Ibid., 33–34.

26. Ibid., 4.

CHAPTER 4: HOMO SAPS

1. Daly, Martin, and Margo Wilson, *The Truth about Cinderella: A Darwinian View of Parental Love* (New Haven, CT: Yale University Press, 1999), 10.

2. Ibid., 16.

3. Ibid., 38–39.

4. Ibid., 1–5.

5. "Killer and Victims: Interview of Martin Daly and Margo Wilson on Homicide," *Human Ethology Bulletin* 11, no. 4 (December 1996): 4, 5.

6. Daly and Wilson, *Truth about Cinderella*.

7. Ibid., 38.

8. Ibid., 7.

9. Gould, Stephen Jay, "Biological Potentiality vs. Biological Determinism," in *Ever Since Darwin: Reflections in Natural History*, 251–260 (New York: Norton, 1977), 257.

10. Daly and Wilson, *Truth about Cinderella*, 24.

11. Ibid., 27.

12. Ibid., 28.

13. Ibid., 30.

14. Ibid., 32.

15. Ibid., 31.

16. Ibid., 63.

17. Ibid., 66.

18. Daly, Martin, and Margo Wilson, "Crime and Conflict: Homicide in Evolutionary Psychological Perspective," *Crime and Justice* 22 (1997): 51.

19. Daly, Martin, and Margo Wilson, *Homicide* (New Brunswick, NJ: Transaction Publishers, 1988), 7.

20. Ibid., 2.

21. Wilson, Margo, Martin Daly, and Antonietta Daniele, "Familicide: The Killing of Spouse and Children," *Aggressive Behavior* 21 (1995): 276.

22. Daly, Martin, and Margo Wilson, "Male Sexual Proprietariness and Violence against Wives," *Current Directions* 5, no. 1 (Feb. 1996): 4.

23. Ibid., 2.

24. Ibid., 5.

25. Ibid., 7.

26. Wilson, Daly, and Daniele, "Familicide."

27. Ibid., 287.

28. Ibid., 287–288.

29. Ibid., 289.

CHAPTER 5: POSSESSION

1. Unless otherwise noted in the text, all information in this chapter was obtained through several personal interviews with co-workers, clients, and friends of William Parente, along with police and court records and information from investigators that is available to the public and was widely reported in news reports.

CHAPTER 6: DEVASTATION

1. Unless otherwise noted in the text, all information in this chapter was obtained through personal interviews with clients of William Parente, and from police and court records available to the public and widely reported in news reports.

2. *In the Matter of the Petition of Jeffrey E. Deluca, Public Administrator of Nassau County, as Administrator of the Estate of William Parente*, Surrogate's Court of the State of New York, Nassau County, March 30, 2012.

3. *Application of Joseph A. Mazzarella for Full Letters of Administration in the Estate of Betty Ann Parente, Stephanie Ann Parente, Catherine Ann Parente*, Surrogate's Court of the State of New York, Nassau County, December 21, 2009.

4. *In the Matter of the Petition of Eric P. Milgrim, Public Administrator of Nassau County, as Temporary Administrator of the Estate of William M. Parente, Deceased*, Surrogate's Court of the State of New York, Nassau County, June 3, 2010.

5. *Stipulation in the Matter of the Proceedings of Joseph A. Mazzarella, as Administrator of the Estate of Betty Ann Parente, In the Matter of the Proceedings of Eric P. Milgrim, Public Administrator of Nassau County, as Administrator of the Estate of William Michael Parente, Administration Proceeding, Estate of Stephanie Ann Parente and of Catherine Ann Parente*, Surrogate's Court of the State of New York, Nassau County, December 23, 2010, 10.

6. Ibid., 19.

CHAPTER 7: DEATH BY THE NUMBERS

1. Richard J. Gelles and Murray Arnold Straus, *Intimate Violence: The Causes and Consequences of Abuse in the American Family* (New York: Simon and Schuster, 1989), 51.

2. Unless otherwise noted, information about the Christopher Foster case was gathered through police statements and records, phone interviews with friends, and several news reports.

3. *The Millionaire and the Murder Mansion*, directed by Nick Poyntz, 2009.

4. Violence Policy Center, "American Roulette: Murder-Suicide in the United States," 4th ed. (Washington, DC: Violence Policy Center, May 2012), 13.

5. Violence Policy Center, "American Roulette: Murder-Suicide in the United States," 3rd ed. (Washington, DC: Violence Policy Center, April 2008), 13.

6. Violence Policy Center, "American Roulette," 4th ed., 8.

7. Ibid., 6.

8. Ibid., 8.

9. Ibid.

10. Violence Policy Center, "American Roulette," 3rd ed., 8.

11. Violence Policy Center, "American Roulette," 4th ed., 8.

12. Websdale, Neil, *Familicidal Hearts: The Emotional Styles of 211 Killers* (New York: Oxford University Press, 2010), 259.

13. Wood, Joanne N., et al., "Local Macroeconomic Trends and Hospital Admissions for Child Abuse, 2000–2009," *Pediatrics* 130, no. 2 (Aug. 2012): 358.

14. Ibid., 360.

15. US Department of Defense Casualty Status, March 25, 2013, http://www.defense.gov/news/casualty.pdf.

16. UNICEF, "A League Table of Child Maltreatment Deaths in Rich Nations," *Innocenti Report Card* 5 (Florence, Italy: UNICEF Innocenti Research Centre, Sept. 2003), 4.

17. Ibid., 7.

18. Ibid., 2.

19. Ibid., 11.

20. Children's Bureau, "Child Maltreatment 2011" (Washington, DC: Department of Health & Human Services, Administration for Children and Families, Administration on Children, Youth and Families, Children's Bureau, 2012), 56.

21. Ibid., 19.

22. Ibid., 20.

23. Ibid., 56–57.

24. Ibid., 59.

25. Zimmerman, Francie, and James A. Mercy, "A Better Start: Child Maltreatment Prevention as a Public Health Priority," *Zero to Three* (May 2010): 5.

26. Finkelhor, D., et al., "Violence, Abuse, and Crime Exposure in a National Sample of Children and Youth," *Pediatrics* 124, no. 5 (Oct. 2009): 1.

27. Children's Bureau, "Child Maltreatment 2011," 56.

28. US Government Accountability Office, "Child Maltreatment: Strengthening National Data on Child Fatalities Could Aid in Prevention" (Washington DC: Report to the Chairman, Committee on Ways and Means, House of Representatives, July 2011), cover findings.

29. Ibid., 16.

30. Ibid., 2.

31. Ibid., 21.

32. Ibid., cover findings.

33. Ibid., 13.

34. Ibid., 25.

35. Ibid., 31.

36. Ibid., 34–35.

37. Cooper, Alexia, and Erica L. Smith, "Homicide Trends in the United States, 1980–2008: Annual Rates for 2009 and 2010" (Washington, DC: Bureau of Justice Statistics, Nov. 2011), 20.

38. Ibid., 21.

39. Medina, Sheyla P., et al., "Tracking Child Abuse and Neglect: The Role of Multiple Data Sources in Improving Child Safety," *Evidence to Action* (Fall 2012): 1.

CHAPTER 8: TRAIL OF TEARS

1. Unless otherwise noted, all information about the following crimes was obtained from police and court records and police statements that are available to the public and were reported widely in the news.

2. "Missing Child's Body Found in Dumpster," WREG Memphis, July 3, 2012, http://www.wreg.com/2012/07/03/missing-3-year-old-boy-found/.

3. "No Parent Should Ever Have to Say a Final Goodbye to a Young Child," WNCT, July 13, 2012, http://www.wnct.com/story/21013377/no-parent-should-ever-have-to-say-a-final-goodbye-to-a-young-child.

4. Quotes from experts and researchers here are all from personal interviews with the author.

5. UNICEF, "Measuring Child Poverty: New League Tables of Child Poverty in the World's Rich Countries," *Innocenti Report Card* 10 (Florence, Italy: UNICEF Innocenti Research Centre, 2012), 10.

6. Ibid., 3.

7. Burstain, Jane, testimony before the Subcommittee on Human Resources of the Committee of Ways and Means, US House of Representatives, June 12, 2011.

8. Fang, Xiangming, et al., "The Economic Burden of Child Maltreatment in the United States and Implications for Prevention," *Child Abuse and Neglect* 36, no. 2 (Feb. 2012): 156.

9. Zimmerman, Francie, and James A. Mercy, "A Better Start: Child Maltreatment Prevention as a Public Health Priority," *Zero to Three* (May 2010): 5.

CHAPTER 9: CONTROL FREAK

1. Nibley, Preston, *Brigham Young: The Man and His Work* (Salt Lake City: Deseret 1937), 119–23.

2. All information in this chapter was gathered from police and court records available to the public and reported widely in the news, interviews with family and friends, and e-mails written by Susan.

CHAPTER 11: GONE

1. All information in this chapter was obtained in interviews with family and friends of Susan Cox Powell, and from police and court records available to the public and widely reported in the news.

2. "FBI Expert: Why Police Raided Josh Powell's Home," *Today Show*, NBC, August 26, 2011.

3. Washington State Department of Social and Health Services, Children's Administration Child Fatality Review, Charles Powell, Braden Powell, April 26–27 and June 8, 2012.

CHAPTER 12: THIS MODERN LIFE

1. This narrative of the William Beadle family annihilation is based on accounts in newspaper articles and letters written at the time, a poem, and the last will and testament written by William Beadle in a collection from the Wethersfield Historical Society of Wethersfield, Connecticut, with excerpts quoted in Smart, James R., *A Life of William Beadle* (self-published senior thesis, Princeton University, 1989) and the book by Mitchell, S. M., *A Narrative of the Life of William Beadle*, 4th ed. (Greenfield, CT: 1805).

2. Mitchell, *Narrative of the Life of William Beadle*, 6.

3. Smart, *Life of William Beadle*, 8–9.

4. Mitchell, *Narrative of the Life of William Beadle*.

5. Fitzgerald, N. K., "Towards and American Abraham: Multiple Parricide and the Rejection of Revelation in the Early National Period" (master's thesis, Brown University, 1971).

6. "Fresh Advices from Our Correspondent," *London Intelligencer*, October 14, 1755.

7. Cohen, Daniel A., "Homicidal Compulsion and the Conditions of Freedom: The Social and Psychological Origins of Familicide in America's Early Republic," *Journal of Social History* 28, no. 4 (Summer 1995): 725.

8. Websdale, Neil, *Familicidal Hearts: The Emotional Styles of 211 Killers* (New York: Oxford University Press, 2010), 26–27.

9. Ibid., 33.

10. Ibid., 44.

11. Ibid., 21.

12. Ibid., 139.

13. Ibid., 154.

14. Ibid., 155.

15. Ibid., 176.

16. Ibid., 177.

17. Ibid., 176–177.

18. List, J., with Austin Goodrich, *Collateral Damage: The John List Story* (New York: iUniverse Incorporated, 2006): 45–47.

19. Ibid., 281.

CHAPTER 13: MASKED

1. This account is based on police and court records and transcripts; interviews with investigators, lawyers, and Scott and Laci Peterson's friends; and several weeks covering Scott Peterson's murder trial for the *New York Daily News*.

2. "Behind Closed Doors," *People*, June 2, 2003.

3. Cleckley, Hervey, *The Mask of Sanity: An Attempt to Reinterpret the So-Called Psychopathic Personality* (New York: CV Mosby, 1941), 369–370.

4. McGinness, Joe, *Final Vision* (New York: Byliner, 2013).

5. McGinness, Joe, *Fatal Vision* (New York: Signet Books, 1984), 104–105.

6. Ibid., 140–141.

CHAPTER 14: CLASH

1. Unless otherwise noted, all information about the murder of Jessica Mokdad is based on police and court records available to the public and an interview with Jessica's mom, Wendy Wasinski.

2. "Outraged and Outrageous," *New York Times*, October 8, 2010, sec. MB, 1.

CHAPTER 15: INFIDEL

1. Hirsi Ali, Ayaan, *Infidel* (New York: Free Press 2008), xxii.

2. AHA Foundation, http://theahafoundation.org/about/ (May 8, 2012).

3. "Muslim Women Face Threat in US," *USA Today*, March 5, 2012.

4. "Culture of Discrimination: A Fact Sheet on 'Honor' Killings," Women's Human Rights Program, Amnesty International USA.

5. "Honor Thy Father: The Inside Story of the Young Muslim Woman 'Honor Killed' by Her Father Because He Believed She'd Become Too Americanized," *Phoenix New Times*, April 1, 2010, 1.

6. All information about the Shafia murder case is from police and court records and transcripts available to the public.

7. "Should We Call It Honor Killing?" *Montreal Gazette*, January 31, 2012.

CHAPTER 16: WHAT TO DO

1. Kauppi, Anne, "Filicide, Intra-Familial Child Homicides in Finland 1970–1994," (PhD diss. in health sciences, University of Eastern Finland, 2012).

2. European Child Safety Alliance, "Finland," *Child Safety Country Profile* (Europe: European Child Safety Alliance of EuroSafe, June 2012).

3. Gelles, Richard J., *The Third Lie* (Walnut Creek, CA: Left Coast, 2011), introduction.

4. Gelles, Richard J., *The Book of David: How Preserving Families Can Cost Children's Lives* (New York: Basic Books, 1996), ix.

5. Ibid., 9.

6. Ibid., 21–22.

7. Ibid., 171.

8. "The Coordination & Integration of Fatality Reviews: Findings from the National Invitational Meeting, a Report to the Maternal and Child Health Bureau, Health Resources Services Administration US Department of Health and Human Services," Michigan Public Health Institute, July 2012.

9. UNICEF, "A League Table of Child Maltreatment Deaths in Rich Nations," *Innocenti Report Card* 5 (Florence, Italy: UNICEF Innocenti Research Centre, Sept. 2003), 21–22.

10. Ibid., 23.

11. Ibid., 30.

BIBLIOGRAPHY

Arrington, Leonard J. *Brigham Young: American Moses.* New York: Vintage Books, 2012.

Barthell, Valerie R., and Kathleen M. Shelton. "Familicide: Risk Factors, Characteristics of the Offender, Characteristics of the Crime of Familicide, and the Prevalence of Suicide following Familicide." *Sociological Perspectives: The Undergraduate Sociological Journal at the University of New Hampshire* 14 (Spring 2009). http://www.unh.edu/sociology/media/pdfs-journal2009/1-Barthell-Shelton2009.pdf (accessed Feb. 15, 2012).

Buss, David M. *The Murderer Next Door: Why the Mind Is Designed to Kill.* New York: Penguin Books, 2006.

Calhoun, John B. "Population Density and Social Pathology." *Scientific American* 206 (1962): 139–148.

Capote, Truman. *In Cold Blood: A True Account of a Multiple Murder and Its Consequences.* New York: Vintage Books, 1965.

"Child Deaths Due to Maltreatment." Hearing before the Subcommittee on Human Resources of the Committee on Ways and Means (H.R.), 112th Cong. 1 (July 2011). Testimony of Theresa M. Covington, M.P.H. Director, National Center for the Review and Prevention of Child Deaths.

Children's Bureau. "Child Maltreatment 2011." Washington DC: Department of Health & Human Services, 2011.

Child Welfare Information Gateway. *Child Abuse and Neglect Fatalities: Statistics and Interventions.* Washington, DC: US Department of Health and Human Services Children's Bureau, 2009.

————. *Child Abuse and Neglect Fatalities 2010: Statistics and Interventions.* Washington, DC: US Department of Health and Human Services Children's Bureau, 2012.

Cleckley, Hervey. *The Mask of Sanity.* St. Louis, IL: CV Mosby, 1976.

Cohen, Daniel A. "Homicidal Compulsion and the Conditions of Freedom: The Social and Psychological Origins of Familicide in America's Early Republic." *Journal of Social History* 28, no. 4 (Summer 1995): 725–764.

Cooper, Alexia, and Erica L. Smith. "Homicide Trends in the United States, 1980–2008: Annual Rates for 2009 and 2010." Washington, DC: Bureau of Justice Statistics, Nov. 2011.

Crier, Catherine. *A Deadly Game: The Untold Story of the Scott Peterson Investigation.* New York: Harper, 2005.

255

Daly, Martin, Karen A. Wiseman, and Margo Wilson. "Women with Children Sired by Previous Partners Incur Excess Risk of Uxoricide." *Homicide Studies* 1 (1997): 61–71.

Daly, Martin, and Margo Wilson. "An Assessment of Some Proposed Exceptions to the Phenomena of Nepotistic Discrimination against Stepchildren." *Annales Zoologici Fennici* 38 (2001): 287–296.

———. "Discriminative Parental Solicitude and the Relevance of Evolutionary Models to the Analysis of Motivational Systems." In *The Cognitive Neurosciences*, ed. Michael Gazzaniga, 1269–1286. Cambridge, MA: MIT Press, 1995.

———. "The Evolutionary Psychology of Marriage and Divorce." In *Ties That Bind: Perspectives on Marriage and Cohabitation*, ed. Linda J. Waite, Michelle Hindin, Elizabeth Thomson, Christine Bachrach, and Arland Thornton, 91–110. Hawthorne, NY: Aldine de Gruyter.

———. "Family Violence: An Evolutionary Psychological Perspective." *Virginia Journal of Social Policy and Law* 8 (2001): 77–121.

———. *Homicide*. New Brunswick, NJ: Transaction Publishers, 1988.

———. "Is the 'Cinderella Effect' Controversial? A Case Study of Evolution-Minded Research and Critiques Thereof." In *Foundations of Evolutionary Psychology*, ed. Charles Crawford and Dennis Krebs, 383–400. Mahwah, NJ: Erlbaum, 2008.

———. "Lethal and Nonlethal Violence against Wives and the Evolutionary Psychology of Male Sexual Proprietariness." In *Violence against Women: International and Cross-Disciplinary Perspectives*, ed. Russell P. Dobash and Rebecca E. Dobash, 199–230. Thousand Oaks, CA: Sage Publications, 1998.

———. "Male Sexual Proprietariness and Violence against Wives." *Current Directions* 5, no. 1 (Feb. 1996): 2–7.

———. *Sex, Evolution, and Behavior*. 2nd ed. Belmont, CA: Wadsworth Publishing, 1978.

———. "Some Differential Attributes of Lethal Assaults on Small Children by Stepfathers versus Genetic Fathers." *Ethology & Sociobiology* 15 (1994): 207–217.

———. "Stepparenthood and the Evolved Psychology of Discriminative Parental Solicitude." In *Infanticide and Parental Care*, ed. Stefano Parmigiani and Frederick S. Vom Saal, 121–134. Chur, Switzerland: Harwood Academic Publishers, 1994.

———. *The Truth about Cinderella: A Darwinian View of Parental Love*. New Haven, CT: Yale University Press, 1999. First published 1998 by Weidenfeld & Nicolson.

———. "Violence against Stepchildren." *Current Directions in Psychological Science* 5 (1996): 77–81.

DeVore, Irven. "Male Dominance and Mating Behavior in Baboons." In *Sex and Behavior*, ed. Frank Beach, 266–289. New York: John Wiley and Sons, 1965.

Dobash, R. Emerson, and Russell P. Dobash. *Rethinking Violence against Women*. Thousand Oaks, CA: Sage Publications, 1998.

Durham, Michael S. *Desert between the Mountains: Mormons, Miner, Padres, Mountain Men, and the Opening of the Great Basin, 1772–1869*. New York: Henry Holt, 1995.

European Child Safety Alliance. "Finland." *Child Safety Country Profile*. Europe: European Child Safety Alliance of EuroSafe, June 2012.

Fang, Xiangming, Derek S. Brown, Curtis S. Florence, and James A. Mercy. "The Economic Burden of Child Maltreatment in the United States and Implications for Prevention." *Child Abuse and Neglect* 36, no. 2 (Feb. 2012): 156.

Finkelhor, D., H. Turner, R. Ormrod, and S. L. Hamby. "Violence, Abuse, and Crime Exposure in a National Sample of Children and Youth." *Pediatrics* 124, no. 5 (Oct. 2009): 1–14.

Fischer, Craig, ed. "Critical Issues in Policing Series: Violent Crime and the Economic Crisis: Police Chiefs Face a New Challenge (Part I)." Washington, DC: Police Executive Research Forum, 2009.

Fitzgerald, N. K. "Towards an American Abraham: Multiple Parricide and the Rejection of Revelation in the Early National Period." Master's Thesis, Brown University, 1971.

Fleeman, Michael. *Inside the Laci Peterson Murder*. New York: St. Martin's Press, 2003.

Fossey, Dian. "Infanticide in Mountain Gorillas with Comparative Notes on Chimpanzees." In *Infanticide*, ed. Glenn Hausfater and Sarah Blaffer Hrdy, 217–235. New York: Aldine, 1984.

Francis, Monte. *By Their Father's Hand: The True Story of the Wesson Family Massacre*. New York: Harper, 2007.

Gelles, Richard J. *The Book of David: How Preserving Families Can Cost Children's Lives*. New York: Basic Books, 1996.

———. *Intimate Violence in Families*. 3rd ed. Thousand Oaks, CA: Sage Publications, 1997.

———. *The Third Lie: Why Government Programs Don't Work—And a Blueprint for Change*. Walnut Creek, CA: Left Coast, 2011.

Gelles, Richard J., and Claire Pedrick Cornell, eds. *International Perspectives on Family Violence*. Lexington, MA: LexingtonBooks, 1983.

Gelles, Richard J., and Jane B. Lancaster, eds. *Child Abuse and Neglect: Biosocial Dimensions*. New Brunswick, NJ: AldineTransaction, 1987.

Goodall, Jane. "Life and Death at Gombe: Violence Never Seen before Erupts among Africa's Chimpanzees in the Continuing Chronicle of Their Behavior by a Pioneer Observer." *National Geographic* (May 1979): 592–621.

Gould, S. J. "Biological Potentiality vs. Biological Determinism." In *Ever Since Darwin: Reflections in Natural History*, 251–260. New York: W. W. Norton, 1992.

Hausfater, Glenn, and Sarah Blaffer Hrdy, eds. *Infanticide: Comparative and Evolutionary Perspectives*. New Brunswick, NJ: AldineTransaction, 1984.

Hirsi Ali, Ayaan. *Infidel*. New York: Free Press, 2007.

Hrdy, Sarah Blaffer. *The Langurs of Abu: Female and Male Strategies of Reproduction*. Cambridge, MA: Harvard University Press, 1977.

———. *Mother Nature: Maternal Instincts and How They Shape the Human Species*. New York: Ballantine Books, 1999.

———. *Mothers and Others: The Evolutionary Origins of Mutual Understanding.* Cambridge, MA: Belknap, 2009.

———. *The Woman That Never Evolved.* Cambridge, MA: Harvard University Press, 1999.

Jay, Phyllis C. "Aspects of Maternal Behavior among Langurs." *Annals of the New York Academy of Sciences* 102 (1962): 468–476.

———. "The Common Langur of North India." In *Primate Behavior: Field Studies of Monkeys and Apes,* ed. Irven DeVore, 197–249. New York: Holt, Rinehart, and Winston, 1965.

———. "The Indian Langur Monkey (*Presbytis entellus*)." In *Primate Social Behavior: An Enduring Problem,* ed. Charles H. Southwick, 114–124. Princeton, NJ: Van Nostrand, 1963.

———. "Mother-Infant Relations in Free-Ranging Langurs." In *Maternal Behavior in Mammals,* ed. Harriet L. Rheingold, 282–304. New York: John Wiley and Sons, 1963.

———. "The Social Behavior of the Langur Monkey." PhD diss., University of Chicago, 1963.

Junger, Sebastian. *A Death in Belmont.* New York: Harper Perennial, 2007.

Kauppi, Anne. "Filicide, Intra-Familial Child Homicides in Finland 1970–1994." PhD diss., University of Eastern Finland, 2012.

Kauppi, Anne, et al. "Maternal and Paternal Filicides: A Retrospective Review of Filicides in Finland." *Journal of the American Academy of Psychiatry and the Law* 38, no. 2 (June 2010): 229–238.

Knight, Brad. *Laci Peterson: The Whole Story.* Lincoln, NB: iUniverse, 2005.

Lawick, Hugo van, and Jane van Lawick-Goodall. *Innocent Killers.* Boston: Houghton-Mifflin, 1971.

Lawick-Goodall, Jane van. "The Behavior of Free-Living Chimpanzees in the Gombe Stream Reserve." *Animal Behavior Monograph* 1 (1968): 165–311.

———. *In the Shadow of Man.* Boston: Houghton-Mifflin, 1971.

Levin, Jack. *Serial Killers and Sadistic Murderers: Up Close and Personal.* Amherst, NY: Prometheus Books, 2008.

Lorenz, Konrad. *On Aggression.* New York: Mariner Books, 1974.

Loseke, Donileen R., Richard J. Gelles, and Mary M. Cavanaugh, eds. *Current Controversies on Family Violence.* 2nd ed. Thousand Oaks, CA: Sage Publications, 2005.

MacDonald, John M. *The Murderer and His Victim.* Springfield, IL: Charles C. Thomas Publisher, 1986.

McCann, C. "Notes on the Common Indian Langur (*Pithecus entellus*)." *Journal of the Bombay Natural History Society* 33 (1928): 192–194.

———. "Observations on Some of the Indian Langurs." *Journal of the Bombay Natural History Society* 36 (1933): 616–628.

McGinness, Joe. *Blind Faith.* New York: G. P. Putnam's Sons, 1989.

———. *Fatal Vision.* New York: Signet Books, 1984.

———. *Final Vision.* New York: Byliner, 2012.

McPhee, Michele R. *Heartless: The True Story of Neil Entwistle and the Brutal Murder of His Wife and Child.* New York: St. Martin's True Crime, 2008.

Medina, Sheyla P., et al. "Tracking Child Abuse and Neglect: The Role of Multiple Data Sources in Improving Child Safety." *Evidence to Action* (Fall 2012): 1–12.

Mitchell, S. M. *A Narrative of the Life of William Beadle.* 4th ed. Greenfield, CT, 1805.

Morris, Errol. *A Wilderness of Error: The Trials of Jeffrey MacDonald.* New York: Penguin Group (USA), 2012.

Rocha, Sharon. *For Laci: A Mother's Story of Love, Loss, and Justice.* New York: Three Rivers Press, 2006.

Stegner, Wallace Earle. *Mormon Country.* Lincoln: University of Nebraska Press, 1942.

Straus, Murray A., Richard J. Gelles, and Suzanne K. Steinmetz. *Behind Closed Doors: Violence in the American Family.* New Brunswick, NJ: Transaction Publishers, 2006. First published 1980 by Anchor Books.

UNICEF. "Child Poverty in Perspective: An Overview of Child Well-Being in Rich Countries." *Innocenti Report Card* 7. Florence, Italy: UNICEF Innocenti Research Centre, 2007.

———. "A League Table of Child Maltreatment Deaths in Rich Nations." *Innocenti Report Card* 5. Florence, Italy: UNICEF Innocenti Research Centre, Sept. 2003.

———. "Measuring Child Poverty: New League Tables of Child Poverty in the World's Rich Countries." *Innocenti Report Card* 10. Florence, Italy: UNICEF Innocenti Research Centre, 2012.

US Government Accountability Office. "Child Maltreatment: Strengthening National Data on Child Fatalities Could Aid in Prevention." Report to the Chairman, Committee on Ways and Means, House of Representatives. Washington DC: GAO, July 2011.

Violence Policy Center. "American Roulette: Murder-Suicide in the United States." 3rd ed. Washington, DC: Violence Policy Center, April 2008.

———. "American Roulette: Murder-Suicide in the United States." 4th ed. Washington, DC: Violence Policy Center, May 2012.

Websdale, Neil. *Familicidal Hearts: The Emotional Styles of 211 Killers.* New York: Oxford University Press, 2010.

Wilson, Edward O. *The Social Conquest of Earth.* New York: Liveright Publishing, 2012.

———. *Sociobiology: The New Synthesis.* Cambridge, MA: Belnap Press of Harvard University Press, 2000.

Wilson, Margo, and Martin Daly. "Lethal and Nonlethal Violence against Wives." *Canadian Journal of Criminology* 37 (1995): 331–361.

Wilson, Margo, Martin Daly, and Antonietta Daniele. "Familicide: The Killing of Spouse and Children." *Aggressive Behavior* 21 (1995): 275–291.

Wilson, Margo, Vessna Jocic, and Martin Daly. "Extracting Implicit Theories about the Risk of Coercive Control in Romantic Relationships." *Personal Relationships* 8 (2001): 457–477.

Wood, Joanne N., et al. "Local Macroeconomic Trends and Hospital Admissions for Child Abuse, 2000–2009." *Pediatrics* 130, no. 2 (Aug. 2012): 358–364.

Zimmerman, Francie, and James A. Mercy. "A Better Start: Child Maltreatment Prevention as a Public Health Priority." *Zero to Three* (May 2010): 4–10.

INDEX

murder
by ax, 158, 163, 164
by beating, 12
by bludgeoning, 12, 71, 87–88, 164
by blunt-force trauma, 117
by car, 167, 225
by carbon-monoxide poisoning,
158
by drugging, 163
by guns, 13, 102–104, 116, 117–18,
118–19, 119, 120, 207
of an intimate partner or spouse,
105
during pregnancy, 13
rationalized as "mercy killings,"
105
shaken baby syndrome, 111, 117,
120
by stabbing, 199–200, 225
by starvation, 12
by strangulation, 196
by suffocation, 12, 196
by throat cutting, 12, 20–26, 116,
118, 163
witnessed by children, 105
murder-suicides, statistics on, 105
Muslims in the United States, 205
Myrack, John, 164

National Association of Social Workers,
238
National Center for Child Death
Review, 238
National Center for the Review and
Prevention of Child Deaths, 239
National Child Abuse and Neglect
Data System (NCANDS), 109–10

National Children's Alliance, 239
National Crime Victimization Survey
(NCVS), 112–13
National District Attorneys Associa-
tion, 238
National Domestic Fatality Review, 238
National Geographic, 53
National Institute of Health, 46–47
National Institute of Justice, 109, 239
natural selection, 165
New York Daily News, 10, 12–13, 174
New York Post, 12, 174
Northern Arizona University, 106, 165
nuclear families, 168

Obaston House estate, 102
On the Road (Kerouac), 186
Organization for Economic Coopera-
tion and Development, 121
Owings, Jovanna, 145

Page, Stephanie, 203
Paramore, Mason, 118–19
parent victims killed by children, 113
Parente, Betty Mazzarella, 9, 77–88
Parente, Catherine, 9, 77–88
Parente, Stephanie, 9, 77–88
Parente, William "Bill," 88
and Betty's breast cancer, 79
and death of mother, 80–81
described, 73–74
as investment advisor, 74–75
and murders of Betty, Catherine,
and Stephanie, 87–88
positioning of family's bodies, 86
and psychic, 80–81
suicide of, 88